The YOUNG EARTH

John D. Morris, Ph.D.

Master Books
P.O. Box 727
Green Forest, AR 72638

The YOUNG EARTH

First printing, June 1994
Fifth printing, August 1996
Sixth printing, March 1997
Seventh printing, May 1998

ISBN: 0-89051-174-8
Library of Congress Catalog Number 94-96176

Printed in the United States of America.

Acknowledgments

I would like to express my gratitude to the following:

Editorial Contributions

Gerald Aardsma	Ken Ham	
Mike Arct	Russ Humphreys	
Steve Austin	Bill Mattox	
Richard Bliss	Henry Morris	
Van Burbach	Harold Ritter	
Brian Cardott	Andrew Snelling	
Art Chadwick	Bill Spear	
Donald Chittick	Jim Stambaugh	
Ken Cumming	Larry Vardiman	
Duane Gish	Carl Wieland	

Layout, Production
Gloria Clanin
Ron Hight

Artwork
Ron Hight
Marvin Ross

Typing
Ruth Richards
Mary Thomas

Proofreading
Merle Meeter

Table of Contents

Foreword

I believe this book is destined to meet a great need "for such a time as this" (Esther 4:14). The issue of origins is crucial to our understanding of the future, and there has been a significant revival of belief in creation, as men and women have realized this fact in recent decades. The frightening glimpses of imminent world catastrophe, and crises of all kinds, should drive every person to a serious confrontation with the meaning of his or her life and destiny.

After all, there are only two basic worldviews—the God-centered worldview and the man-centered worldview, creation or evolution. If there is really a great personal Creator God behind the origin and meaning of all things, then we urgently need to know Him and to order our lives according to His will, as revealed in His inspired Word. If human beings, on the other hand, are simply the end-products of a long process of evolution from the primordial nothingness (as taught today in most secular schools and information media), then "let us eat and drink; for tomorrow we die" (1 Corinthians 15:32).

The decision obviously is one of urgent importance. Our personal lives (and possibly the present world itself) are ephemeral. The worldwide revival of true creationism in recent decades has occurred as more and more people have awakened to the urgency of this decision.

As one who has been directly involved with the creation movement for over fifty years, I can testify to this remarkable growth of intelligent belief in divine creation. There are now many thousands of scientists who have become creationists, and this includes scientists in every field and every nation. Polls show that half of the people in the United States now believe in special creation.

Even though most scientists and other intellectuals still continue to believe in evolution, the facts of science oppose evolutionism, and most people see this, once these facts are shown to them. There is no evidence whatever—past, present, or possible—that *vertical* evolution of one kind of organism into a more complex kind or organism has ever occurred, or ever can occur.

All the changes ever really observed in nature (e.g., different varieties of dogs and cats, different tribes of people) are *horizontal* changes, within fixed limits. Many kinds of creatures have deteriorated and become extinct in human history, but none has ever evolved into a higher kind. Similarly, in the fossil record of the past, there are many examples of deterioration and extinction, but no real transitional fossils from lower kinds to higher, more complex kinds. As far as *possible* evolutionary changes are concerned, the two basic laws of change in nature have been expressed scientifically as the law of conservation of *quantity* and the law of decay of *quality*—that is, the first and second laws of thermodynamics, which seem to indicate that "vertically upward" evolution is impossible.

While such scientific data do not seem to impress the doctrinaire evolutionists who control our scientific and educational establishments, they have convinced great numbers of people—scientists and laymen—that creation is a much better scientific "model" of origins and history than evolution.

As a result, in recent years, organizations studying and promoting scientific Biblical creationism have been established in at least 25 countries around the world. In this country alone, there are probably 100 national, regional, or local creationist organizations. Perhaps the most influential of these (at least judging from the outcries of the evolutionists) is the Institute for Creation Research and its Graduate School of Science. Dr. John Morris, the author of this book, serves ICR as Professor of Geology and Vice President for Outreach, and has established a solid reputation as speaker and writer in this vitally important field of Biblical and scientific creationism.

In addition to the scientific case for creation (which is essentially the same as the scientific case against evolution), there is an overwhelming Biblical case for creation, as well as a moral and social case against evolution, as documented in the many publications of the Institute for Creation Research.

However, there still remains one serious problem, and that is the question of the age of the earth. Evolutionists, realizing that evolution requires immense periods of time to be even marginally feasible, have repeatedly fallen back on the supposed multi-billion-year history of the world as their main defense. Using their assumption of "continuity," or uniformitarianism ("the present is the key to the past"), it is relatively easy for them to find numerous natural processes whose present-day rates of action might suggest long ages of operation to produce the present structure of the world.

The fallacy in this approach, however, at least to a Bible-believing Christian, is that it rejects the divine revelation from the Creator of the world that He did it all in six days several thousand years ago (Genesis 1:1–2:3; Exodus 20:8–11). Further, God defined the word "day" (Hebrew *yom*), the very first time the word was used, as the "light" period in the cyclical succession of light and darkness (Genesis 1:3–5), that has continued regularly ever since that first day.

Some, however, consider the Old Testament as conveying only theological concepts instead of historical facts. But the Lord Jesus Christ, who was actually the Creator of all things (John 1: 1-3; Colossians 1:16) and who therefore knows how it was, completely rejected the long-age notion of the ancient evolutionary philosophers (Stoics and Epicureans). He reminded us that "from the beginning of the creation [not several billion years after the beginning] God made them [i.e., Adam and Eve, citing Genesis 1:27] male and female" (Mark 10:6).

But what about the supposedly scientific indicators of great age for the earth and the universe? Must we choose science *or* Scripture?

No, of course not! The same God who created the world has revealed the Word, and He does not contradict Himself. If there seems to be a problem, one or the other must have been misunderstood. At this point, most scientists and even many Christian leaders opt for the uniformitarian-age estimates of the evolutionists, and either reject the Biblical testimony altogether or else "wrest the Scriptures" (II Peter 3:16) to try to make them accommodate the billions of years demanded by evolutionism.

Since John Morris is my son, I am both pleased and thankful that he has chosen a "more excellent way" in this book, knowing that God has magnified His Word above all His Name (I Corinthians 12:31; Psalm 138:2). John himself is both a scientist and a Christian leader. With a Ph.D. in geological

engineering and many years of personal Bible study, he is eminently qualified to write this book.

He believes, as I do, that God is able to speak plainly, especially on such vital issues as origins, meanings, and destinies. Therefore, the infallible Biblical record of the recent, literal Creation of all things and then the subsequent cataclysmic destruction of the world in the great Flood must be taken as established fact, with all the real data of science (as distinct from the uniformitarian interpretations of these data by fallible scientists) reinterpreted within a creationist context.

That this is the God-honoring (rather than man-honoring) approach is confirmed in the climactic words of the Apostle Peter shortly before he died. "In the last days," he wrote, "scoffers" will be saying that "all things continue as they were from the beginning of creation" (II Peter 3:3,4). This is an explicit prophecy of the latter-day prominence of the doctrine of continuity, or uniformity—which undergirds evolutionism. But then Peter said that they "willingly are ignorant of" two great facts of history. First, there is the special creation of all things "by the word of God," not by continuing natural processes. Second, "the world that then was, being overflowed with water, perished" (II Peter 3:5,6).

Thus, the key to resolving the modern conflict between the Bible and evolutionary uniformitarianism, prophetically given two thousand years ago by the Holy Spirit through the Apostle Peter, is to recognize and apply the two great facts of God's primeval, complete Creation and the subsequent global deluge to the study of Earth's processes and systems.

When this is done, as Dr. Morris has shown in this book with both scientific insight and Biblical conviction, as well as clarity in explanation, these processes and systems provide compellingly strong support for the Biblical revelation of the recent Creation and worldwide Flood. There are no proven scientific evidences that the earth is old, and scores of circumstantial evidences that the earth is young. The only way we can know, for certain, the age of the earth, is for God (who was there!) to tell us. And this He has done! We should believe what He says!

Henry M. Morris
President, Institute for Creation Research

Day 1

Day 2

Day 3

Day 4

Day 5 & 6

Day 6

Introduction

This is, without a doubt, a fascinating time to be a Bible-believing Christian. On the one hand, the forces of evil are running rampant, with the earth seemingly on a collision course with its ultimate destiny. But on the other hand, there has never been a time when more support for the Biblical worldview was available. You might not have heard it in the media, but discovery after discovery confirms the truth of God's Word and the benefits of living according to His guidelines.

Today we can watch as the concept of evolution self-destructs. It has never been well supported by the evidence, and now many scientists are coming forward to point out its weaknesses. Many have recognized the total inability of chance, random processes to produce the incredible complexity we see around us—especially in living systems. Students of earth history have abandoned the creed of former decades, that "the present is the key to the past," and are proposing instead secular theories of past events which sound almost Biblical in their proportions. The problem for Christians is gaining access to this revealing information, for many educators, politicians, and media outlets have joined forces to continue promoting the evolutionary, humanistic, naturalistic worldview.

The American educational system has particularly done a great disservice to many Americans. Not only is its social agenda a disaster, but its academic training has failed. The achievements of American students are lagging behind those of other developed countries. Many important facts and ideas are censored out of the classrooms, and students are seldom taught how to *think* about the material they *do* see. Instead, they are taught certain "facts" and theories—expected to remember them and repeat them on a test—but skills in gathering and interpreting data are neglected.

This is especially true when dealing with ideas about the past. The idea of evolution has come to be so firmly entrenched in our educational system that most people merely assume it is true. Scientific facts are placed within this interpretive scheme. End of discussion! Remember and repeat. Never mind the fact that no one has ever seen evolution take place,

nor have the fossils documented evolutionary trends in the past. Scientific law refutes the whole idea, and it's contrary to logic. Many people intuitively suspect it's not true, but still "believe" it anyway, because it's all they've been taught. "All educated people believe in evolution," they're told. "Only ignorant, bigoted, Christian fundamentalists still deny it."

If people were taught to think, taught to recognize the difference between scientific facts, which can be observed in the present, and ideas about the past which can be used to interpret the facts, then the issue would clear up, for the intellectually honest, anyway. SAT scores would climb once again as *science* classes spend more time on *science*, and less on ideas about evolutionary "history."

Even many Christians are ensnared in the trap of not thinking critically. In the Bible they read that God created all things in six days. They've come to know the Lord and love and trust His Word, but they've heard that "all educated people know that evolution has been proven." And so, they find themselves in a dilemma. Creation or evolution, the Bible or science? "Since science is true, and since it disagrees with the Bible, then Scripture must be untrue," they think.

Several options present themselves. A frequent response is to believe in creation at the appropriate times, but to believe evolution at other times, and try not to think about the inconsistency.

Or maybe the two are somehow compatible. Maybe God used evolution to create. Maybe the days of Genesis are long periods of time. Maybe evolution occurred in a "gap," then that original world was destroyed, and God re-created in six days. Maybe, maybe— "well I'm just not going to think about it. I'll stay in the New Testament."

But those doubts. Where do the dinosaurs fit in with Scripture? Where did Cain get his wife? Where did the races come from? What about the Ice Age? How did all those animals fit in Noah's Ark? Where did all the water come from to cover the mountains? And where did it go? Reasoning from an evolutionary mindset, there are no good answers to these questions. And so, many think, maybe

Scripture has errors. Maybe it can't be trusted.
Maybe even the New Testament can't be trusted.

The result: a weak church, with weak, doubting
Christians. Young people from Christian homes and
good churches who go off to college and come back
doubting and defeated or worse. Pastors who don't
teach the whole Scripture. Denominations that go
liberal. Seminaries that teach a smorgasbord of
ideas—"choose whichever compromise you like; we
can't know the truth."

The Institute for Creation Research (ICR) exists to
address these issues. Its purpose is to study the
evidence and give better interpretations, consistent
with Scripture, and to discover new scientific truth
where it can. But perhaps most of all, ICR's desire is
to teach people how to think about the past, and how
to interpret scientific and historical data from a
Scriptural perspective and to get it right! We've seen
how evolution has been used as an excuse to
disbelieve the Gospel, and this roadblock needs to be
removed.

**Descent from a
Common Ancestor**

GEOLOGIC TIME SCALE

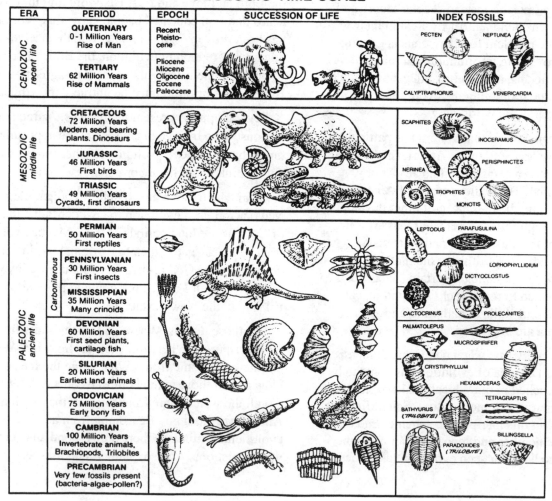

ERA	PERIOD	EPOCH	SUCCESSION OF LIFE	INDEX FOSSILS
CENOZOIC *recent life*	**QUATERNARY** 0-1 Million Years Rise of Man	Recent Pleistocene		PECTEN, NEPTUNEA, CALYPTRAPHORUS, VENERICARDIA
	TERTIARY 62 Million Years Rise of Mammals	Pliocene Miocene Oligocene Eocene Paleocene		
MESOZOIC *middle life*	**CRETACEOUS** 72 Million Years Modern seed bearing plants. Dinosaurs			SCAPHITES, INOCERAMUS
	JURASSIC 46 Million Years First birds			NERINEA, PERISPHINCTES
	TRIASSIC 49 Million Years Cycads, first dinosaurs			TROPHITES, MONOTIS
PALEOZOIC *ancient life*	**PERMIAN** 50 Million Years First reptiles			LEPTODUS, PARAFUSULINA
	PENNSYLVANIAN 30 Million Years First insects *Carboniferous*			LOPHOPHYLLIDIUM, DICTYOCLOSTUS
	MISSISSIPPIAN 35 Million Years Many crinoids			CACTOCRINUS, PROLECANITES
	DEVONIAN 60 Million Years First seed plants, cartilage fish			PALMATOLEPUS, MUCROSPIRIFER
	SILURIAN 20 Million Years Earliest land animals			CRYSTIPHYLLUM, HEXAMOCERAS
	ORDOVICIAN 75 Million Years Early bony fish			BATHYURUS (TRILOBITE), TETRAGRAPTUS
	CAMBRIAN 100 Million Years Invertebrate animals, Brachiopods, Trilobites			PARADOXIDES (TRILOBITE), BILLINGSELLA
	PRECAMBRIAN Very few fossils present (bacteria-algae-pollen?)			

In recent years we have noticed an incredible interest in creation thinking. Individual Christians and families have become desperate for good teaching on the subject. Evolutionism and humanism have become so pervasive and so distasteful that more and more Christians no longer feel comfortable with compromise.

Our most popular seminar series is called "Back-to-Genesis," and that's the theme of much that we do here at ICR. We're all scientists, but we're also Christians. We love science, but we also love the Lord, our Savior Jesus Christ, and His Word. We encourage Christians to go "Back to Genesis," to see the *true* history recorded there and then interpret the scientific data relating to the unobserved past in submission to Scripture.

We don't spend the majority of the time in our seminars presenting new and different data. Instead, we take the same data as used by our evolutionary colleagues (i.e., dinosaur fossils, racial differences, geologic deposits etc.) and interpret them from a Biblical perspective. We have found that the Ph.D. scientist needs exactly the same teaching as the high school youngster. All of us need encouragement to think right! To think in terms of Biblical fundamentals!

The scientist already knows the data, and will immediately see how it should be reinterpreted. The lay person will remember those evolution lectures and TV specials and recognize the error. Committed Christians rejoice to get their questions answered and doubts removed, to get the monkey of evolution off their backs. "God's Word is true! It can be trusted, even in these difficult areas of science and history."

This book represents an outgrowth of my "Back to Genesis" lecture on "The Age of the Earth." At the end of each lecture, folks always rush up and ask where my material is in print. Numerous ICR books deal with this vital question (among others), but there seemed to be a need for a book which focused on both the data supporting a young earth and the way data are interpreted.

Presenting that lecture always frustrates me. As a geology professor, there's so much I want to say, so many examples to use. But in a 45-minute lecture, it just can't happen. Here in the book, much more information and much more support has been included, although much more could still be added.

This book does not pretend to be a complete technical treatment on the age of the earth. It hopefully provides a good lay understanding of the general subject, in such a way as to be of use to both lay and technical readers. It does, however, cover numerous important subjects, even technical subjects. My desire is that all readers will not only learn new information, presented in a non-threatening format, but a new and helpful way to think about the information as well.

This is not to say that the material is presented in a less-than-correct manner. We serve the God of Truth, and *must* be both truthful and careful in all our study.

You will note that some of the references I've cited will be to other creationist books, where more complete discussions of pertinent points are made, and where original sources are given. I would very much like to see each reader introduced to the wealth of good creationist books and articles, including my own. On other occasions, I have included a reference to a particular technical source for a deeper understanding. On still other occasions, I will merely report on my own field work and observations, and thus *no* references may be given, if not published elsewhere.

Another question many people often ask after a lecture is where can they get copies of my overheads. And so, I've endeavored to make the book "user friendly," to provide the graphics, sketches, and many quotes in a large format, so that overhead transparencies could be made directly from the book for use in teaching situations. I would encourage each reader and creation speaker to acquire his own slides and examples from personal observation and investigation. The evidence for Creation, the Flood, and the young earth, rightfully interpreted, is everywhere. Hopefully, this book will inspire many to do just that. And hopefully it will also inspire many Christian geologists to join the work and solve some of the remaining problems for the young earth concept. I don't claim, by any stretch of the imagination, to have all the answers. What I do claim is to have access to the Book giving the framework for solving the problems. Let's proclaim what we do know, propose a model based on the Biblical framework, continue to solve the remaining problems, and correct any flaws in our understanding as we go.

Before we start into the discussion, it probably would be helpful to give some definitions, so questions in the reader's mind can be avoided. You'll notice that even these definitions and graphics are user friendly, designed less for completeness than for ease of teaching.

Biblical Creationism: Supernatural creation of all things in six literal days by the God of the Bible.

The Biblical Creation Model

1. Special Creation of all things by God in six solar days.

2. The Curse on all things because of sin. All things are dying.

3. The global Flood of Noah's day. Deposited rocks and fossils.

The Creation Model

1. Supernatural origin of all things. Design, purpose, interdependence, information.

2. Net basic decrease in complexity over time. Limited horizontal change.

3. Earth history dominated by catastrophic events.

Scientific Creationism: Each basic category of life appeared abruptly, without descending from an ancestor of a different sort. Much variation within a category is expected, but each possessed genetic limits to its variability, and thus exhibited stasis.

Stasis: The tendency of types of organisms to remain unchanged over time, "static," or "stationary" with respect to evolutionary progress.

Catastrophism: There have been episodes in the past which occurred at rates, scales, and intensities far greater than those possible today, or which were of an entirely different nature than those of today.

Evolution: The idea that all of life has come from a common ancestor through a process of modification over time. Thus man and the apes are thought to have descended from an ape-like common ancestor. All vertebrates came from fish, which in turn came from an invertebrate. All life descended from a single-celled organism which arose spontaneously from non-living chemicals. Changes occurred through natural processes, including mutation, natural selection, and genetic recombination.

The Evolution Model

1. Naturalistic origin of all things. Chance, random mutation, natural selection.

2. Net basic increase in complexity over time. Unlimited vertical change.

3. Earth history dominated by uniform events. Neo-catastrophism.

Macro-evolution: Large hypothetical changes which occur in an individual or in a population of organisms which produce an entirely new category or novel trait. These changes have never been observed to occur within living populations.

Micro-evolution: Small adaptations within a population of organisms which allow a certain trait to be expressed to a greater or lesser degree than before; variation within a given category. These are regularly observed to occur within living populations.

Mutations: Changes in the genetic material of an organism, potentially expressed in offspring. Many times a single mutation affects more than one trait. While some are neutral, many are lethal. No beneficial mutations have been observed.

Natural Selection: The process observed within populations of organisms which selects those traits best suited for a given environment. This conservative process tends to maintain the *status quo*, and never produces new genetic material.

Punctuated Equilibrium: Macro-evolution on a rapid pace. Invoked to explain and allow for evolution in the absence of fossil transitional forms.

Uniformitarianism: There have never been episodes occurring in the past of a dramatically different rate or character than processes possible today. "The present is the key to the past."

Geologic Column: Hypothetical column of fossils, with ancient ones on the bottom, more recent ones on top. Does not exist in complete form in nature, except as a trend. Index fossils are thought to be unique to individual eras, periods, and systems. Sometimes called the *Geologic Time Scale*, it's a statement of evolutionary dogma.

Index Fossils: While almost every stratum of rock contains many of the same basic fossil types, i.e., clams, coral, etc., certain individual organisms or variations are thought to have existed in only a brief period of supposed geologic time, and thus can be used to determine the layer's age.

Neo-catastrophism: Natural catastrophes occurred in the past, which, while of great intensity and scale, were no different in character from processes possible today. These catastrophes were episodic, separated by long periods of uniformity. Popular among geologic thinkers today.

Theistic Evolution: Essentially the same as atheistic evolution in its relation to scientific data. God may have either started the evolution process, then left it to natural processes, or may have guided the evolution process.

Progressive Creation: Sometimes called the Day-Age Theory. The days of Genesis were long periods of time, roughly equivalent to the geologic ages. Each basic category of life was created by supernatural intervention at various times throughout the ages.

Framework Hypothesis: The idea that the Bible, when it speaks of things historic or scientific, is to be understood in a theological sense only, assuming that God was involved, but not actually as recorded. Genesis is not to be taken as factual history. This view is very popular in many modern evangelical seminaries, and allows theologians to accept evolution fully.

Local Flood Theory: The teaching that the Flood of Noah's day covered only the Mesopotamian River Valley—a major flood, but not global. This view (or its counterpart, the Tranquil Flood theory, which says that the Flood was global but had no discernible effect, i.e., no erosion, no rocks, no fossils) is a necessary part of any compromise with evolution or old earth ideas, since the world's rock and fossil record is usually mis-interpreted as evidence for evolution and an old earth.

Evolutionism: The application of evolutionary ideas in the public arena. Includes concepts such as social Darwinism, man is an animal, animal rights equivalent to human rights, low view of human life, etc.

New Age Thinking: The modern equivalent of ancient pantheism, melding evolution science with Eastern mysticism, espousing a one-world government, a combination of all religions, and evolution*ism* in society.

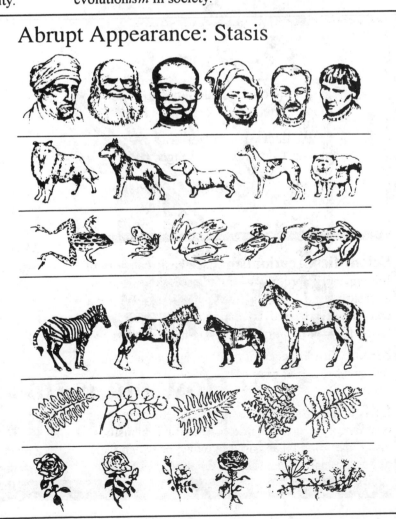

Abrupt Appearance: Stasis

How old is this Rock?
How old is this *Fossil*?

Chapter 1
What Do the Rocks Say?

How many times have you opened the newspaper and read an article describing the discovery of a new fossil, archaeological find, or underground fault? After describing the nature of the discover, the article explains how scientists are so thrilled with its confirmation of evolutionary theory. An age is reported, perhaps millions or hundreds of millions or even billions of years. No questions are raised concerning the accuracy of the date, and readers may feel they have no reason to question it either.

Did you ever wonder how they got that date? How do they know with certainty something that happened so long ago? It's almost as if rocks and fossils talk, or come with labels on them explaining how old they are and how they got that way.

As an earth scientist, one who studies rocks and fossils, I'll let you in on a little secret. My geologic colleagues may not like me to admit this, but rocks don't talk! Nor do they come with explanatory labels.

I have lots of rocks in my own personal collection, and there are many more in the ICR Museum. These rocks are well cared for and much appreciated. I never did have a "pet" rock, but I do have some favorites. I've spent many hours collecting, cataloging, and cleaning them. Some I've even polished and displayed.

But what would happen if I asked my favorite rock, "Rock, how old are you?" "Fossil, how did you get that way?" You know what would happen — NOTHING! Rocks don't talk! They don't talk to me, and I strongly suspect they don't talk to my evolutionary colleagues either! So where then do the dates and histories come from?

The answer may surprise you with its simplicity, but the concept forms the key thrust of this book. I've designed this book to explain how rocks and fossils are studied, and how conclusions are drawn as to their histories. But more than that, I've tried to explain not only how this endeavor usually proceeds, but how it *should* proceed.

Before I continue, let me clearly state that evolutionists are, in most cases, good scientists, and men and women of integrity. Their theories are precise and elegant. It is not my intention to ridicule or confuse. It is my desire to show the mind trap they have built for themselves, and show a better way. Let me do this through a hypothetical dating effort, purely fiction, but fairly typical in concept.

How It's Usually Done

Suppose you find a limestone rock containing a beautifully preserved fossil. You want to know the age of the rock, so you take it to the geology department at the nearby university and ask the professor. Fortunately, the professor takes an interest in your specimen and promises to spare no effort in its dating.

Much to your surprise, the professor does not perform carbon-14 dating on the fossil. He explains that carbon dating can only be used on organic materials, not on rocks or even on the fossils, since they too are rock. Furthermore, in theory it's only good for the last few thousand years, and he suspects your fossil is millions of years old. Nor does this expert measure the concentrations of radioactive isotopes to calculate the age of the rock. "Sedimentary rock, the kind which contains fossils," he explains, "can not be accurately dated by radioisotope methods. Such methods are only applicable to igneous rocks, like lava rocks and granite." Instead, he studies only the *fossil's* shape and characteristics, not the rock. "By dating the fossil, the rock can be dated," he declares.

For purposes of this discussion, let's say your fossil is a clam. Many species of clams live today, of course, and this one looks little different from those you have seen. The professor informs you that many different clams have lived in the past, the ancestors of modern clams, but most have now become extinct.

Next, the professor removes a large book from his shelf entitled *Invertebrate Paleontology*, and opens to the chapter on clams. Sketches of many clams are shown. At first glance many seem similar, but when you look closely, they're all slightly different. Your clam is compared to each one, until finally a clam nearly identical to yours appears. The caption under the sketch identifies your clam as an *index fossil*, and explains that this type of clam evolved some 320 million years ago.

With a look of satisfaction and an air of certainty, the professor explains, "Your rock is approximately 320 million years old!"

Notice that the rock itself was not examined. It was dated by the fossils in it, and the fossil type was dated by the assumption of evolutionary progression over time. The limestone rock itself might be essentially identical to limestones of any age, so the rock can't be used to date the rock. The fossils date the rock, and evolution dates the fossils.

You get to thinking. You know that limestones frequently contain fossils, but some seem to be a fine-grained matrix with no visible fossils. In many limestones the fossils seem to be ground to pieces, and other sedimentary rocks, like sandstone and shale, might contain no visible fossils at all. "What do you do then?" you ask.

The professor responds with a brief lecture on stratigraphy, information on how geologic layers are found, one on top of the other, with the "oldest" ones (i.e., containing the oldest fossils) beneath the "younger" ones. This makes sense, for obviously the bottom layer had to be deposited before the upper layers, "But how are the *dates* obtained?" "By the fossils they contain!" he says.

It turns out that many sedimentary rocks can't be dated all by themselves. If they have no fossils which can be dated within the evolutionary framework, then "We must look for other fossil-bearing layers, above and below, which can help us sandwich in on a date," the prof says. Such layers may not even be in the same location, but by tracing the layer laterally, perhaps for great distances, some help can be found.

"Fortunately, your rock had a good fossil in it, an *index* fossil, defined as an organism which lived at only one time in evolutionary history. It's not that it looks substantially more or less advanced than other clams, but it has a distinctive feature somewhat different from other clams. When we see *that* kind of clam, we know that the rock in which it is found is about 320 million years old, since *that* kind of clam lived 320 million years ago," he says. "Most fossils are *not* index fossils. Many organisms, including many kinds of clams, snails, insects, even single-celled organisms, didn't change at all over hundreds of millions of years, and are found in *many* different layers. Since they didn't live at any one particular time, we can't use *them* to date the rocks. Only *index* fossils are useful, since they are only found in one zone of rock, indicating they lived during a relatively brief period of geologic history. We know that because we only find them in one time period. Whenever we find them, we date the rock as of that age."

Let me pause in our story to identify this thinking process as circular reasoning. It obviously should have no place in science.

Instead of proceeding from observation to conclusion, the conclusion interprets the observation, which "proves" the conclusion. The fossils should contain the main evidence for evolution. But instead, we see that the ages of rocks are determined by the stage of evolution of the index fossils found therein, which are themselves dated and organized by the age of the rocks. Thus the rocks date the fossils, and the fossils date the rocks.

Back to our story. On another occasion, you find a piece of hardened lava, the kind extruded during a volcanic eruption as red hot, liquid lava. Obviously, it contains no fossils, since almost any living thing would have been incinerated or severely altered. You want to know the age of this rock too. But your professor friend in the geology department directs you to the geophysics department. "They can date this rock," you are told.

Your rock fascinates the geophysics professor. He explains that this is the kind of rock that can be dated by using *radioisotope dating techniques*, based on precise measurements of the ratios of radioactive isotopes in the rock. Once known, these ratios can be plugged into a set of mathematical equations which will give the *absolute* age of the rock.

Unfortunately, the tests take time. The rock must be ground into powder, then certain minerals isolated. Then the rock powder must be sent to a laboratory where they determine the ratios and report back. A computer will then be asked to analyze the ratios, solve the equations, and give the age.

The geophysicist informs you that these tests are very expensive, but that since your rock is so interesting, and since he has a government grant to pay the bill, and a graduate student to do the work, it will cost you nothing. Furthermore, he will request that several different tests be performed on your rock. There's the *uranium-lead* method, the *potassium-argon* method, *rubidium-strontium*, and a few others. They can be done on the whole rock or individual minerals within the rock. They can be analyzed by the *model* or the *isochron* techniques. All on the same rock. "We're sure to get good results that way," you are told. The results will come back with the rock's *absolute* age, plus or minus a figure for experimental error.

After several weeks the professor calls you in and shows you the results. Finally you'll know the true age of your rock. Unfortunately, the results of the different tests don't agree. Each method produced a different age! "How can that happen on a single rock?" you ask.

The uranium-lead method gave 500 ± 20 million years for the rock's age.

The potassium-argon method gave 100 ± 2 million years

The rubidium-strontium model test gave 325 ± 25 million years

The rubidium-strontium isochron test gave 375 ± 35 million years.

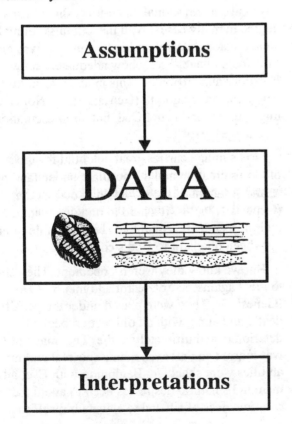

Then comes the all-important question. "Where did you find this rock? Were there any fossils nearby, above or below the outcrop containing this lava rock?" When you report that it was just below the limestone layer containing your 320 million year old fossil, it all becomes clear. "The rubidium-strontium dates are correct; they prove your rock is somewhere between 325 and 375 million years old. The other tests were inaccurate. There must have been some leaching or contamination." Once again, the fossils date the rocks, and the fossils are dated by evolution.

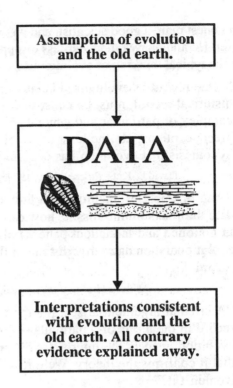

Our little story may be fictional, but it is not at all far-fetched. This is the way it's usually done. An interpretation scheme has already been accepted as truth. Each dating result must be evaluated—accepted or rejected—by the assumption of evolution. And the whole dating process proceeds within the backdrop of the old-earth scenario. No evidence contrary to the accepted framework is allowed to remain. Evolution stands, old-earth ideas stand, no matter what the true evidence reveals. An individual fact is accepted or rejected as valid evidence according to its fit with evolution.

Let me illustrate this dilemma with a few quotes from evolutionists. The first is by paleontologist Dr. David Kitts, a valued acquaintance of mine when we were both on the faculty at the University of Oklahoma. While a committed evolutionist, Dr. Kitts is an honest man, a good scientist, and an excellent thinker. He and many others express disapproval with the typical thinking of evolutionists.

"...the record of evolution, like any other historical record, must be construed within a complex of particular and general preconceptions, not the least of which is the hypothesis that evolution has occurred."

David B. Kitts, *Paleobiology*, 1979, pp. 353, 354.

"And this poses something of a problem: If we date the rocks by the fossils, how can we then turn around and talk about patterns of evolutionary change through time in the fossil record?"

Niles Eldridge, *Time Frames*, 1985, p. 52.

"A circular argument arises: Interpret the fossil record in the terms of a particular theory of evolution, inspect the interpretation, and note that it confirms the theory. Well, it would, wouldn't it?"

Tom Kemp, "A Fresh Look at the Fossil Record," *New Scientist*, Vol. 108, Dec. 5, 1985, p. 67.

In God's Image

Is circular reasoning the best science has to offer? Are better decisions possible? Are scientists doomed forever to run in this circle? Is the human mind capable of more?

The Bible reveals that hope exists. In fact, even "the invisible things of Him from the creation of the world are *clearly seen*, being understood by the things that are made, even His eternal power and Godhead, so that they are without excuse (Romans 1:20). Thus, by studying the creation—the things that are made—we ought to be able to accurately determine certain things, especially the fact that things were made by something or Someone separate from the creation, an entity that was *not* made in the same fashion as everything else. The character of the creation reveals the character of its Maker.

Surely this means that the natural man, using his or her own senses and reasoning ability, is capable of correct observations and interpretations, perhaps within certain limits, but indeed an observer is "without excuse" in concluding that the creation has no maker, or that the maker is part of the creation. At least some understanding of the character of the creator, "even His eternal power and Godhead,"

should result. But the tenor of the passage indicates that people don't always come to the right conclusion, a truth obvious from our own experience. What is wrong? What has happened?

The Bible teaches that humankind is created "in the image of God" (Genesis 1:27). Man is not God, nor is man omnipotent, omniscient, or omnipresent, but being God's image brings certain abilities and characteristics. What does God's image entail?

The image of God does not refer to God's physical body. On occasion, God took on human flesh in order to reveal Himself to man, especially when Jesus Christ "took upon Him the form of a servant, and was made in the likeness of man" (Philippians 2:7), but also at times in the Old Testament (Genesis 18, 24, etc.). On other occasions, Scripture talks of His arm or face or hand in communicating God's attributes or actions, discussing them in terms understandable by humans, but not implying that God has a physical body, for "God is a Spirit" (John 4:24).

Rather, the "image of God" refers chiefly to the fact that man possesses personal, rational, and moral qualities and has a God-consciousness, making him totally distinct from the animals. Much of man's physical and emotional make-up is shared (to a lesser degree in many cases) with the animals. Animals were created "after their kind," but man was created "in God's image," somehow adequately reflecting His glory and attributes. This image was in the beginning "very good" (Genesis 1:31). Notice that man was not and is not God, but a representation of His image.

God's image carries great potential for the study of God's creation and the accurate understanding of it, and Adam and Eve were told to do just that (Genesis 1:26,28). It's hard to imagine what they and their descendants would have been capable of had they been obedient to God's command.

But we know they weren't obedient. They chose to rebel against their Creator and incurred His wrath (Genesis 3). They were placed under the penalty of death, and along with all of creation began to deteriorate and ultimately to die. The image of God was marred so that even man's spiritual and rational abilities were shackled. Beginning with Eve, all of mankind's natural desire has been to avoid the consequences of sin and to elevate himself to a position of power, refusing to acknowledge God as Creator. Little wonder that today Adam's descendants so often conclude falsehood. "Because, when they knew God, they glorified Him not as God, neither were thankful, but became vain in their imaginations, and their foolish heart was darkened. Professing themselves to be wise, they became fools" (Romans 1:21,22). "The fool hath said in his heart, there is no God" (Psalm 14:1), for "the god of this world hath blinded the minds of them which believe not" (II Corinthians 4:4). They walk "in the vanity of their mind, having the understanding darkened, being alienated from the life of God through the ignorance that is in them, because of the blindness of their heart" (Ephesians 4:18).

This incomplete reasoning ability and lack of a complete desire for truth, coupled with lack of access to or unwillingness to discover and discern all the relevant data, as well as imperfect logical tools, leads to "science falsely so called" (I Timothy 6:20).

In principle, the marred image of God is capable of discovering truth, but in practice man seldom, if ever, accomplishes this in an ultimate sense. God exists, creation occurred, but can we truly understand it as it needs to be understood? Dim approximations are about the best we usually achieve.

A good rule of thumb to follow perhaps is to separate valid observations from interpretations of those observations, especially if the interpretation process involves an anti-God component.

Man, in the image of God, can make valid observations, although necessarily incomplete in most cases. A scientist can measure the precise abundance of elements in a rock, and can discern its stratigraphic position among other rock strata. The scientist can describe and catalog the fossils present and compare them to other fossils. But since the deposition and timing of the rocks and fossils weren't observed, interpreting the ages and origins is much more difficult, if possible at all, and many times interpreters resort to circular reasoning.

Is There an Alternative?

How should a creationist react to circular reasoning? In fact, how should a scientist of any persuasion react to circular reasoning? Obviously,

with skepticism and even rejection, as did the three evolutionists just quoted. Circular reasoning has no place in science. We *can* do better.

The key is understanding our assumptions held at the start. Is the assumption of evolution necessary to do science? Despite the pronouncements of some modern-day evolutionists, obviously not! Are other assumptions possible? Yes! Can good science be done without an exclusive commitment to naturalism? Certainly! How can we determine which assumption set is correct?

Before discussing this, let me clarify something that too few people recognize, and evolutionists seldom admit. Science operates in the *present*, and in a very real sense is limited to the present. Scientific theories must involve, among other things, the *observation* of data and process which exist in the present. But who has ever seen the long-ago *past*? Rocks and fossils exist in the *present*. We collect them, catalog them, study them, perform experiments on them—all in the present! The scientific method is an enterprise of the *present*.[1]

Theories must also be *testable* and potentially *falsifiable*, (i.e., there must be some conceivable test which could prove them wrong). But who could disprove an idea about the past? What test could be run to conclude that evolution (or creation) is impossible?

Another requirement for good science is *reproducibility*. This means that observations made today of a particular event or object will be the same as observations of an equivalent event or object tomorrow. Similar events will yield similar results and similar observations.

Events which occurred only once might have been observed, and their results studied, but they can't be repeated. But some events, which occurred only once (such as the origin of the earth), may not have been observed at all. When scientists have only the *results* of an event or its after-effects to study, a full reconstruction of the one-time event (sometimes called a singularity) is lacking.

Let me explain further this difficult concept. I am not trying to discredit science; I'm only trying to show its limitations. For example, geology is science.

1 Of course, observations and records dating from within human history are usable, to the extent that the observers are deemed reliable.

Studying the nature of existing rocks and fossils and the processes which produce or alter them—that's science. Predictions of the future of the rock are another matter. Likewise, historical geology—the reconstruction of the unobserved past of rocks and fossils—that's also another story. The same difficulty exists in biology, ecology, astronomy, archaeology, etc.

Note that evolution, if it ever occurred, did so in the unobserved *past,* and each supposed stage only occurred *once*. No one ever saw the origin of life from non-living chemicals. No one has ever seen any type of organism give rise to a completely different type (macro-evolution). No one has ever even *claimed* to have seen meaningful evolutionary changes take place. The minor variations (micro-evolution) in plant and animal groups (e.g., DDT resistance in insects, shift in dominant color of peppered moths, etc.) which do occur in the present are not evolutionary changes. In fact, since creation allows for adaptation and variation *within* created kinds, small changes are perfectly compatible with creation theory as well, and certainly not the proof of evolution. Major changes (macro-evolution) have *never* been scientifically observed, and thus the theory of evolutionary descent from a common ancestor has not been and could never be proven scientifically. How could you ever run a test to see if it happened in the past? Or how could you ever prove that it didn't happen in the past? Evolution is a belief system some scientists hold about the past, and they use this view of *history* to interpret the evidence in the present.

Likewise, creation, if it ever occurred, did so in the unobserved past. It is not going on today. No human observer has ever seen creation take place. Thus, creation has not been, nor could it ever be, scientifically proven. It, too, is a belief some scientists have about the past.

Note: Appealing to Scriptural authority for proof, while appropriate for Bible-believing Christians, does not constitute *scientific* proof, in a modern sense, which requires observation and repeatability. But face it, if Scripture is truly God's Word, and since He is reliable, then we *can* have confidence in it.

By the way, how do we come to the notion that Scripture is authoritative and its Author reliable?

Many books have been written on this subject, each one taking a slightly different approach, and I don't pretend to have the final word. For our purposes, suffice it to say that our confidence in Scripture does not spring from nowhere, nor is it a blind leap of faith. We all live in a real world, and deal with realities not always falling into any neat philosophical framework. We can and do observe which ideas make sense to us—which ones seem to work. If an idea repeatedly fails, or lacks common sense, we reject it.

Scripture makes many statements which are testable and potentially falsifiable. And each time we investigate, we find it to be true, or at least possibly true if we had all the data and complete reasoning skills. Even though many detractors have claimed otherwise, never has a charge against Scripture stood up under close and objective scrutiny. We see Scriptural teachings work in medicine and economics and science and history. We see prophecies come true long after they were made. We see societies and families thrive if guided by Biblical principles, as do legal, governmental, and educational institutions. Scriptural values such as love, honesty, and truthfulness witness in our spirits that they are correct.

In short, Scripture works! We see it provide useful results and good fruits in every realm. Other systems and teachings don't work nearly as well. This does not prove Scripture—we must still believe it by faith. And we must always be willing to fine-tune our interpretation of it as our understanding grows, but we have every reason to accept it as God's true and authoritative Word. So, while we can't scientifically *prove* Scripture, it is, at least, valid for us to hold the faith position that Scripture is true, and applicable in all areas. And since Scripture speaks of a recent creation, it provides us with a basic scientific model which can guide our research and understanding, a model which warrants consideration in the market place of ideas. But, because it involves one-time events in the past unobserved by humans, Creation cannot be scientifically proven.

Thus, both evolution and creation are outside the realm of empirical science, inaccessible to the scientific method. Neither is observable or repeatable. They are in the category of singularities, one-time events. It is not illegitimate for a scientist, who exists in the present, and conducts his or her science in the present, to wonder, "What happened in the unobserved past to make the present, which is observed, get to be this way?" Scientists can then try to reconstruct history in the most logical way possible, but no historical reconstruction can be proven (or disproven). Any view of origins must be held ultimately by faith.

Having said that, let me also say that as a scientist I am totally convinced that the creation view of history is correct. I'm a Christian, a child of God, a fact which I know to be true beyond a shadow of a doubt, but which likewise I can't prove scientifically. I know the Creator personally and trust His account of past events. After all, He was there, and in fact He was doing it all! His record, the Bible, doesn't give me all the scientific details, but it does provide the general framework which guides my own scientific study. I'm convinced it's an accurate record of real events.

A Christian's Resource

All other factors being equal, a Christian, reasoning from a Scriptural position, has greater potential for understanding these things than the non-Christian, who starts the process with a non-Biblical (i.e., false) worldview. This is due to the fact that the Christian has input from a source not available to the non-Christian—the Holy Spirit. Jesus taught that when "The Spirit of truth is come, He will guide you unto all truth . . . He shall glorify Me" (John 16:13).

The presence of the Spirit does not guarantee a right conclusion, for even a Christian is subject to practical limitations. Even Christians still live in a sin-dominated world, and bear the *marred* image of God. Getting saved doesn't change that. Furthermore, we all live in a society which brainwashes its citizens with a secular viewpoint, and we experience difficulty in ridding our minds of ingrained error. And how about personal sin? While we can be forgiven and victory gained over wrong habits, sin still clouds our thinking processes and inhibits the Holy Spirit from complete control.

But a Christian can start from the right perspective, and many times he receives enlightenment from the Spirit in varying degrees. Through the work of the Spirit, the recognition of truth can be realized by inner conviction and

Spirit-directed thinking processes. We must always be willing to grow in understanding and change our opinion as more information comes in and our maturity in Christ deepens, but Christians at least have greater potential to arrive at truth than the non-Christian.

By adopting the view of ancient history given in Scripture, a Christian is then able to study the *results* of Creation, the plant and animal types that were created. We can study the *results* of the Flood of Noah's day, which certainly laid down the majority of the earth's sedimentary rocks which contain fossils. Although we did not witness the Creation or the Flood, we are convinced they really happened in history, and can attempt to interpret the *present* evidence, the results of *past* events, within a true historical framework. In this way, we can fill in the gaps in our knowledge, more fully understand the past, and make sense of the present.

On the other hand, if the Bible is correct, and the Creation, the Curse, the Flood, the Dispersion at Babel really happened, what occurs when someone assumes an evolutionary history instead? Obviously, if one *denies* true history, and accepts a false view by assumption, any attempt to reconstruct history is doomed to failure. It will not only be wrong, it will be inferior to a reconstruction based on *real* events, and it will neither be internally consistent nor scientifically satisfying. The data won't fit very well, but it cannot be absolutely disproved. There will always be a story which can be told about the evidence.

Keep in mind that facts are facts, evidence is evidence. All too often, Christians who believe in creation only by faith are afraid to look at the facts. Many are afraid they might find something which will contradict their faith, so they choose not to look.

But we should never be concerned that facts, which exist in the present, will be incompatible with our assumptions about the past. Facts are like rocks, they don't talk, they must be interpreted by one's assumptions. When I was in graduate school, the professors frequently admitted, "There is no such thing as a value-free fact." Especially when it comes to unobserved history. Facts must be interpreted: they must be placed within an existing world view before they have much meaning at all. A Christian must try to discover *God's* interpretation of the facts. We must also be willing to fine tune our presuppositions as our understanding grows in both science and Scripture. Truth does exist, and we must strive, with God's help, to overcome our limitations and discern it with diligent study.

To make matters worse, raw facts or data relating to the unobserved past can usually be interpreted in more than one way, within more than one world view, although both interpretations can't be true. Like the fossil mentioned at the start of this chapter. That fossil clam *can be* interpreted by an evolutionary historical reconstruction as a clam type that supposedly evolved from other animal types and ultimately single-celled organisms. In this view, it lived 320 million years ago, and its descendants either became extinct or they descended into modern clams.

Or, it can be interpreted by the creation historical reconstruction, as an animal deposited in sedimentary material during Noah's Flood, but which was a descendant of the original clams in the clam "kind" created on day five of Creation Week. Other clams survived the Flood, and their descendants survive to this day.

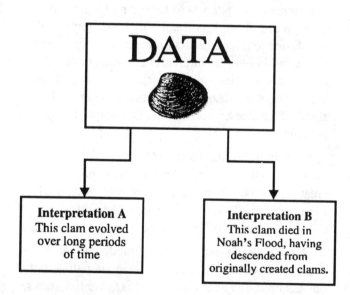

In this scheme, the Christian/creationist accepts by faith God's record of creation. Contrary to what some might think, the scientific research that stems from a creation view is anything but trivial and sterile. The details of the view are yet to be fully worked out, and much is to be learned. But, if the events in Scripture really happened, we have a chance to reconstruct the specifics of a particular

fossil deposit correctly, while those who deny history have no chance at all. They are forever doomed to tell and retell an inferior reconstruction that offends our logic and makes a farce of the present.

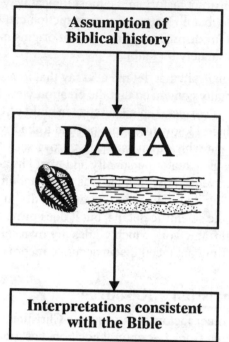

The Christian should stand in submission to Scripture in every area of life, including science and reconstructions of the past. We must interpret scientific data within the framework given there.

Can the Matter Be Resolved?

Since neither view of history can be scientifically proved or disproved, what hope is there? Will the creation/evolution debate go on forever, or can it be resolved? Can it even be resolved in the mind of a particular individual?

Recently, I was lecturing at a seminar when a representative of the local atheist group showed up. He had brought a young man, a university graduate student. They sat in the front row, right below where I stood, and whispered and gestured at my comments, calling attention to themselves and their disgust. (I suppose they hoped to discredit me and my statements, but they were so obnoxious that many, who may not have been on my side to start with, wanted nothing to do with *their* position, whatever it was. Intending to thwart my effectiveness, they were actually a big help.)

As the lecture ended, many people gathered around to ask questions. The two atheists shoved their way to the front, and the younger man fired one question after another. He appeared to have been coached by the older. I tried to be polite, but each time he saw I had an answer for his last question, he interrupted and asked another. Finally, I challenged him (i.e., them) to give me his hardest question and then listen while I answered, if I could.

The older man, himself a professor with a long history of "fighting creationism" as he put it, inadvertently got to the crux of the matter. He said he didn't like creationism because it disagreed with all the "great" scientists of our day, Stephen Gould, Carl Sagan, Isaac Asimov, etc. My view was different from theirs; therefore, I must be wrong.

But his main point was that my view mixed science and religion, and we all know that only naturalistic (read atheistic) evolution is science, but creation is religion.

Evidently he had not been listening to my lecture. Over and over again, I had insisted that my interpretations were not held by the majority of university scientists, and that I had specifically been giving another interpretation. I had pointed out that I didn't disagree with scientific data, just the religious opinions (i.e., naturalistic opinions) of some scientists about those data and their reconstructions of unobserved history. I had specifically pointed out that the modern "definition" of science is improper, self-serving, and harmful. Furthermore, I had shown many data censored by my evolutionary colleagues, facts which do not fit an evolutionary view very well at all and which were therefore usually ignored. But I had not disagreed with the *facts*!

The place we differed was in the *interpretation* process. I had started from a different assumption set, performed good scientific research on the data, and derived an interpretation consistent with my world view. In my lecture, I had *insisted* that my presuppositions were different from those of many scientists. But, when I asked him to find fault with my interpretations given my assumptions, he got strangely silent. The only thing he would say was to repeat the oft-repeated charge that science has no room for the supernatural, and that I couldn't be a scientist if I believed in God.

He was unwilling to consider my assumptions as possibly legitimate, but admitted he couldn't fault my science or my interpretations. Strangely enough, the young man didn't return for the rest of the seminar, but the older man sat through it all without another outburst.

Until a person is willing to talk on an assumption or presuppositional level, there can be little movement on this issue. The facts are roughly compatible with both models of history. Good science can be done by both groups, and the resulting interpretations can be consistent within each model, although quite different from each other.

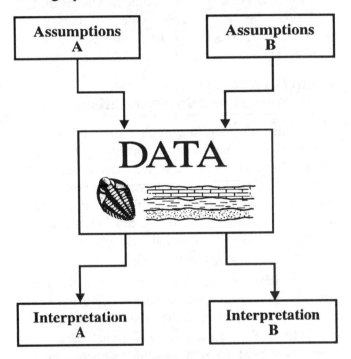

This schematic drawing illustrates the point well. It actually works for many situations, even in the present. This is how you get political liberals and conservatives for example.[2]

Where Are You Coming From?

As we've seen, the Christian's assumption set should come from a careful and honest interpretation of Scripture, guided by the Holy Spirit, and in submission to its teachings. The evolutionist's assumption set comes primarily from an unnecessarily high assessment of the ability of scientists to discern truth. Finite men, with access to

2 I am indebted to my friend Dr. Donald Chittick for helping firm up my thinking in this area. This schematic is adapted from his excellent book *The Controversy* (Multnomah Press, 1984).

only a portion of the total data, with fallible logical tools, and who weren't present to make the necessary observations, can hardly expect to fully understand the past. Humankind, created in the image of God, can do many things, but there are limitations.

I have found that most evolutionists believe in evolution simply because that's the only concept they've ever been taught. Their mentors, from high school on up, have drilled into them the false notion that only "ignorant fundamentalists"— "flat-earthers"—believe in creation. So they reject it without investigation. They've never heard a credible case for creation, and so they perpetrate the lie that evolution is the only legitimate view. This fallacy is furthered by the redefinition of science as *naturalism*, which denies the possibility of creation.

Comets:
Assumptions and Interpretations

Consider this interesting application of the two models. We observe comets in our solar system in an elliptical orbit around the sun. We observe that on each swing around the sun, a comet loses some of its mass. By measuring the mass of the comets and the amount of loss over time, we can conclude that many comets (especially those which make frequent passes) are not extremely old.

Young-earth advocates have interpreted this to imply a young solar system. If the solar system were many millions of years old, the short-period comets would have all ceased to exist. But since those comets still exist, the solar system must be young. Seems simple enough.

But those who insist on an old solar system hold that position in spite of the evidence from comets. They acknowledge that the present comets must be young, but are convinced the solar system is old. They propose a hypothetical storehouse of comets in the outer reaches of the solar system, too far out to see with telescopes or to measure with any sensing device. They call this hypothetical (read imaginary) cloud of comets the Oort Cloud, after the one who first proposed it. Oort claimed that inter-stellar events occasionally dislodge a piece of material from this otherwise stable cloud, propelling it into a near solar orbit, furnishing our solar system with an inexhaustible supply of comets.

Did you follow the logic? Assumption: The solar system is old. Observation: Comets live for only a short time. Conclusion: Youthful comets are continually coming in from a far-away unseen source.

When young solar-system advocates bring up the age of comets, old solar-system advocates say, "Oh, we've solved that. Comets are replenished from the Oort Cloud." Thus the observations play second-fiddle to the assumptions. Without getting a person to question the assumption, you'll seldom get him to question the imaginary Oort Cloud.

Resolution becomes even more difficult when dealing with proposed one-time events of the long-ago past, events outside the realm of scientific observation.

Note: Observations made by careful observers in the past, such as Newton and Pasteur for example, are legitimate. One must always discern the difference between scientific data and interpretations of those data, and the observed past and unobserved, inferred past. By the way, many of the founding fathers of science, including the two "giants" mentioned above, were Bible-believing Christians and creationists, and did their study from a Scriptural world-view. I recommend *Men of Science: Men of God*, by Henry M. Morris, 1982, for brief biographies of many such scientists.

Unfortunately, evolutionists seldom even admit they have presuppositions. They present their view of history and their interpretations as if they were observed facts. Students and laymen alike are either snowed by "professionals" or intimidated into acceptance of a world view with its philosophical and religious implications without even knowing what has happened. Most people believe in evolution because most people believe in evolution. That's all they've ever been taught. If creation is even mentioned, it's ridiculed and unfairly caricatured. Thus, evolution is assumed, not proved, and creation is denied, not refuted.

Nevertheless, comparison, evaluation, and rational discussion *are* possible if both parties recognize their assumptions and their own interpretation process. You won't get very far with someone who won't even admit he has presuppositions. But, let's look at how we can and should proceed.

Predicting the Evidence

Having completed the formal statement of each model, "predictions" can be made. These are not predictions of the future, but, instead, predictions about the data. In effect, each adherent must say, "If my assumptions are correct, I predict that when we look at the data, we will see certain features." The model which better "predicts" the evidence is the one more likely correct. But, neither can be ultimately proved or disproved.

We evaluate the predictions by looking for internal inconsistencies. Does the model shoot itself in the foot? Does the model need secondary modifications in order to be consistent? Furthermore, does it fit all the data? Are there facts which just don't seem to fit at all? Finally, on a more basic and intuitive level, does the model in question work where the rubber meets the road? Does it make good common sense, or does it require imaginary components? Can I live with its implications? Does it satisfy my personal need for purpose and hope? Does it lead to a suitable and pragmatic philosophy of life? This process of evaluation allows us to select an appropriate model, one that works in science and in life.

I make three claims for the creation model. I don't claim it is *scientifically* proven, but I do claim that (1) it handles the data in an internally consistent fashion; it does not contradict itself; (2) it does so in a way clearly superior to the evolution model; and (3) it forms the basis of a life which satisfies and works.

> ### Predictions of the
> # Evolution Model
>
> 1. Transitional forms
> 2. Beneficial mutations
> 3. Things getting better
> 4. New species

Marxist Assumptions

In 1990, I had the distinct privilege of journeying to Moscow on a lecture tour, speaking on university campuses and at scientific research institutes. I was

there just before communism was displaced. Change was in the wind.

> ### Predictions of the
> # Creation Model
>
> 1. Separate, distinct kinds
> 2. Intelligent design in nature
> 3. Tendency for decay
> 4. Extinction of species

One lecture was given to several hundred biology faculty and students at the University of Moscow. I had come to suspect that Russian students had one interesting advantage over American students. Whereas in America, students are all too often expected to memorize what the professor has taught and then to give it back on a test, Russian students tend to think presuppositionally. (Perhaps Russian students have grown up reading Tolstoy and playing chess, while American students read comic books and play video games—after they have memorized their lessons.) Russians of that time openly admited their atheism and their naturalistic view of science, while many American students and professors hold naturalism by default, without knowing it. Thus, to a greater degree than in America, Russians seem to be prone to think presuppositionally, and to be less intimidated when confronted with another model.

However, at that time Russians were totally steeped in evolutionary thinking. Communism rests unalterably on atheism, and that's all this present generation had heard until the communist government collapsed. Evolution provided the communistic world view with an air of scientific credibility.

Parenthetically, I remember one of my graduate students at the University of Oklahoma, who, as a young man growing up in Iran under the Shah's regime, had turned to communism. A leader in the Student Communist Party, he was taken to Moscow for a year's saturation in communist thought. Do you know what they taught him? Not Marx. Not Lenin. For the whole year they just filled him with evolution! Evolution is a necessary foundation for Marxism. Evolution is true, and all things come from natural processes (materialism is the Marxist word for this). Evolutionary process through time is inevitable, and Marxism is claimed to be the most highly evolved social and political system.

Before going on, let me tell you something else about the Russian people. They tend to be very quiet, almost stoic in lecture settings, but certainly respectful of authority figures (such as a guest professor). I suspect for 70 years they hadn't been allowed to show much emotion. The result was that I had little audience response during my lecture.

At any rate, my talk was focused on the presuppositional nature of science and the legitimacy of the creationist presupposition set and the scientific logic of its resulting interpretations. I used the schematic drawing of Assumptions A and B yielding Interpretations A and B respectively, and got little response, although I could see they were listening intently.

Until, that is, I showed them a revised schematic, with only one assumption set and only one interpretation. I pointed out that this was the way it was in Russia, this was how they were being taught. Remarkably, there were heads nodding all over the room. They recognized it!

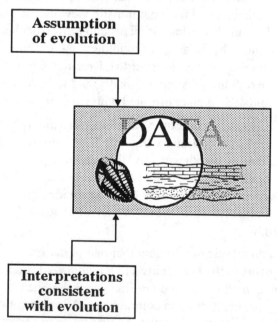

Assumption of evolution

Interpretations consistent with evolution

Encouraged by this response, I claimed, through the interpreter, "This is not education; this is brainwashing!" Together they burst into a nervous laughter of recognition. Warming to the occasion, I said "This is adherence to the party line!" I thought they

never would quit laughing and talking among themselves. They recognized their education and themselves in that chart, and didn't like what they saw. From then on, students and faculty alike listened intently to the presentation of a creationist worldview consistent with itself and the real world. Reporters thronged me as soon as I was through, and a story and even my itinerary for the rest of the tour was carried in *Pravda*, the first time such a thing had ever been done.

Incidentally, my tour was partially sponsored by the Moscow chapter of the Gideons. They had just received a shipment of Bibles—the Book students had been warned about, but had never seen.

As my lecture ended, having presented only logical and scientific information which pointed toward creation, the students had thought it through. "With this evidence for creation, there must be a God. Who is this God? How can I know Him?" many called. They rushed the platform with questions, nearly all of a spiritual nature. And the Gideons were there, opening boxes of Bibles and passing them out. The liberating light of creation has great power, even in the midst of darkness.

Conversely, evolutionary ideas have brought much sorrow. Without question, Marxism is founded on evolution and naturalism. Marx considered Darwin's book, *Origin of Species*, to give his view of evolution in the social realm scientific credibility. He offered to dedicate his book, *Das Kapital*, to Darwin. In the name of evolution, unthinkable evils have been perpetrated, especially in Marxist and totalitarian countries. Even many of our Western social ills are the result of a society which has adopted evolution, rejecting the Creator's authority over their lives and actions. "Ideas have consequences," as they say, even ideas about the past.

Even more remarkably, in 1993 I had occasion to speak to a packed crowd of 2700 government bureaucrats, university students, and Communist Party officials in Beijing, China. Believe it or not, the government had requested Christian professionals to come and address the possible benefits of Christianity to China. I had helped organize the conference, identify the lecture topics, and select the speakers. I was scheduled to discuss the benefits to science of a creationist worldview.

Throughout the months of preparation, the government canceled many of the presentations, including mine, on several occasions. But each time, mine was reinstated because of the primary role I was playing in conference preparations. They were quite concerned about my talk but were reluctant to lose face by canceling it. Finally, the night before the conference, it was canceled again. The communist organizers deemed my talk a frontal assault on their worldview, and rightly so.

But, in final negotiations, since I was already listed in the printed programs, they offered to let me speak if I refrained from mentioning creation, evolution, Christianity, or the Bible. They approved me to lecture if I agreed to speak only about my own personal geologic field research. Since all the other talks of substance had been totally canceled, and this was the only opportunity to present anything, I agreed. I presented a slide lecture on the 1980 eruption of Mount St. Helens, and its implications in interpretations of unobserved geologic events of the past. Some of these startling evidences are discussed later in this volume.

My presentation, however, included a little more than just interpretations of the past. I showed how my *American* education, at all levels up through my Ph.D. program had been incomplete. Much information, such as we had discovered at Mount St. Helens had been *censored* out of my education, indeed, out of all geologic education. These new "catastrophic" ideas were proving quite helpful in geology. Censorship of information and ways of thinking from students produces harmful effects, both to the student and to the country involved in such brainwashing.

The Communist Party dignitaries on the front row knew what I was saying and who I was talking to. They appeared furious, a fact which was later related to me in no uncertain terms. On the other hand, the students were delighted. They were hearing things that had been kept from them. And the scientists—as soon as the lecture was over, I was surrounded by several, including the director of the Academy of Science, and questioned at length over these new ideas, (which they themselves had never heard). They unofficially invited me back to speak at universities and even join them on a field trip to Tibet to see if catastrophism would help in locating oil and minerals. The only ones who approve of censorship and brainwashing are those who have a worldview to protect—in this case an atheistic worldview based on evolution.

We must get away from thinking of evolution as a science. It's a philosophical world-view about the past, loaded with religious implications, which historically and presently exists in a frantic attempt to explain the fact that we are here without a Creator/God. It results in bad science, a denial of true history, and much misery to people and nations who have adopted it.

May God grant *this* nation a return to light and logic before it is too late.

Forced to Make a Choice

Chapter 2

What Does the Bible Say?

Many Christians would readily agree that large-scale evolution has not occurred, especially as it applies to the origin of mankind, but also for the basic plant and animal types. Those who have carefully thought about it with an open mind can easily see that the fossil record gives no support to the concept of descent of all life from a common ancestor. Likewise, the trend of change is not toward innovation and introduction of more complexity in living things, but rather toward deterioration and extinction. It is inconceivable to most Christians that the incredible design and order that we see in the universe, especially in plants and animals, could have come about by mere natural processes, mindless and random.

Furthermore, evolution is essentially the atheistic explanation for origins, doing away with the need for God. From Darwin to the present day, evolutionists use it to explain how we got here without a Creator, and, therefore, to justify a lifestyle without accountability to God. To those who don't hold an atheistic worldview, the exclusion of God from any involvement in earth history is unreasonable. Thus, most committed Christians tend to shy away from embracing naturalistic evolution too tightly. And, of course, Christians of all persuasions believe in Scripture (albeit in many varying degrees), and Scripture clearly presents God as Creator.

> A man who has no assured and ever present belief in the existence of a personal God or of a future existence with retribution and reward, can have for his rule of life, as far as I can see, only to follow those impulses and instincts which are the strongest or which seem to him the best ones.
>
> *The Autobiography of Charles Darwin,* 1887, as republished by The Norton Library, p. 94.

But the age of the earth is a different matter. Somehow it has become acceptable for Bible-believing Christians to adopt the idea of a five billion year old earth. Many evangelical Christians would claim that God *has* created, using special creative processes (agreeing that God did not use "theistic evolution," a concept which relies on either totally natural processes or on very minor input by God). But they would also claim that He accomplished His work of creation over billions of years as supposedly recorded in the rock and fossil record. This position usually accepts as authoritative the results of radioisotope dating, and either ignores the Biblical genealogies and other passages which speak to the age question, or claims that they refer only to the relatively recent timing of the origin of true man (i.e., Adam, who they feel was the first living creature with an eternal spirit, unlike "pre-Adamic" hominids or supposed ape men).

But this leads to a host of theological problems, some of which are discussed in the pages to follow. For example, to the consistent old-earth "creationist," Neanderthal Man, who lived long ago according to evolution theory and radioisotope dating methods, was only a human-like animal, who talked, painted pictures, buried his dead, etc., but who had no eternal spirit, and was not related to modern man. Holding this and other unorthodox conclusions, many born-again Christians accept the old-earth view, usually because that's all they have ever been taught.

> This spirit-man into whom God breathed life (Genesis 2:7) would correspond to what scientists identify as modern man. In other words, modern man is distinct from all the other animals, including hominids that preceded him, in that he is a spirit-being....
>
> The Bible indicates, that the first spirit-man, Adam, was created about 15,000 years ago, give or take 10,000 years. Science gives a similar date for the appearance of modern man.
>
> Hugh Ross, Genesis One: A Scientific Perspective, p. 13.

The contention in this book is that the earth is only thousands of years old, not billions, just as a straight-forward reading of the Bible indicates, and that the rocks and fossils are fully compatible with the Biblical evidence. Furthermore, since all Scripture is inter-related, the age of the earth has important theological implications, as we shall see.

Two Views Very Different

The old-earth and the young-earth views are extremely different in their conclusions. They simply are not saying the same thing. Attempts to straddle the fence and accept them both will be unsatisfying—scientifically and Scripturally.

The Bible, if we allow it to speak for itself, tells of a creation period of six solar days, during which the entire universe was created in a "very good" state.

Note: The term "solar day" need some explaining. Strictly speaking, it refers to the time for one rotation of the earth on its axis, today approximately 24 hours, resulting in a day/night sequence. But according to Genesis 1, whereas light and the day/night cycle were created on day one, the sun wasn't created until day four, so there was no sun during the first three days. In Scripture, however, there is no differentiation between the length of the first three days and the last three, and the entire week is referred to as being "6 days" long, followed by a day of rest. For convenience, therefore, I use the term "solar day" to refer to a day quite similar to ours.

This creation soon came under the death sentence, due to the rebellion of Adam against God's authority. Later, the earth's surface was restructured by the world-wide Flood of Noah's day. I feel that the Bible does not give a precise date for creation (as clearly shown by the fact that nearly every scholar who has tried to calculate such a date from Scripture has arrived at a different number), but that it does give a "ball park" age for the earth of just a few thousand years. Even if one inserts every possible time gap in the genealogies and elsewhere (which is clearly not warranted), the time of the creation of Adam would be no longer ago than, say, 12,000 years (most likely, closer to 6,000 years). Beyond that, Scripture has been stretched to where it has little meaning.

How Much Time Elapsed Before Adam?

The length of time for the creation-week days has been demonstrated conclusively by many Bible-believing scholars to be only six solar days.[1] As has been pointed out, the Hebrew word *yom*, translated "day," *can* have a variety of meanings, and sometimes can mean an indefinite period of time. It occurs over 2000 times in the Old Testament, and it almost always certainly means a solar day, and always *could* mean a solar day. But, when uncertainty arises, the Bible must be used to interpret itself, most specifically the context of the word, other usages of the word, and other passages on the same subject. For the following several reasons, I am convinced that the context and the way in which the word "day" is used in Genesis 1 implies a literal solar day.

When the Hebrew word *yom* is modified by a number, such as "*six* days," or the "*third* day" (as it is some 359 times in the Old Testament outside of Genesis 1),[2] it *always* means a literal day. Furthermore, the words "evening and morning," which *always* mean a true daily evening and morning, define *yom* some thirty-eight times throughout the Old Testament outside of Genesis 1. There are several good words in Hebrew which mean "time," or an indefinite period, which the writer could have used, but *yom* was chosen, the *only* Hebrew word which can mean a solar day. Thus, in all cases, the use of the language implies a literal meaning for *yom*. Why would Genesis 1 be the exception? These facts, plus the general tenor of the passage, plus the summary verses in Genesis 2:1–4, will not allow any other meaning. Genesis 1:1–2:4 was obviously intended to give a chronology of events that really happened, just as written.

Perhaps the most definitive passage was written by God's own finger on a slab of rock so that we couldn't get it wrong. The fourth of the Ten Commandments regards resting on the Sabbath Day:

---

1 For an excellent discussion of this, see *The Genesis Record,* by Dr. Henry Morris, a scientist and careful Bible scholar. This well-received commentary on Genesis contains much insight into early earth history, both from the Bible and from science.

2 Along with many other scholars, Mr. Jim Stambaugh, theologian and ICR librarian, has done much original research on this. Some of his results, which although mentioned here, have not yet been fully published. But see his article in the ICR newsletter *Acts and Facts,* "The Meaning of 'Day' in Genesis," Impact Article No. 184. A free subscription to *Acts & Facts* can be obtained from ICR at P.O. Box 2667, El Cajon, CA 92021. Also see his series of articles in *Creation Ex Nihilo Technical Journal,* published by Creation Science Fellowship, especially Vol. 5, No. 1, 1991, pp. 70–78. It can be ordered from Creation Science Ministries at P.O. Box 6330, Florence, KY 41022.

Remember the sabbath day, to keep it holy. Six days shalt thou labor, and do all thy work: But the seventh day is the sabbath of the LORD thy God: in it thou shalt not do any work, thou, nor thy son, nor thy daughter, thy manservant, nor thy maidservant, nor thy cattle, nor thy stranger that is within thy gates: For in six days the LORD made heaven and earth, the sea, and all that in them is, and rested the seventh day: wherefore the LORD blessed the sabbath day, and hallowed it.

Exodus 20:8–11

In this passage, God instructs *us* to work six days and rest one day because *He* worked six days and rested one day—during which week He created the heavens, the earth, the sea, and all things in them. The word "remember" in Hebrew, when used as a command, as it is in verse 8, always refers back to a *real* historical event. And "for" in verse 11 is usually translated "because." It too refers back to a *real* historical event. Thus, the days of our *real* work week are equated in duration to the *real* days of creation. Same words, same modifier, same sentence, same slab of rock, same Finger which wrote them. If words mean anything, and if God can write clearly, then creation occurred in six solar days, just like our days.

Furthermore, when the plural form of *yom* is used, *yamim*, as it is over 700 times in the Old Testament, including Exodus 20:11, it *always* means a literal, solar day. How could God, the Author of Scripture, say it any more plainly? He did it all in six solar days!

The passage in Exodus also clears up another mystery. "If God is omnipotent, surely He is capable of creating the entire universe instantaneously. Why did He take six days?," some ask. The answer is, to provide a pattern for our work week. We are to work six days and rest one, just as He did. The seventh day rest is a commemoration of His perfect work of creation.

Old-Earth Creationists

Christian writers who attempt to accommodate long ages into Biblical history, recognize the obvious meaning of *yom* as a literal day, but claim that "science has proven the old earth and, therefore, Scripture must be interpreted to fit it." Consider the

---

3   Young, Davis A., *Christianity and the Age of the Earth*, 1982, p. 25.

How Long Is a Day?

- The word "day" (Hebrew *yom*) can have a variety of meanings.

    A solar day
    Daylight
    Indefinite period of time

- Occurring 2291 times in the Old Testament, it almost always means a literal day.

- When used in the plural form *yamim* (845 times), it always refers to a literal day.

- When modified by numeral or ordinal in historical narrative (359 times in the Old Testament outside of Genesis 1), it always means a literal day.

- When modified by "evening and/or morning" (38 times outside of Genesis 1) it always means a literal day.

- Context of Genesis 1 is a tight chronology.

- Forms basis for our work week of 6 literal days (Exodus 20:11).

- Proper interpretation is a solar day, not an indefinite time period.

testimony of old-earth advocate Dr. Davis Young, Christian geology professor at Calvin College.

It cannot be denied, in spite of frequent interpretations of Genesis 1 that departed from the rigidly literal, that the almost universal view of the Christian world until the eighteenth century was that the Earth was only a few thousand years old. Not until the development of modern scientific investigation of the Earth itself would this view be called into question within the church.[3]

Recognizing that the historic view of the church was "young-earth creation," Dr. Young has chosen not to hold it. He started out his career as a young earth creationist, "evolved" into an old-earth creationist, then a theistic evolutionist, and now teaches that since the old earth and evolution have been "proven" by science, Scripture must contain little factual scientific or historic content. He recommends we even stop trying to incorporate evolution into Scripture, and adopt "The Framework Hypothesis," wherein one simply allegorizes places in Scripture where it appears to present facts about the past. He now advocates gleaning only "spiritual" implications from Genesis, not historic or scientific implications.

In a summary statement of his position,[4] Dr. Young gives seven "Conclusions and Suggestions for the Future," of which two are given below:

> Literalism and concordism are failed enterprises that evangelicals should abandon (p. 291).... In future wrestling with "geologically relevant" texts such as Genesis 1–11, evangelical scholars will have to face the implications of the mass of geologic data indicating that the earth is extremely old, indicating that death has been on earth long before man, and indicating that there has not been a global flood (p. 295).

> Approaches to Genesis 1 that stress the contemporary cultural, historical, and theological setting of ancient Israel are potentially fruitful (p. 302).

> I suggest that we will be on the right track if we stop treating Genesis 1 and the flood story as scientific and historical reports.... Genesis is divinely inspired ancient near eastern literature written within a specific historical context that entailed well-defined thought patterns, literary forms, symbols and images" (p. 303).

Next, consider the opinion of Wheaton College biologist Dr. Pattle P. T. Pun. Dr. Pun believes in creation (sort of), but advocates that God created over billions of years, and claims to be among the most conservative professors on the Wheaton science faculty. Note what he says about the Scriptures:

> It is apparent that the most straightforward understanding of the Genesis record, **without regard to all the hermeneutical considerations suggested by science** [emphasis added], is that God created heaven and earth in six solar days, that man was created in the sixth day, that death and chaos entered the world after the Fall of Adam and Eve, that all of the fossils were the result of the catastrophic universal deluge which spared only Noah's family and the animals therewith.[5]

While Dr. Pun insists he believes in inerrancy, it seems obvious from this quote that Scripture cannot be trusted in a straightforward sense. It must be understood within the hermeneutic of secular science, even though it is obvious, even to him, that a literal interpretation was intended by the author.

Note: Hermeneutics is the methodology by which Scripture is interpreted. I hold to a historical, grammatical hermeneutic which seeks to discern the actual meaning the author was communicating to the reader. Dr. Pun advocates one based on secular science for early earth history.

Here's another statement by old-earth advocates, Bradley and Olsen. Note that they agree that the Scriptures, in context, seem to point to a young earth. But, as is apparent in the last sentence, they have adopted, for *other* reasons, the idea of the old earth. They imply that since science has proven the old earth, and since Genesis 1 and Exodus 20:11 are describing its creation, these Scriptural passages that seem to be describing a recent creation should not be understood in a literal sense.

> The Hebrew word *yom* and its plural form *yamim* are used over 1900 times in the Old Testament. In only sixty-five of these cases is it translated as a time period other than a day in the King James Version. Outside of the Genesis 1 case in question, the two hundred plus occurrences of *yom* preceded by an ordinal, *all* refer to a normal twenty-four hour day. Furthermore, the seven-hundred plus appearances of *yamim always* refer to a regular day. Thus, it is argued [by young-earth creationists, ed.] that the Exodus 20:11 reference to the six *yamim* of creation must also refer to six regular days.

> These arguments have a common fallacy, however. There is no other place in the Old

---

4 Dr. Young's latest thinking is explained in his two-part series "Scripture in the Hands of Geologists," Parts One and Two, *The Westminster Theological Journal*, Vol. 49, Vol. 1 Spring, 1987, pp. 1–34, and Vol. 2, Fall, 1987, pp. 257–304.

5 Dr. Pattle P. T. Pun, *Journal of the American Scientific Affiliation*, March 1987, p. 14.

Testament where the intent is to describe events that involve multiple and/or sequential, *indefinite* periods of time.[6]

Recognizing that every rule of interpretation points to a literal meaning of "day," these scientists (sincere Christians and anti-evolutionists) insist that Genesis 1 and other creation passages are the only exceptions to the rule that the "context defines the meaning of a word."

How do these authors know that Genesis 1 is describing "multiple and/or sequential, indefinite periods of time"? They do *not* develop that opinion from Scripture. They are convinced of it through the interpretations of scientific data by some secular scientists. Thus, they must force long ages into Scripture, placing opinions of scientists above the clear meaning (even to them) of God's Word.

But Scripture does speak clearly. The question is not "What does it say?," but "Does it really mean what it says?" and "Will I believe it?"

Most secular scientists think that young-earth advocates are wrong, but they have little regard for Scripture and have probably never been exposed either to proper Biblical interpretation technique or to good scientific data in support of the young earth. From their way of thinking, the old-earth idea must be true, regardless of what the Bible says. But what must they think when they see supposedly Bible-believing creationists distort the Bible and the normal Christian way of Biblical interpretation in order to embrace something clearly refuted by God's Word? As the Hebrew scholar Dr. James Barr (who does not claim to be a Bible-believer) recognizes:

> Probably, so far as I know, there is no professor of Hebrew or Old Testament at any world-class university who does not believe that the writer(s) of Genesis 1–11 intended to convey to their readers the ideas that (a) creation took place in a series of six days which were the same as the days of 24 hours we now experience (b) the figures contained in the Genesis genealogies provided by simple addition a chronology from the beginning of the world up to later stages in the biblical story (c) Noah's flood was understood to be world-wide and extinguish all human and animal life except for those in the ark. Or, to put it negatively, the apologetic arguments which suppose the "days" of creation to be long eras of time, the figures of years not to be chronological, and the flood to be a merely local Mesopotamian flood, are not taken seriously by any such professors, as far as I know.[7]

Dr. Barr, recognized as being one of the world's leading Old Testament Hebrew scholars, makes no claim to believe Scripture in a historical sense, yet he forthrightly insists that any worthwhile scholar would rightly conclude that the Genesis narrative

---

6   Bradley, Walter L. and Olsen, Roger in "The Trustworthiness of Scripture in Areas Relating to Natural Science," *Hermeneutics, Inerrancy, and the Bible,* 1984 (Academic Books, Grand Rapids), p. 299.

7   Letter to David Watson from James Barr, 1984.

was intended to be understood literally, and that it speaks of a recent creation and a global flood. If a non-believing scholar has such a high regard for Genesis, how much more should "Bible-believing" Christians take Genesis seriously?

"Long" Days Don't Help

To top it off, even *if* the days of Genesis *were* long periods of time, and if Genesis is giving, in *any* sense, a historical account of creation, the problem still remains. As it turns out, the order of creation given in the Bible differs markedly from the order of appearance of things in the evolutionary view. The two are simply not telling the same story. Any attempt to harmonize the two always results in severe twisting of Scripture. Perhaps Dr. Young, quoted above, is more consistent, arguing that the Biblical Genesis account contains no actual historical information.

things according to the standard evolutionary chronology and geologic time scale.

For example, the Bible says that fruit trees bearing fruit were created early on Day Three, while oceanic life, even the invertebrates, didn't appear until Day Five. This order is opposite in evolution, for marine invertebrates evolved early, while fruit trees are much more recent. By claiming that Day Five extended from Day Two through Day Six, and that Day Three extended from Day Two through Day Five, he can rearrange the order to fit. By undergoing such manipulative gymnastics, Scripture no longer has any meaning, for it can fit *any* reconstruction of the past. Dr. Ross's diagram, redrawn here, has proven offensive to Bible-believers.

Dr. Young once proposed a similar scenario, and his graph of overlapping days is nothing short of repugnant. He evidently no longer holds this view,

Overlapping Days

Thus we have a difficult time understanding and appreciating the lengths to which old-earth advocate, Christian astronomer Dr. Hugh Ross goes in his efforts to reinterpret Scripture to fit what some secular scientists insist is true. He proposes that the "days" of Genesis were not only long periods of time, long enough to allow for the billions-of-years-old universe and earth, but also "overlapping." By this he means that each "day" overlapped onto "days" before and after it, and thereby he "solves" the obvious mismatch between the order of creation as given in the Bible and the order of appearance of

having given up on the idea of the historicity of Genesis, but it illustrates the lengths to which one must go to harmonize the Bible with evolution and the old earth.

Dr. Ross has even claimed that Scripture *necessarily* teaches the old earth, and he says that he decided to become a Christian only when he was satisfied that Scripture fit in with the Big-Bang and old-earth ideas. (He now aggressively defends the Big Bang as God's method of creation, even though many secular astronomers are casting about for another theory which fits the observed evidence better.)

Contradictions in Order Between the Biblical View and the Secular View

Biblical Order of Appearance	Evolutionary Order of Appearance
1. Matter created by God in the beginning	1. Matter existed in the beginning
2. Earth before the sun and stars	2. Sun and stars before the earth
3. Oceans before the land	3. Land before the oceans
4. Light before the sun	4. Sun, earth's first light
5. Atmosphere between two water layers	5. Atmosphere above a water layer
6. Land plants, first life forms created	6. Marine organisms, first forms of life
7. Fruit trees before fish	7. Fish before fruit trees
8. Fish before insects	8. Insects before fish
9. Land vegetation before sun	9. Sun before land plants
10. Marine mammals before land mammals	10. Land mammals before marine mammals
11. Birds before land reptiles	11. Reptiles before birds
12. Man, the cause of death	12. Death, necessary antecedent of man

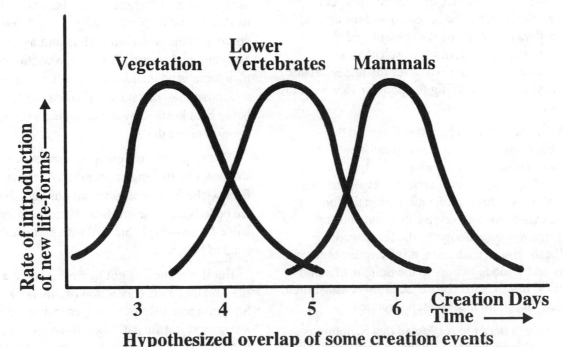

Hypothesized overlap of some creation events
(Redrawn from Hugh Ross; Genesis One: a Scientific Perspective, 1983)

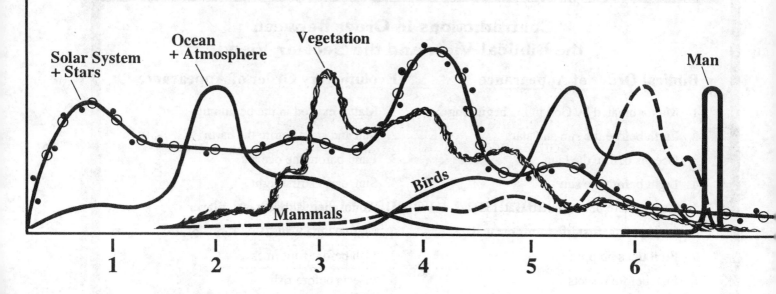

Creative Events of the Six Days of Creation

(Redrawn from Davis Young; *Christianity and the Age of the Earth*, 1982)

Whatever the popular view among secular scientists, some Christians, especially those trained in science, feel they must adopt it, because after all, how could science be wrong? Perhaps it's peer pressure, the desire to be accepted and recognized by one's colleagues. Perhaps it's a misplaced understanding of the abilities of scientists to reconstruct the past. But whatever the reason, many Christians insist on holding the popular viewpoint of "science."

Unfortunately, it doesn't stop there. To the Bible-believing Christian, science must be compatible with Scripture, and so the two are combined somehow. As it concerns evolution and old-earth ideas, this combination takes the form of theistic evolution, progressive creation, the gap theory, the day-age theory, or the framework hypothesis. But in each case, it is Scripture that suffers and is made to bow to the opinion of some scientists. But then, of course, scientists change their view and Scripture must be reinterpreted.

How much better to recognize that Scripture is truth, and that incomplete scientific data must be interpreted within a Scriptural framework. With Scripture as our presuppositional stance, we can do

better science, guided by the witness of the Holy Spirit within us. But we must acknowledge that precision in Scriptural interpretation sometimes escapes us, and that scientific observations can help us understand difficult passages. By doing so, we can continue to improve our understanding of both Scripture and science as research continues. Even then there is no guarantee we will arrive at a full understanding, but at least it keeps the Christian from being held hostage by the changing "scientific" opinion of the day.

This trap can have grievous consequences. We shouldn't be looking to science to "prove" the Bible—the Bible doesn't need our help. Nor should we be looking to scientific opinion to interpret the Bible for us—the Bible will interpret itself. We just need to believe it.

But if it's true, it's got to work, the evidence must fit! And that's the contention of this book. Use Scripture and a Biblical understanding of the past to interpret scientific data. Do all things in submission to God's Word. And when we do, we find that the evidence is not only compatible with Scripture, it also supports it and encourages our faith.

Assumption

The Bible is God's Word

↓

Certain faulty *interpretations* of
some secular scientists mistaken for
DATA

Naturalism • Evolution • Old Earth

↓

Interpretation
of Bible to fit "proven" science

- Theistic Evolution
- Day Age Theory
- Progressive Creation
- Gap Theory
- Framework Hypothesis
- Local Flood

Faulty thinking process employed
by many Christians.

Chapter 3
The Two Views Contrasted

Despite pronouncements by Ross, Pun, Davis, and others, the old-earth/universe view differs markedly from the straightforward concept of creation as understood from Scripture alone. According to the Big-Bang concept (which is coming under more and more criticism these days), the universe began some ten to twenty billion years ago with an explosion. Prior to that time, all the matter and energy in all the universe were condensed into a super-dense "cosmic egg" about the size of an electron. Some cosmologists now claim that even the "egg" originated "as a quantum fluctuation in a vacuum," i.e. "evolution *ex nihilo*," from nothing.

moving mass into huge "lumps," leaving the majority of space quite empty.

Within the interior of stars, hydrogen and helium were supposedly fused into heavier atoms. In the course of time, some of these stars underwent nova and super-nova explosions, flinging the elements into space. The exploded remnants of such stars eventually coalesced into "second-generation" stars containing minor concentrations of those heavier elements. In time, the process repeated. Our sun is thought to be a "third-generation" star, and the planets and people consist of left-over interstellar stardust, which escaped the sun's gravitational pull and remained in orbit. Our solar system dates back about five billion years, according to this view.

In this scenario, life arose spontaneously from non-living chemicals about three to four billion years ago, and multi-cellular life some one billion years ago. Life increased in complexity until man evolved around one to three million years ago. Modern man and civilization date back only a few thousand years—a seeming afterthought in the cosmic timetable.

Some time later, an instability arose and the egg exploded, first in a very short-lived "cold big whoosh" and then a "hot big bang," initially producing sub-atomic particles and then fusing some particles into hydrogen (then some into helium) gas atoms. Eventually, the hydrogen gas, instead of expanding radically outward, as would be expected in an explosion, somehow began to coalesce into stars, galaxies, and super clusters of galaxies concentrating the still

Scripture and Genealogies

The Bible, on the other hand, places creation in six literal days only a few thousand years ago, with man, the "Image of God," the goal from the very start. This date derives mostly from summing up the time spans given in Scriptural genealogies.

By adding up the numbers found in the genealogy given in Genesis 5, as found in all English Bibles based on the Massoretic text, we find that only 1656 years passed from the Creation to the Flood. These genealogies consist of the age of each Patriarch at the birth of his son, through whom the patriarchal line was passed, the years the father lived after the son was born, and the summation of both, providing the total age of each father at death. Because of the correct addition of the numbers given, and no hint elsewhere in Scripture that generations are missing, it is concluded by most conservative Bible scholars that the total of 1656 years accurately reflects the time span between Creation and the Flood, allowing for the possible rounding off of numbers and birthdays within a particular year.

The Evolutionary View of History

1. Most recent "Big Bang," 10–20 billion years ago.

2. Our Solar System, 5 billion years ago.

3. Single-celled organisms, 3–4 billion years ago.

4. Multi-celled organisms, 1 billion years ago.

5. Humankind, 1–3 million years ago.

6. Modern Civilization, 5–10 thousand years ago.

It must be admitted that the Septuagint Text, the Greek translation of the Hebrew Bible used in Israel at the time of Christ, places the number at about 2300. While both cannot be correct, for the purposes of old-earth/young-earth discussions, the difference can be considered trivial.

Note: The various extant copies of the Massoretic Text, from which our English Old Testament is translated, give exactly the same numbers in the genealogies of Genesis 5. The Septuagint, on the other hand, has numerous variants. Taking the maximum number for each link in the genealogy yields a maximum of 2402 years between Creation and Flood. Taking each minimum number gives a time span of 1307 years. The most reliable Septuagint Texts give 2262 years. Josephus, the Jewish historian who lived at about the time of Christ, followed the most reliable Septuagint figures. The Samaritan Pentateuch, another ancient manuscript, yields a span of 1307 years. Whatever the manuscript of choice, there is no support for adding much time to Genesis 5.[1]

Noah to Abraham

The next two intervals are less well defined. Genesis 10 provides a list of the early descendants of Noah's three sons, Japheth (vv. 2–5), Ham (vv. 6–20), and Shem (vv. 21–32). These are repeated exactly in I Chronicles 1:8–23. Genesis 11 amplifies and extends the lineage of Shem, and furnishes age spans from Noah to Abraham (vv. 10–32), (with the names exactly reproduced in I Chronicles 1:24–28). Adding up the numbers in Genesis 11 yields 292 years from the Flood to the birth of Abraham. But the total is not nearly as "tight," lacking the summary totals of Genesis 5.

Note: As in Genesis 5, the Septuagint Chronologies of Genesis 11 are varied. For the time span from the Flood to Abraham, they range from a minimum of 292 years (matching the Massoretic) to a maximum of 1513 years—the most accepted variant registering 942. This figure matches that from the Samaritan Pentateuch and approximates that given by Josephus, 952.[2]

Furthermore, by comparing the list with that in Luke, we find one discrepancy in the line from Noah to Abraham, for in Luke 3:36 the name "Cainan" is added as Shem's grandson. Many scholars offer good explanations for the difference (most likely, a late

---

1   See Paul J. Ray, "An Evolution of the Numerical Variants of the Chronogenealogies of Genesis 5 and 11," *Origins*, Vol. 12. No. 1, pp. 26–37, 1985.

2   See Ray, op cit.

error in copying Luke's Gospel, with a scribe erroneously adding the name "Cainan," properly found in Luke 3:37 to Luke 3:36 by mistake), but we must admit that the time span cannot be fixed with absolute certainty.

However, even if one puts a large gap of time between *each* father-son listing, (i.e., say great-grandfather to great-grandson instead of father to son), it still doesn't stretch the total more than a few thousand years. Thus, it doesn't help solve the discrepancy between the secular view and the Biblical view.

Abraham to David

To go from Abraham to dates well established in the Bible and in archaeology, say in the time of David, is also somewhat subjective. Most scholars conclude that Abraham lived about 2000 B.C., but uncertainties in the date of the Exodus and the time of the Judges make it possible, as proposed by some, that either a much shorter or much longer time is implied. Indeed, an expanded chronology might seem to yield more compatibility with the scale developed by secular archaeology apart from Scriptural input. Please understand, I am *not* advocating a longer time span. I suspect that it is the secular chronology which needs revision. However, although we must admit the possibility of some uncertainty as to the exact dates, the "young-earth" doctrine of Scripture is not in question here.

Even if we stretch it and stretch it to accommodate every possible longer period, the numbers only increase by a few thousand years, an insignificant increase as far as evolution is concerned.

Thus we can derive a "most probable" range of dates, all of which fall into the "young-earth" position.

	Min.		Max.
From Creation to the Flood	1656	to	2400
From the Flood to Abraham	300	to	4000
From Abraham to Christ	2000	to	4000
From Christ to Present	2000	to	2000
Total Range of Dates	6000	to	12,000

My own conviction is that the true age is probably on the order of 6000 years or so. But in order to make a *correct* statement, one in which we can have confidence, we should give the age of the earth as a range of approximate dates. Remember, even a 12,000-year-old earth is a *young* earth, as far as our discussions of creation/evolution, young-earth/old-earth are concerned.

But what can be made of the billions of years of history required by evolution? Suffice it to say that if the Bible is right, the old-earth concept is wrong. And vice versa. If the earth is old, the Bible is wrong. The only point of general agreement between old- and young-earth views is that modern civilization began just a few thousand years ago, with the introduction of writing and recorded history (i.e., the only history we *know* is true).

Comparing the Two

These two viewpoints are so divergent and different in their predictions that we ought to be able to test between them and see from the data, which one is more likely correct, and I think we can.

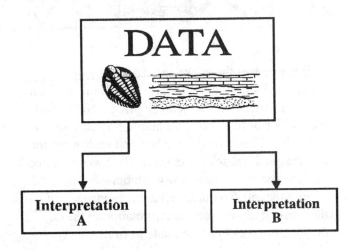

As already mentioned, both camps are in substantial agreement as to the dating of *true* history, *i.e.*, recorded, human history. But before Abraham's day we get into the realm of geology, and as we've seen, rocks are somewhat generic with respect to time. They do *not* come with labels on them telling us how old they are. They *do* come with certain densities, fossil content, mineral isotope ratios, etc. Both old-earthers and young-earthers recognize exactly the same facts about the observed *present* nature of the rocks. But in discussing the unobserved past, these facts must be interpreted within one's view of history. When proposing an age or a method of origin, scientists are trying to answer the question: "What happened in the unobserved past to make the observed present get to be this way?'' I have started calling these efforts "historical reconstructions." The data gathering and analysis are empirical science, but historical reconstructions, however legitimate, are a totally different enterprise.

It is true that the rocks and fossils *can be* interpreted within the old-earth viewpoint, with some degree of success. They can be made to fit. In fact, the rocks can fit within any number of old-earth scenarios. This is obvious when one recognizes that the accepted age for the earth in 1900 was only about 100 million years, and now evolutionists date it 50 times as great! No matter what the evidence and what the "politically correct" interpretation of the day may be, the rocks can be made to fit it.

Note: Don't ask me for specifics, but I get the feeling, with new ideas coming along in astronomy to replace the Big Bang, essentially proposing an infinitely old universe, that some major revisions in the "age" of the earth are coming too. But, not to worry, the rocks are generic enough to accommodate any new date

The rocks can *also* be interpreted, however, within the young-earth viewpoint. They are compatible with either (although less compatible with the old earth, I believe). Neither the old-earth idea, nor the young-earth idea can be scientifically proven by geologic observations, and, likewise, neither can be disproven.

Many Bible-believing creationists, including myself, hold to the young-earth view. I am convinced that the Word of God specifically indicates that Creation took place only thousands of years ago, and that the world's surface was subsequently restructured by a world-wide Flood in the days of Noah. If these events represent true history, any attempt to reconstruct history which denies these truths will surely fail.

While neither can be proven or disproven, these two views can be compared to see which one fits the data better and is therefore more likely correct. I am convinced, that when they are compared, the Creation/Flood/young-earth model will be found not only to fit the data quite well, it will fit the data much better than does the old-earth/evolutionary model.

Those committed to a completely naturalistic viewpoint of history can perhaps be expected to adopt the old-earth model. But a Christian, one who believes in the existence of an all-powerful God and claims to believe in Scripture, should never feel compelled to adopt this naturalistic, un-Scriptural, and quite inferior way of thinking. Instead, a Christian should feel very uncomfortable relegating God to the long-ago and far-away, and making Him responsible for the ages-long evolutionary process, wasteful, bloody, and unGodly as it is.

As always, if we begin our reasoning process with Scripture, and interpret the scientific data from a Scriptural perspective, we will not only find our interpretation scientifically compelling, but personally satisfying, intuitively correct, and clearly preferable to those deriving from a viewpoint which denies true history.

Importance of the Issue

Interestingly enough, the scientific view of creation (as opposed to evolution) doesn't necessarily depend on young-earth ideas. Many Christians who certainly don't believe that all life came from a common ancestor through descent with modification, and strongly hold that the Creator God specifically created each basic category of plant or animal, have accepted the old-earth position. They are "creationists" (of a sort), but old-earthers. Unfortunately, this viewpoint entails many Biblical problems and, therefore, should, in my opinion, be rejected. Did death and bloodshed occur before sin? What was the omniscient God's purpose in creating dinosaurs and other now-extinct animal types? Furthermore, compromising on this issue does not yield acceptance among secular academics, for they demand strict naturalism. There is no benefit to the Christian in this compromise.

On the other hand, the old-earth concept is a *necessary* part of evolution. Everyone agrees that evolution is an unlikely process, involving millions and millions of favorable mutations, fortuitous environmental changes, etc. Only as one shrouds evolution in the mists of time does it become respectable. If the earth is billions of years old, there is enough time for unlikely events to occur, or so it is thought.

Consider this incredible quote from George Wald, a well-known evolutionary spokesperson:

> Time is in fact the hero of the plot....given so much time the 'impossible' becomes possible, the possible probable and the probable virtually certain. One has only to wait: time itself performs miracles.
>
> George Wald ,"The Origin of Life," in *Physics and Chemistry of Life*, 1955, p. 12.

Time has become a vast rug under which all the problems of evolution are swept. (See illustration on p. 34.)

But, a realistic look at the evidence insists that time does not perform miracles, nor has real evolution ever happened. The fossil record shows no evidence that any basic category of animal has ever evolved from or into any other basic category. The laws of statistics show that favorable mutations are so improbable that they will most likely never even happen *once* in twenty billion years, let alone happen millions of times. The laws of science absolutely preclude evolution, pointing towards degradation of life's complex systems, and not toward evolutionary integration. The more time there is, the more *extinction* and the more *harmful* mutations will occur—de-volution not evolution. Time is the *enemy* of evolution, rather than its hero.

But, of course, if the earth is only thousands of years old, then evolution becomes even more foolish. Thus, the idea of the old earth is necessary for the evolutionary viewpoint, but belief in the young earth is not absolutely necessary to believe in the special creation of plants and animals. However, strictly speaking, belief in the young earth *is* necessary for a truly Biblical point of view. The "old-earth creationists," whose spiritual salvation is not in question here, embrace an inconsistent way of thinking about God, the Bible, and the past.

A Functionally Mature Creation

It has been pointed out that when God created, He must have created things with at least a superficial appearance of history or process involved in their formation. For instance, when God created fruit trees, they were mature fruit trees with fruit already on them (Genesis 1:11). When He created animals, they were able to swim or fly or walk (vv. 14–25). When He created Adam, Adam was a mature, full-grown man, not a baby or an embryo. Indeed, it would be impossible to create functioning organisms which didn't have a superficial appearance of a prior history. (Even an embryo has a history.)

I stress the word "superficial" because I suspect that if modern scientists had been able to examine Adam immediately after he had been created, they might have been able to discern that he had just been created, that he had not lived a life of, say, twenty-five years or so. Certainly they would have found no decay in his teeth, no calcification in his bones, no cholesterol in his arteries, and no defective genes. Careful investigation might have shown that the only way he could be in that state was to be newly created, that he showed no objective evidence of deterioration caused by age. *Superficially*, he appeared to be a grown man. He was functionally mature, but only minutes old. The same could probably be said for the plants and animals.

Similarly, the stars were created for the purpose of being seen on earth, to accomplish the purpose of measuring time (Genesis 1:14–19). In order for God's purpose to have been fulfilled, the light would have either been created enroute and arrived immediately, or perhaps the speed of light was initially nearly infinite, or perhaps the stars were not so far away, or perhaps the structure of space has been changed, or something. However it got here, the light from the sun and stars had to be here on earth in order for God's purpose in creation to be fulfilled.

Note: old-earth/universe advocates such as Hugh Ross hold that the stars predate the earth by billions of years, even though Scripture reveals that they weren't created until Day 4. But the Hebrew construction, as well as the context, makes a straightforward understanding of Genesis 1 preferable. For a good discussion of this, see "Star Formation and Genesis 1," ICR Impact Article No. 251, May 1994, by Jim Stambaugh.

But, of course, if God is capable of creating a star, He is also able to create light. This would probably be an "easier" job than creating ripe fruit on a newly created fruit tree. For some reason, this issue remains a real problem to many Christians, who are willing to accept the creation of a fruit-bearing fruit tree, but cannot conceive of the creation of stars with light already here. But it should be no problem if we understand the nature of God and His creative power. This is not deceptive, as some have charged, but the inevitable result of the creation of a functionally mature creation. Furthermore, He told us *when* He created, in case we were inclined to make an error of judgment. In fact, since He told us He created things *recently*, if Creation were really long ago, then He deceived us in His Word.

Most importantly, we dare not make the error of limiting God to that which we see occurring today. Creation Week was different in every respect from today. The omnipotent, omniscient Creator was using creative processes which He is no longer using, and which are certainly not happening on their own. God even told us that His work of creation is *"finished"* (Genesis 2:1), no longer going on. Perhaps some recognizable processes were occurring (e.g., gravity), but we cannot even limit *them* by today's experience. Christians need to rest in the certain knowledge that the Creation episode is beyond our present experience, and the only way we can know about it is for the Creator to tell us. We can study the *results* of creation, but we can't study the actual event or the processes used.

At the end of Genesis 1 God declared His entire creation to be "very good" (v. 31). In order for it to have been so good, it would have to be functionally mature, ready to accomplish God's purposes in creation. As we study the *results* of creation today, we see that the evidence is perfectly compatible with the Scriptural record. The data don't *prove* Genesis, but they do support and confirm it. In general, the facts of science fit quite nicely with what we would expect if Scripture is correct.

God knew that this superficial appearance of history could be misunderstood by those not having access to the originally created state, or not having the patience to study it, and so He told us in His Word when this was accomplished. Today, some scientists, attempting to discern the age of things, deny the possibility of Creation, and having denied truth, come to a wrong conclusion. If one denies the possibility of a functionally mature Creation, he or she will perhaps mistake that functional maturity for age.

Aspects of a Mature Creation

Partial List

- Continents with top soil
- Plants bearing seed
- Fruit trees bearing fruit
- Land with drainage system
- Rocks with crystalline minerals
- Rocks with various isotopes
- Stars visible from earth
- Marine animals adapted to ocean life
- Birds able to fly
- Land animals adapted to environment
- Plants and animal in symbiotic relationships
- Adam and Eve as adults
- All "very good"

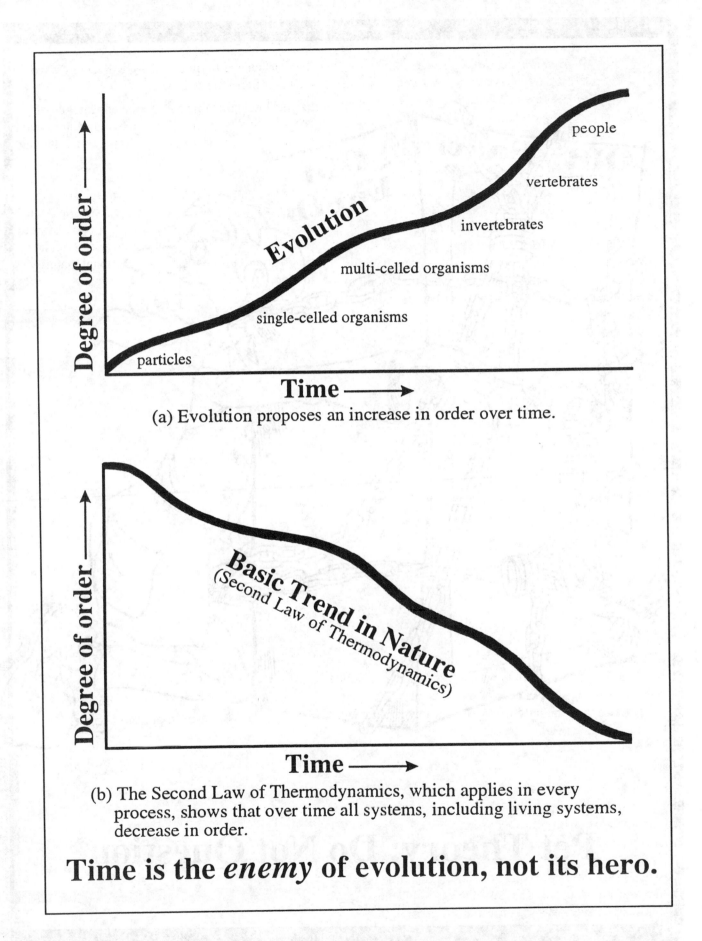

(a) Evolution proposes an increase in order over time.

(b) The Second Law of Thermodynamics, which applies in every process, shows that over time all systems, including living systems, decrease in order.

Time is the *enemy* of evolution, not its hero.

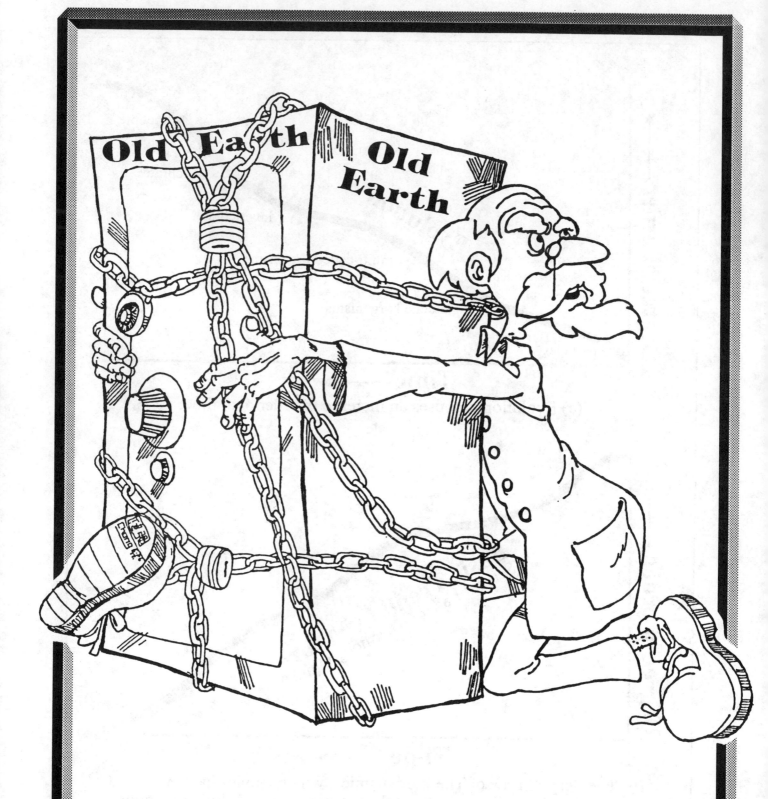

Pet Theory: Do Not Question

Chapter 4
Dating Methods

In this chapter we want to answer those newspaper and magazine articles, those television specials, and those classroom lectures which insist that a particular rock or fossil has been discovered which dates to 3 million years or 700 million years or 2 billion years or whatever. Few people stop to think about how these dates are derived. How do the scientists determine the "age of a rock?," and is this method reliable?

As we have seen, the assumption of evolution is used to arrange the fossils in an evolutionary sequence, which in turn evaluates all other dates, no matter how they are derived. But let's see where those other dates and ages come from.

Actually, every dating method involves the same basic procedure. The concept behind them is not difficult. Keep in mind that rocks, fossils, and *systems* (geologic layers) don't come with labels on them revealing their age, and yet these phenomena must be *interpreted*. There may be, and in fact generally is, more than one legitimate way to interpret the data.

Under normal circumstances, the dating method proceeds in the following manner:

1. The scientist will observe the present state of the rock or system which is to be dated.
   (This is science, dealing with the present.)

2. The scientist will measure the rate of a process presently operating within that system.
   (This also is science.)

3. The scientist must then assume certain things about the past history of this rock or system.
   (This is model building, setting up assumptions in order to reconstruct unobserved history.)

4. The scientist will calculate how long it would take for that present process, operating throughout the unobserved past, to produce the present state of things in that system. (This is interpretation of observed data based on assumptions about the unobserved past.)

A Parable

Let me illustrate this procedure with a parable. Parables can be used to shed light on complex concepts, and while the concept of dating is not terribly difficult, it is new to many people, making a parable appropriate. Let me call this "The Parable of the Potato Basket."

Suppose that as a scientist, you entered a lecture hall to attend a scientific lecture. As you arrived, you saw me up on the platform with a basket of potatoes on the table in front of me (sketch 1). As you sat down you noticed that as the second hand of the wall clock reached twelve, I reached into the basket, pulled out a potato, peeled it, and put it back in the basket. As the second hand reached twelve once again, I repeated the process. You observe me peeling potatoes for ten minutes and, finally, you ask yourself the question, "I wonder how long this nut's been doing that?"

Sketch 1

45

The question you have just asked is exactly the same question that a scientist asks when investigating the "age" of a rock or system. "How old is this rock?" "How long has this tree been growing?" "How long has this river delta been building up?"

How are you going to determine how long I've been peeling potatoes? Obviously, you would come up and count the peeled potatoes. Suppose you counted 35 peeled potatoes. You have thus observed the present state of the system (the number of peeled potatoes, 35). And you have measured the process rate (the rate of potato peeling, one per minute). Both of these observations are scientific observations, dealing with the present. You would likely conclude that the system has been in operation for thirty-five minutes.

Is that the *correct* age of the system? Well, maybe.

Let's step back and think for a moment. In order to derive such a conclusion, you must make certain assumptions about the unobserved past. These assumptions are critical to your conclusion.

The first thing that one must assume about the past is that the rate of potato peeling has been constant throughout the whole history of the potato basket. Scientifically, all you really know is that I've been peeling potatoes at one per minute for the last ten minutes. You simply don't *know* what my rate of potato peeling was before you came in. Perhaps I'm getting better at it and only now can peel a potato each minute, whereas before it took me longer. Or perhaps I'm getting tired and slowing down. By observing the present rate, you don't necessarily know the rate in the past, and you have no firm basis on which to assume that the rate of potato peeling has been constant. Perhaps your assumption of constant peeling rate is reasonable, but is it right?

Note: Actually, the first assumption you must make is that time runs in a smooth, linear fashion, but I don't want to get into that!

The next assumption you have to make or the question you must answer is "Have any peeled potatoes been added to or taken away from the basket throughout its whole history?" If so, then your calculation would be misleading. For all you know, someone has sabotaged the experiment by adding several peeled potatoes to the basket, so that some of the peeled potatoes now in the basket didn't get there through the observed process of potato peeling (sketch 2). Likewise, you must assume that no one, including the government, has come in and removed some of my hard-earned peeled potatoes. Again, you have absolutely no way of *knowing* just by looking at the potato basket (Sketch 3).

Sketch 2

46

Sketch 3

We must continually remind ourselves what is going on in a dating process—any dating process. Strict scientific observation can only get us started. We are able to observe the present state of things. And we are able to measure the rate of a relevant process. But establishing a date for the unobserved origin of something requires making assumptions regarding unobserved *history*, to a great degree inaccessible to empirical science. It is not illegitimate for a scientist to speculate on such things, but it would be better for scientists to approach it with a little more humility. Unfortunately, the results of historic speculations are usually presented as unquestioned fact, and students, or tourists at the national parks, or interested persons watching a TV special or reading the newspaper are sometimes intimidated into accepting a politically correct view of history as if it were scientific fact.

There's another question that you must answer, and that is "Were there any peeled potatoes in the basket at the start?" Perhaps when I came in with the basket, there were already several peeled potatoes in it, and therefore the time determination is incorrect. Again, you have no certain way of knowing, except by asking me or another witness who was present at the start, and then you wouldn't really know if you were told accurate information (sketch 4).

These three assumptions, i.e., (1) regarding the constancy of the process rate, (2) regarding the degree to which the system has been isolated from the environment, and (3) regarding the initial conditions of the system, are inherent in *any* dating process. *Correct* assumptions in each must be made in order to proceed to a *correct* answer, unless specific, accurate knowledge about the past is known.

Sketch 4

Trees and Tree Rings

Let me illustrate once again, with a more realistic example, that of determining the age of a tree.

We all know that certain trees form tree rings at the rate of one per year, with very few exceptions. Much can be inferred from tree rings, based on years of careful study. For instance, in a wet year the tree grows faster than in a dry year, leaving a wider ring. A year of disease or insect infestation will show up as an abnormal ring. Frost damage can be seen, and a protracted cold spell during the normal growth season may even produce a second ring in one year, but those are usually recognizably different from normal rings. By documenting weather patterns and other variable conditions and cataloging tree-growth responses in the observed past, scientists have developed confidence in deciphering the past of a particular tree.

Let's say that we examine a particular tree, and it is found to have 250 tree rings. We document that no unusual atmospheric or geologic occurrences capable of altering normal tree growth are recorded in the most recent 250 years, and therefore the rate of tree-ring formation was likely constant, at one per year, throughout the life of the tree. We could even observe how the tree had responded to various dated episodes during its lifetime. Furthermore, we could properly assume that nothing had happened which

had somehow robbed the tree of a tree ring, and that when the tree first formed from a seed, it had no tree rings present.

Because these assumptions are likely correct, we are justified in concluding that the tree is 250 years old. But in a real sense, the only way we could know for sure is if someone gave us an accurate record of the date of tree-planting, and then we would still be somewhat uncertain of the total accuracy of the record. In this case, the age determination of 250 years is quite likely precise, but the point is that the past holds many uncertainties.

Dating Niagara Falls

Let me offer another less obvious example, that of the age of Niagara Falls. The waters of Lake Erie flow over the Niagara Escarpment in spectacular falls which empty into Lake Ontario. The falls are observed to be retreating toward Lake Erie as the cliff is eroded, at a measured rate of 4 (or 5) feet per year, forming a long gorge. This has been stabilized somewhat in recent years by artificial means, but the measurement reflects the natural erosion rate before engineers slowed it. Next we notice that the falls are only seven miles (37,000 feet) from Lake Ontario.

Here's the question: How old is this system? How long has Niagara Falls been eroding the cliff in the up-river direction?

Simple division indicates that the system is on the order of 9,000 years old, but is that the correct determination? As we've seen, there are some assumptions involved, including a constant rate of erosion, no major alterations of the dynamics of the system, and that the erosion started at the *end* of the gorge, as the tilt of the land caused the water to run faster and do its erosive job.

But what if there were more water in the past? And what if the rock were more easily eroded? I suspect that in the centuries after the Flood there would have been much more water, and the (then)

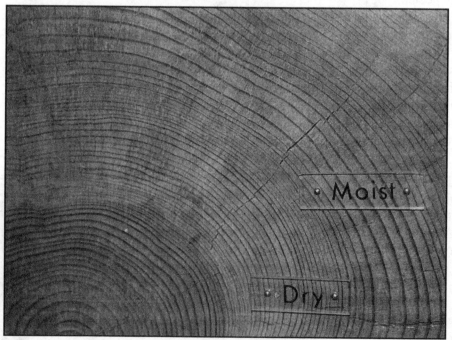
Tree rings accurately record, with very few exceptions, the years of the tree's history. fairly recently deposited strata

48

would have been softer, more easily eroded. And in all likelihood, the Ice Age followed the Flood, with major changes in precipitation and run off as well as in acidity of the water. And do we really know where the original mouth of the gorge was? Very likely, the true age of this waterfall system is younger than the simple calculation indicates, but obviously we can't truly know.

Interestingly enough, Charles Lyell visited Niagara Falls in 1841 while promoting his concept of uniformity of geologic processes throughout the past,[1] a concept largely abandoned by geologists today. He was anxious to find geologic features which would take more time to form than the Bible would allow. Although local residents insisted that the falls were retreating at a rate of at least three feet each year, he estimated the rate at only one foot per year, even though he observed it for only a brief time. Thus, he charged that the Bible was in error, for Niagara Falls would take 35,000 years to form.

Obviously, assumptions about the unobserved past dominate the dating process.

In the chapters to follow, numerous evidences for the young earth are given. Even though certainty can't be reached, the claim will be made that the total evidence is much more compatible with the young-earth model than with the old-earth. Such is the case with Niagara Falls. The age calculated as based on sound observations is quite compatible with the Biblical time scale, especially when factors concerning the recent Flood and subsequent Ice Age are considered.

The youthful age of the falls and its gorge doesn't support the concept of vast ages, despite the wishful thinking and dishonest calculations of adherents.

Unfortunately, Lyell's rigged calculations were believed by many, and played a significant role in the abandonment of the popular Ussher chronology. In a similar way, bogus claims abound today, and still lead to disbelief of the Bible—and even of God.

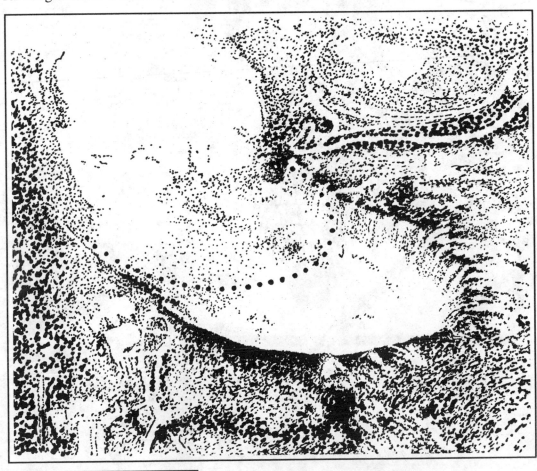

Niagara Falls as it appears today, showing the gorge caused by erosion over the years. The dotted line shows where the Falls were in Lyell's day.

---

1   For an excellent discussion of this, see *In the Minds of Men* by Ian Taylor, 1987, p. 81.

Chapter 5
Radioisotope Dating

C certainly many people think radioisotope dating has proved that the earth is billions of years old and that this family of dating methods can determine the age of ancient rocks. However, just as with the potato basket and every other system, the concepts suffer from various problems and unprovable assumptions.

It must be stated before we begin to look at these methods, that the only rocks which can be dated by this method are igneous and metamorphic rocks, rocks which once were extremely hot and which since have cooled into solid rock. This would include rocks such as basalt (a type of solidified lava), rocks which are now quite hard, but once were in a hot, liquid or semi-liquid condition. Advocates propose that melting resets the age clock to zero and that the date given through this method reflects the time elapsed between the cooling of the rock and the present.

Generally speaking, sedimentary rocks, such as limestone, sandstone, and shale, cannot be dated with radioisotope schemes. (There are a few proposed schemes which have been proposed as potentially able to determine the "age" of certain minerals or crystals contained within sedimentary rocks, but these are far less reliable, are seldom considered helpful, and are not discussed here).[1] Sedimentary rocks, by definition, are laid down as sediments by moving fluids, are made up of pieces of rock or other material which existed somewhere else, and were eroded or dissolved and redeposited in their present location. In other words, the rock material itself would have been from a previously existing older source, and no dating would be accurate because of redeposition. Such fossil-bearing rocks are dated ultimately by the index fossils contained therein, which, of course, are organized, arrayed, and dated by the assumption of evolution (which, I contend, is a *false* assumption).

The first radioisotope dating technique which was well studied and which has formed the basis for all of the others, utilizes the fact that uranium-238, an unstable radioactive element, decays spontaneously into lead-206. Old-earth advocates don't think that uranium-238 and other radioactive elements formed here on earth, but instead result from the fusing together of smaller atoms in the interior of stars, and were flung out into space during past supernova events. Both larger and smaller atoms are presumed to be part of the inter-stellar stardust which coalesced to form the earth billions of years ago. As shown in

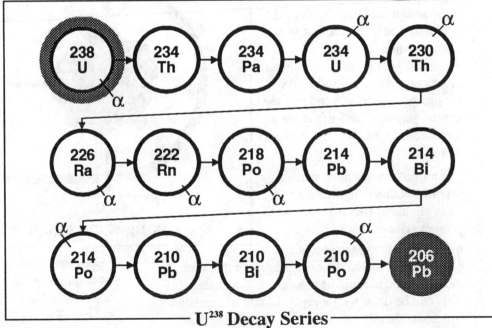

U²³⁸ Decay Series

the accompanying diagram, uranium-238 changes into thorium-234 through what is called *alpha* decay. The alpha particle actually has mass and decreases the mass of uranium, changing it to equal the mass of

---

1 For a good review of the strengths and weaknesses of these proposed methods, see the standard textbook by Gunter Faure, *Principles of Isotope Geology*, 2nd edition, 1986, particularly pp. 74–80.

thorium-234. Other types of decay, including *beta* decay, don't substantially reduce the mass. Thus, thorium-234, in turn, changes into protactinium-234, which changes into uranium-234, which, in turn, changes into thorium-230, and on down the line, through various isotopes of radium, radon, polonium, lead, and bismuth, finally arriving at the stable atom lead-206. Each time an atom changes into another type of atom, it gives off a certain amount of energy, the level of which can be measured, and the specific decay-episode recognized. Uranium, in this process, is called the "parent" material, which eventually produces the "daughter" material, lead, after passing through the various intermediate stages.

The rate at which uranium changes into lead through its intermediate steps is measurable and has been accurately measured for the last several decades. It is referenced by its "half-life," the time it takes for half of a given number of uranium-238 atoms to turn into lead-206. Actually, each of the intermediate steps has its own characteristic half-life, the sum of which provides the complete half-life from beginning to end. As it turns out, for uranium-238, nearly all of the total half-life is in that first step from uranium-238 to thorium-234, the rest being much more rapid decay episodes. As we proceed, keep in mind that the measurement of half-life is not a measurement of *time*, but of the *rate* of decay.

Simplistically stated, when a scientist wants to age-date a rock, he or she must first measure the present state of that rock. This means measuring the amount of each of the affected isotopes present in that rock, including the amount of uranium-238 and lead-206. This can be done with a great amount of precision. Since we already know the rate of decay of the parent uranium into the daughter lead, we can begin the process of answering the question, How old is this rock? How long, in other words, would it take for this amount of decaying uranium to produce the amount of lead present?

But do we thus derive the *true* age of the rock? As you might suspect, the assumptions inherent in any dating effort call into question the age calculated.

The First Assumption

The first assumption regards the constant decay rate. Is it scientifically reasonable to assume that the decay rate hasn't changed over billions of years when we've been measuring it for only the last several decades? To be sure, the decay rate hasn't changed during the time when accurate measurements have been possible. Scientists have performed all sorts of experiments trying to encourage the rate to change, and using conditions likely to occur in nature, but it hasn't been observed to change more than by a very small fraction. But since the half-life of uranium-238 to lead-206 is 4.51 billion years (in other words, a very slow process), is it reasonable to assume that the half-life has been constant throughout the assumed multi-billion year past?

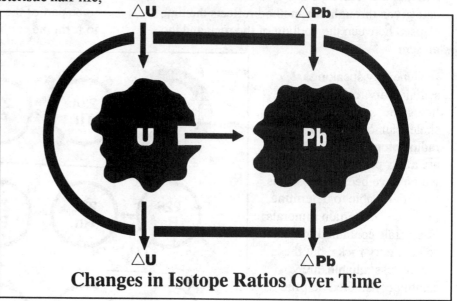

Changes in Isotope Ratios Over Time

Between you and me, I'm not going to challenge that assumption, at least until more is known. I think it's a reasonable assumption, given the fact that we know of no normal conditions that would change the decay rate to any significant degree. There are a few clues in nature that, perhaps, the decay rate has changed in the past,[2] but these are subject to a variety of interpretations, and as of yet, have not convincingly established a changing decay rate. For

---

2   See for example the report in *Science News*, 8 Jan. 1994, p.16, where the half-life of tritium was altered by about 30%.

purposes of discussion, I'm willing to grant (with reservations) the probability that the decay rates of the major isotopes used in dating have remained the same throughout the past.

The Second Assumption

The second assumption is a little less reasonable. This is one that assumes that neither the parent nor the daughter concentrations (nor any of the intermediate products, some of which are highly-mobile gases) have been altered throughout the entire history of the rock (except by radioactive decay) or that the amount of loss or gain can be known. This assumption has some serious problems.

It is true that when scientists gather a specimen for analysis in a laboratory, they attempt to find one which shows no evidence of having been contaminated through leaching by ground-water or other processes throughout its history. Great care is taken in this. A specimen which shows such evidence would not be considered proper for analysis. One would hope that the results obtained on good specimens would be reasonable and consistent, since all questionable specimens were already screened out.

Nothing could be further from the truth, however. Many, many times, when specimens are dated, the resulting answers don't agree with each other or with any other estimate gained from the fossils or from stratigraphic analyses. If the results came back "wrong," the results from the tests are thrown out, and a charge of "contamination" is levied. But these are the specimens which have *already* been culled for any evidence of contamination.

Let me give an example. Dr. Andrew Snelling, ICR Adjunct Professor in Geology, studied the published dates and isotope ratios from a uranium deposit in Australia. He wrote in his conclusion:

> The above evidence conclusively demonstrates that the U/Pb system, including its intermediate daughter products, especially Ra and Rn, has been so open with repeated large scale migrations of the elements that it is impossible to be sure of the precise

status/history of any piece of pitchblende selected for dating. Even though geochronologists take every conceivable precaution when selecting pitchblende grains for dating, in the light of the above evidence, no one could be sure that the U and Pb they are measuring is "original" and unaffected by the gross element movements observed and measured. Those pitchblende grains dated have always contained Pb, both within their crystal lattices and as microscopic inclusions of galena, making it impossible to be sure that all the Pb was generated by radioactive decay from U. In addition, the pitchblende grains don't have uniform compositions so that "dating" of sub-sections of any grain would tend to yield widely divergent U/Pb ratios and therefore varying "ages" within that single grain. A logical extension of these data and conclusions is to suggest, as others already have, that U/Pb ratios may have nothing to do with the age of a mineral. So that in spite of the "popular" dating results looking sensible, the evidence clearly indicates that these dates are meaningless.[3]

My question is, if leaching and contamination can occur which cannot be visibly detected, how do we know that they haven't occurred in other clean looking samples whose answers happen to come

Assumptions of Radioisotope Dating

1. **Constant decay rate.**
2. **No loss or gain of parent or daughter.**
3. **Known amounts of daughter present at start.**

3   Snelling, Andrew, "The Age of Australian Uranium," *Creation Ex Nihilo* Vol. 4, No. 2, 1981, pp. 44–57.

back in agreement with what the examiner thought they *should* be?[4]

The Third Assumption

The third assumption is the real Achilles' heel of radioisotope dating. This is the one that considers the original quantity of the various isotopes, particularly the daughter product. If some of the daughter material is present at the start, the rock would already appear to be old, when in fact it was just formed. It would have a superficial appearance of history.

This assumption comes close to being able to be tested, because rocks which can be dated are forming now. We can gather samples, for example, from recent eruptions and date them. If the dating process is accurate, then the date derived should be almost equivalent to zero, or too young to be measured. In the scientific literature, research results have been reported where rocks of known age have been dated. In almost every case the "age" of these recent lavas has come back from the lab in terms of excessively *high* ages, not essentially *zero* as one would predict.

Let me give a few examples. Sunset Crater, in northern Arizona, is known to be a recent volcano. Indian artifacts and remains are found within the rocks formed by the volcanic eruption, first in the form of lava flows, then cinder showers. Few of the inhabitants seem to have been killed by the eruption, but their villages and agricultural sites were buried. The Indians hastily moved to a safer location, but took with them the tale of the mountain's activity, some 900 years ago. Tree-ring dating accurately dates the eruption to about 1065 A.D.

The two lava flows have been dated by the potassium-argon method. Much to everyone's surprise, the lava flows gave "ages" of 210,000 and 230,000 years![5] The explanation? The "date is too old because of excess argon." Well, it's true that higher levels of argon-40 are present than were expected, but that's not much of an explanation.

A similar error could be cited from the eruption of Mt. Rangitoto in New Zealand, dated by radiocarbon studies of destroyed trees of less than 300-year-age. But potassium-argon put the date at 485,000 years.[6]

Numerous volcanic eruptions have occurred on Grand Canyon's north rim since the Canyon was eroded, within the last one million years at most. But in almost every case, the hardened lavas date excessively old.

A Grand Canyon volcano of much interest is Vulcan's Throne, which has yielded the "youngest" potassium-argon date in Arizona, of 10,000 years.[7] This designation seems appropriate, since the eruption postdates all the rocks in the Canyon. But what of the date? Native American legends recall the eruption of volcanoes in this vicinity, and Indians have been in the area only a few thousand years at most. (More on the dating of volcanic rocks on the Canyon rim later in this chapter.)

An additional "age" determination was made on the mineral olivine contained within the lava at Vulcan's Throne. Olivine is known for its low potassium concentration, and is seldom used for dating, but when the test was run, it again showed an excessively high concentration of argon for this amount of potassium, thus yielding an "age" of

Basalt at Grand Canyon. How old is this rock?

---

4   See Woodmorrappe, John, "Radiometric Geochronology Reappraised," *Studies in Flood Geology*, Institute for Creation Research, 1993, for a compilation of many unusable dating results.

5   Dalrymple, G. B., "40 Ar/36 Ar Analyses of Historical Lava Flows," *Earth and Planetary Letters*, Vol. 6, 1969, pp. 47–55.

6   McDougall, I., et al., "Excess Radiogenic Argon in Young Subaerial Basalts from Auckland Volcanic Field, New Zealand," *Geochemica et Cosmochemica Acta*, Vol. 33, 1969, pp. 1485–1520.

7   Reynolds, S. J., et al., "Compilation of Radiometric Age Determinations in Arizona," *Arizona Bureau of Geology and Mineral Technology Bulletin 197*, 1986, p. 8.

117± 3 million years![8] Some explain this away by claiming the mineral was contained within a "pod," which may have become incorporated into the lava flow from a deeper source at the time of eruption. Thus, this "pod" was unable to give up its excess argon, it is claimed, and retained evidence of its older age. Fair enough, but as we have seen, even molten rocks don't always "reset the clock" to zero. When does the method work, and on what basis can one determine which specimens are valid just by looking at the field evidence? And how do we know that even the 10,000 year specimen didn't retain excess argon?

Kilauea east rift, Sept. 1977, Hawaii

Investigators have many times acquired anomalous dates by the potassium-argon method as well as other methods. Consider the tests run on historic lava flows in Hawaii.[9] Rocks from the Kaupelehu Flow, Hualalai Volcano, known to have erupted in 1800–1801, were dated with a variety of methods on several different minerals and inclusions. Although too "young" to have produced much radiogenic argon or helium, the rocks contained large quantities of these gases dispersed throughout. The article reports 12 dates, ranging from 140 million years to 2.96 billion years! The dates average 1.41 billion years! The authors go to great lengths to try to explain them away, claiming primarily that, as it rose, the magma brought with it older material from deep inside the earth, but the authors are unable to explain how the gases were retained, and why the different gases and minerals give such different "ages."

The same article reports similar findings from Salt Lake Crater on Oahu, thought to be "less than one million years old." One of the methods produced an age of "less than 400,000 years," which they call the "real" age, but the other sixteen ranged from 2.6 million to 3.3 billion, with an average of 845 million! Again, an effort is made to explain away the calculated ages, but the point is, the use of the various methods produced results which didn't agree with known dates, didn't agree with each other, and were bizarre. In each of these volcanic events on land, daughter material was present at the start, giving anomalously old "ages," even though the daughter gases could have easily escaped into the atmosphere, thus producing "younger" dates.

But what about volcanic events in the oceans? Does the water pressure make a difference? As you might expect, deep-ocean basalts have been analyzed, with predictably confusing results.

One such investigation[10] involved Mt. Kilauea, again on Hawaii, where lavas erupted into the deep ocean which "are very young, probably less than 200 years old." Repeated runs on samples taken from 4680m in depth gave a potassium-argon "age" of 21 ± 8 million years. From a depth of 3420m, the calculated "age" was 12 ± 2 million years, while those from 1400m produced an age of zero years (the correct answer, i.e., too young to measure), even though all the samples were from the same lava flow. Evidently, excessive argon was trapped inside the rock by pressures in the deep ocean, and even grinding the rock to an extremely fine particle size didn't release the gas. The authors point to the correlation between depth and apparent age, and caution against using ages obtained from

8   Damon, P.E., and others, "Correlation and Chronology of the Ore Deposits and Volcanic Rocks," *U.S. Energy Commission Annual Report, No. C00-689-76*, 1967, p. 82.

9   Funkhouser, John G., and Naughton, John J., "Radiogenic Helium and Argon in Ultramafic Inclusions from Hawaii," *Journal of Geophysical Research*, Vol. 73, No. 14, July 1968, pp. 4601–4607.

10 Nobel, C. S., and Naughton, J. J., "Deep-Ocean Basalts: Inert Gas Content and Uncertainties in Age Dating," *Science*, Vol. 162, 11 Oct. 1968, pp. 265–266.

deep-ocean basalts, but the problem remains. Even though this trend is known to exist, and efforts are made to minimize its effects, many investigators to this day regularly use and/or cite potassium-argon results on ocean-floor basalts, among other things, to "prove" slow rates of sea-floor spreading.

And what do we make of the fact that oceanic lavas from shallow depths gave up their excess argon when lavas on land did not? If investigators routinely apologize for their findings and explain them away, what good is the method? It seems that whenever igneous rocks form today, they usually have daughter elements already present and already *appear* to be somewhat "old." If this assumption doesn't work on those times when we *can* check it, how can we be confident that it works on those occasions when we *cannot* check it?

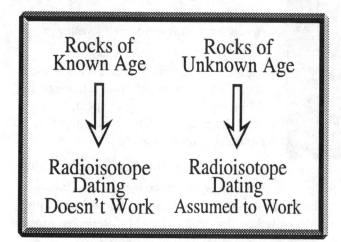

Rocks of Known Age → Radioisotope Dating Doesn't Work

Rocks of Unknown Age → Radioisotope Dating Assumed to Work

As we have seen, assumption number one is essentially the assumption of uniformity, which is known to be unreliable in normal geologic processes, but which seems to be a reasonable (although not necessarily correct) assumption in these atomic processes. Assumption number two is a little more troublesome, because buried in it is the idea that nothing has ever happened to the earth's crust which would have dramatically opened these rocks to the environment. But it would not be surprising if, during the time of Noah's Flood, the earth's crust was in such turmoil that contamination or leaching would have been a very common occurrence. Assumption number two, therefore, is to a great degree, the assumption that catastrophes such as the Flood of Noah's day have not occurred. Even local catastrophes, which are now well accepted by all

geologists, would disturb the uniformity of the geologic process in the areas affected.

Assumption number three, as we have seen, fares poorly when tested, and is probably completely wrong. Furthermore, it is essentially the denial of the possibility of Creation!

A Denial of Creation

Let me illustrate. The Bible says: On Day One, "God created the heavens and the *earth*" (*Genesis 1:1*). On Day Three, the continents were called forth from the world ocean (v. 9). Certainly rocks existed which were either created directly by God or formed during these early processes.

If a scientist were to come along on Day Eight and gather a specimen of this newly created rock, the rock would actually be only a few days old. (For this illustration, let us assume that the radioactive isotopes began to decay immediately after they were created.) If the rock were then taken into a laboratory and dated with the set of assumptions discussed above, how old would that rock appear to be? The question is, when God created the earth, was there any lead-206 present? Or was the concentration of lead abnormally high? If so, the rock would possess a superficial appearance of a history from the very start, if one assumes that excessive lead-206 comes only from uranium decay.

The Bible says that at the end of the Creation period the creation was "very good." Would lead atoms have been present? I suspect so. The various isotopes of lead are indeed "very good," because lead has had many more applications of use for mankind throughout history than uranium, which has been of use only in recent decades. In order for the earth to be "very good," it would certainly include lead, and likely the various isotopes of lead as well. I suspect the rocks would appear "old" (using these questionable assumptions to date them), even though they were newly created.

This is *not* an act of deception on God's part. The Bible is very clear that Creation took place only several thousand years ago, just in case we are inclined to misinterpret the array of isotopes. And, as already stated, if the earth *is* very old, then God *has* deceived us, for His revealed Word teaches plainly that His world is young! But, keep in mind that the radioisotope dating concept assumes that much, if not all, of the "daughter" isotopes came from parent decay, and thus denies the power of God to create a variety of isotopes. In other words, it denies truth, and, therefore, can only arrive at error.

The Fourth Assumption

There's another assumption which is an over-arching backdrop for the whole method, and that is the assumption that the earth is at least old enough for the present amount of radiogenic lead in a specimen to have been produced by present rates of uranium decay. If we knew that the earth was old, the possibility exists that radioisotope dating could help us determine exactly how old, but it is useless in testing *between* old earth and young earth. It *assumes* the old earth.

To sum up, the concept of radioisotope dating assumes uniformity. It assumes that there has never been any world-restructuring catastrophe. It assumes there has never been any supernatural creation, and it assumes the earth to be old.

So we see that this method uses questionable and Biblically incorrect assumptions, and one might suspect that the results obtained from this approach would not be very useful, and indeed it is not. As can be seen from individual articles reporting results and from listings of dates obtained, many times the laboratory results are found to be bizarre, not agreeing with what was suspected, not agreeing with each other, not agreeing with the "ages" of nearby fossils, and not agreeing with stratigraphic analyses. Such results are, to a significant degree, discarded because they simply don't agree with preconceived notions.

Grand Canyon Dating

Let me illustrate from an area of interest to all scientists, and in particular to those of us at the Institute for Creation Research—i.e., Grand Canyon. My colleague in the Geology Department, Dr. Steve Austin, has led this research effort. His work is summarized in the book *Grand Canyon: Monument to Catastrophe*, ICR, 1994, edited by Dr. Austin.

The layers in the Grand Canyon which are most noticeable, and of great notoriety, are the horizontal, fossil-bearing sedimentary layers, which are *not* datable by radioisotope methods. But there are several layers which are

potentially datable by this family of radioisotope techniques, which include not only the uranium-to-lead method, but also potassium/argon, rubidium/strontium, lead/lead ratio methods, isochron methods, etc.

Two particular rock layers in Grand Canyon can be and have been dated extensively by these methods and to them I'll call your attention. One is called the Cardenas Basalts, a sequence of basaltic layers which is thought to be among the oldest rocks in the Canyon. It has been assigned to the Precambrian system, lying stratigraphically below the fossil-bearing Tapeats Sandstone, assumed in evolutionary thinking to be about 550 million years old.

The other rock consists of basaltic lavas which have been extruded by volcanoes up on the plateau. These volcanoes erupted after the Canyon had been carved, because lava flowed down the Canyon walls and even blocked the river for a time. Native Americans, in all likelihood, witnessed these eruptions, probably dating within the last few thousand years.

Both layers have been well studied, with results published in the geologic literature. In addition, Dr. Austin has gathered fresh samples in an attempt to reproduce the original results, as well as extend the studies. In each study, the accepted radioisotope methods were used, employing the (questionable) assumptions discussed earlier. This extensive study

Grand Canyon, Arizona

thus provides a good test case. Do radioisotope methods accurately determine the age of rocks?

The Cardenas Basalts

The deeply buried Cardenas Basalts were first dated in 1972 by the potassium-argon (K-Ar) method.[11] The isotopic array published was used to calculate an "age" of 853 ± 15 million years, using recently revised values for the decay constants. A later study yielded "ages" of 820 ± 20 and 800 ± 20 million years.[12] Further study produced "ages" of 791 ± 20 and 843 ± 34 million years.[13] Thus, the range of dates, including uncertainties, would place the actual age somewhere between 771 and 877 million years. In each of these tests, only a single isotope analysis of each rock was obtained. The results are referred to as "model" ages.

The Cardenas basalts, one of the oldest rocks in Grand Canyon

Results from "model" age studies are often recognized as *discordant*, not agreeing with other analyses obtained by using a different radioisotope method or not even agreeing with the results of the same test run on a different specimen of the same rock. Other times, the derived isotope dates are *discrepant*, not agreeing with dates obtained by stratigraphic or fossil studies. Frequently, a date will simply be *discarded* if it doesn't fit, and never published at all.

In recent years an effort has been made to minimize the effects of both variations throughout the rock and uncertain assumptions inherent in the "model" age method and to reduce scattered estimates of the age to a single figure upon which more reliance could be placed. Thus, the "isochron" technique was developed, based on multiple analyses of various specimens of both rocks and minerals, all from the same geologic unit. In theory, this method would not only give the true age of the unit, but also determine the amount of daughter material present initially. Confidence in the result grows when the various data points plot along a straight line. The slope of the line gives the age, and the intercept gives the initial condition.

Thus, the five model ages given above can be reformatted as an isochron. The straight line plotted indicates an "age" of only 715 ± 33 million years and the initial amount of argon-40 can be found. Remember that the *model* ages are calculated using the assumption that *no* argon was present at the start. But the newer and better trusted *isochron* method revealed that this assumption was in error, even though the significantly older dates had previously been accepted.

More accurate determinations are thought to result from use of the rubidium-strontium method, which has become quite popular in recent years. Six specimens gathered from the same basalt strata (see footnote #12) yielded an isocron date of 1.07 ± 0.07 billion years, much older than the K-Ar isochron of 715 million years, even though both of them plotted along straight lines. Obviously they can't both be correct. The geologic community has generally accepted the Rb-Sr isochron as correct, and discarded the younger K-Ar dates.

Basalts on the Canyon Rim

Now let's apply the same suite of methods to the recent volcanic rocks on the Canyon's rim. Remember that these plateau basalts are extremely

11 Ford, T.D., et al., "Name and Age of the Upper Precambrian Basalts in the Eastern Grand Canyon," *Geologic Society of America Bulletin*, 83, Jan. 1972, pp. 223–226.

12 McKee, E.H., and Noble, D.C., "Age of the Cardenas Lavas, Grand Canyon, Arizona," *Geologic Society of America Bulletin* 87, Aug. 1976, pp. 1188–1190.

13 Elston, D. P., and McKee, E. H.,"Age and Correlation of the Late Proterozoic Precambrian Grand Canyon Disturbance, Northern Arizona," *Geologic Society of America Bulletin* 93, Aug. 1982, pp. 681–699.

A series of volcanoes erupted after the Canyon was eroded. Some of these basalts date excessively old.

"fresh" looking and are lying on top of all other rocks in the Canyon, and erupted even *after* the Canyon was eroded. Perhaps witnessed by Native Americans, they are easily the most recent rock units in the Canyon.

As mentioned before, one K-Ar model date stands at 10 *thousand* years, with a K-Ar model date of an olivine mineral from the same rock dating at 117 ± 3 *million* years. (Some have proposed that this mineral was from an older "pod" which may have been incorporated into the later lava flow). Other nearby specimens were dated by this method to be 3.67, 2.63, and 3.60 million years old.[14]

When Dr. Austin conducted Rb-Sr studies on five specimens gathered from obviously recent (Quaternary) lava flows in the same area, he obtained an isochron "age" of 1.34 ± 0.04 *billion* years! Obviously this isochron is "discordant" with the K-Ar dates and "discrepant" with the stratigraphic control, which places the entire suite of rocks at less than

a few million years old, most likely in the low *thousands* of years.

Furthermore, these lava flows couldn't possibly be older than the Cardenas basalts, even though both produced equally good isochron plots. The Rb-Sr isochron of the plateau basalts would be called by evolutionists a "fictitious isochron" with the isochron slope having no relationship to real time. Could the isochron derived for the stratigraphically lower Cardenas basalts (which was accepted as accurate) likewise be fictitious? And how does one know? How *could* you know?

Problems with the plateau basalts are magnified when a technique employing the ratio of lead isotopes is used. Fifty-five specimens were analyzed[15],[16] from numerous lava flows throughout the plateau. When the lead-lead results were plotted, they yielded an isochron "age" of 2.6 ± 0.21 *billion* years! This is the oldest figure ever derived, yet it is for the youngest suite of rocks! These specimens came from numerous sources, but they plotted along

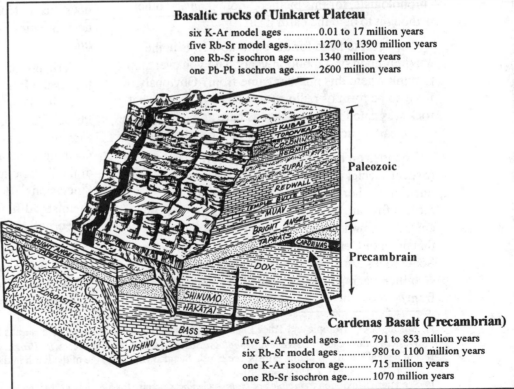

Basaltic rocks of Uinkaret Plateau

six K-Ar model ages	0.01 to 17 million years
five Rb-Sr model ages	1270 to 1390 million years
one Rb-Sr isochron age	1340 million years
one Pb-Pb isochron age	2600 million years

Paleozoic

Precambrain

Cardenas Basalt (Precambrian)

five K-Ar model ages	791 to 853 million years
six Rb-Sr model ages	980 to 1100 million years
one K-Ar isochron age	715 million years
one Rb-Sr isochron age	1070 million years

14 Reynolds, S.J., et al., op. cit., pp. 14,16.

15 Everson, J.E., "Regional Variation in the Lead Isotopic Characteristics of Late Cenozoic Basalts from the Southwestern United States," California Institute of Technology, unpublished Ph.D., Dissertation, 1979, p. 454.

16 Alibert, C., et al., "Isotope and Trace Element Geochemistry of Colorado Plateau Volcanics," *Geochimica et Cosmochimica Acta*, Vol .50, 1986, pp. 2735–2750.

a straight isochron line, attesting to their similar time of origin. This trend was reproduced by Dr. Austin.[17] Surely, "fictitious isochrons" are real, but neither they nor the accepted isochrons seem to be giving the true age of the rocks in question.

It must be admitted that rocks lower in the strata column, typically (but as we have seen, not always), date older than rocks found higher in the column. The *true* ages are not discerned, and the results only selectively reported, but something is going on which is not yet fully understood by creationists or evolutionists. Uniformitarians, in their zeal to establish the old-earth position, misinterpret this enigmatic array of isotopes as evidence for great age. A number of creationists are attacking this problem, and answers may be forthcoming, but until then, surely the Bible-believing Christian need not be intimidated by radioisotope dating.

Age of Meteorites/Earth

The lead-lead method of analysis holds a very prestigious, if obscure, reputation among chronologists, for this method, more than any other, is thought to date the earth itself.

The accepted age for the earth now rests in the neighborhood of 4.6 billion years. Did you ever stop to think where this number came from? Obviously, from some form of radioisotope technique, but what rock was dated? What rock was here at the formation of the earth, such that it could give the earth's age?[18]

Theories on the formation of the earth vary, but all (except special creation) hold that the earth was at one time, either during or after its formation, a molten fireball. No solid material was present. Even early rocks underwent intense metamorphism, so that no dating effort could see back to its formation. Some rocks are now claimed to yield dates of 3.8 or so billion years, but where did 4.6 billion years come from?

The answer? Meteorites! Rocks that fall from the sky. Sometimes these meteorites date at 4.6 billion years or so, usually by using the lead-lead isochron method.[19,20] This age is then transferred to the earth.

Theories on the origin of the solar system propose that the sun and its planets condensed out of interstellar star dust at about the same time. Meteorites are thought by most to be remnants of a planet which broke up after condensing. Therefore, meteorites are of the same age as the earth. To date a meteorite is to date the earth, or so it is claimed. Now, obviously, some things are being assumed here, things that are not known.

A Meteorite Called "Allende"

The meteorite that has received the most attention is a stony meteorite called "Allende" (A-yen-day). This extra-terrestrial rock has perhaps been studied more than any other rock on earth. Numerous radioisotope techniques have been employed in determining its age, but it's the lead-lead dating result which has yielded the date of 4.6 billion years for the meteorite, and thus for the earth. But what does this meteorite really teach? Do the different determinations agree? As you might suspect, *not at all.*

Perhaps the most extensive dating effort[21] studied the results from several radioisotope methods, including Pb-206/U-238, Pb-207/U-235, Pb-207/Pb-206, Pb-208/Th 232, and Sr-87/Sr-86. For each of these methods (and others which did not give meaningful data), the authors identified the "ages" of the "whole rock," of at least 50 different "inclusions" (local concentrations of a particular chemistry different from the general matrix of the meteorite), and of the rock "matrix" itself.

The U-Th-Pb suite of tests on the inclusions yielded much scatter, from 3.91 billion years to 11.7 billion years. The matrix results varied from 4.49 to 16.49 billion years, with 13 out of 18 "ages" being

17 Austin, S.A., "Isotopic and Trace Element Analysis of Hypersthene-normative Basalts from the Quaternary of Uinkaret Plateau, Western Grand Canyon, Arizona," *Geologic Society of America Abstracts with Programs*, 24, 1992, A261.

18 For a good history of dating efforts, see Brush, Stephen G., "The Age of the Earth in the Twentieth Century," *Earth Sciences History*, Vol. 8, No. 2, 1989, pp. 170–182.

19 See Faure's textbook *Principles of Isotope Geology*, op cit., for a review of this evidence and technique, especially pp. 311–312.

20 The earth's age was "proven" at 2 billion years, deduced by "several independent methods," in the 1930's. Many revisions and proposals have been advanced. The views of an early leader in deciphering the presently accepted age based on meteorites are expressed by Patterson, C.C., in "Age of Meteorites and the Earth," *Geochimica et Cosmochimica Acta*, Vol. 10, 1956, pp. 230–237.

21 Tatsumoto, M., Unrch, D., and Desborough, G., "U-Th-Pb and Rb-Sr Systematics of Allende and U-Th-Pb systematics of Orgueil," *Geochemica et Cosmochimica Acta*, Vol. 40, 1976, pp. 616–634.

impossibly high, even though estimates of the amount of original daughter isotopes were subtracted out. This subtraction amount was based on the lead content of another important meteorite, the "Cañon Diablo" troilite. No isochron was possible.

The "Cañon Diablo" troilite has been accepted as containing a representative ratio of radiogenic to non-radiogenic lead, and thus establishes the amount of original daughter material to be subtracted from the total. Of course, the individual atoms are identical and cannot be differentiated by simple inspection. The theoretical amount of original daughter material in all meteorites is thus derived from the "Cañon Diablo" meteorite ratio, the "correct" ratio in turn determined by its concordance with the accepted age of the solar system.

But the fact remains, there is a seeming excess of lead in meteorites, or a deficiency of uranium and thorium. Typically, there is too much lead to have been derived from decay of the uranium and/or thorium present. Thus, some estimate of the original daughter material must be made. Unfortunately, meteorites still tend to give excessively high "ages."

Similarly, the Rb-Sr suite of techniques yielded differing results. (The Sr-87/Sr-86 was the only technique discussed—the results of other methods were deemed too unreliable and were not reported.) The inclusions yielded ages from 0.70 billion years to 4.49 billion years, with most being significantly lower than expected. The matrix ages were reported as 4.60 and 4.84 billion years, even though the best estimates of original daughter material were taken into account. No isochron was possible.

Although the dating of mineral inclusions is considered standard procedure, and the results accepted on many occasions, it is conceivable that discrepancies might arise. Thus, the "whole rock" model age would take precedence. As can be seen from the accompanying table, no agreement was reached, with most values being greater than the assumed age of the solar system, an impossibility

In the discussion portion of the article, the authors gave reasons for the varied results, including anomalous concentrations in the original solar nebula, removal or enrichment of certain isotopes by later disturbance events, movement of mobile elements Rb and Pb from the matrix into the inclusions, large variations of isotope ratios in the individual inclusions, ratios affected by impact on earth, original isolation from the solar nebula. Need I go on? If the results don't fit, explain them away. But how could a 20th-century investigator possibly know what was happening in an isolated corner of the solar nebula five billion years ago? How could anyone have confidence in the few dates accepted? Perhaps they too are contaminated, and the true date is unknown. As it stands, the dates are accepted or rejected based on their agreement with an unprovable view of solar-system formation. The *scatter*, which is very real, seems more impressive and important than the forced agreement with the theory.

"Age" of "Allende"

Pb-207/Pb-206	=	4.50 billion years
Pb-207/U-235	=	5.57 billion years
Pb-206/U-238	=	8.82 billion years
Pb-208/T-232	=	10.4 billion years
Sr-87/Sr-86	=	4.48 billion years

Furthermore, a potassium-argon investigation of "Allende" yielded no help. This study[22] of similar inclusions gave apparent ages averaging 5.29 billion years, again older than the assumed age of the solar system. The suspected cause?—potassium loss in the solar nebula.

At the very least, we can say that the isotope ratios which do exist do not demonstrate conclusively that the earth's age can be known from these methods as presently understood. Even some evolutionists are inclined to agree. Note this concluding quotation:

"We suspect that the lack of concordance [scatter in the data] may result in some part from the choice of isotope ratios for primitive lead, [the original amount assumed for daughter material based on the 'Cañon Diablo' troilite], rather than from lead gain or uranium loss. It therefore follows that the whole of the classic interpretation of the meteorite lead isotope data is in doubt, and that the radiometric estimates of the age of the earth are placed in jeopardy."[23]

22 This study by T. Kirsten, 1980, is discussed in *The Chemical Evolution of the Atmosphere and Ocean,* by Heinrich D. Holland, 1984, Princeton University Press, p. 6.
23 Gale, N., et. al. "Uranium-Lead Chronology of Chondrite Meteorites," *Nature (Physical Sciences)*, Vol. 240, Nov. 20, 1972, p. 57.

But, as we have seen, there is also much selectivity in reporting the data. Many results are discarded, but to the extent that "independent" methods show similar isotope ratios (interpreted as the same age), this could mean that the universe *is* all the same "young" age, all created at about the same time, fully functional, with a God-ordained "very good" array of isotopes.

Radio Halos

Consider some other very intriguing evidence from radioactive elements. In recent years, physicist Robert Gentry has called our attention to an unusual phenomenon which he interprets as pointing to the *instantaneous* creation of certain granites. His conclusions have been published in scientific journals and in his book *Creation's Tiny Mystery*.[24]

Scientists have long known that when each particular radioactive atom decays, it gives off energy at a characteristic level. This energy burst damages the mineral matrix in which the atom rests, and the size of the damaged zone reflects the level of energy released. Because uranium atoms (for purposes of this discussion) are usually found within certain minerals as inclusions of billions of atoms (which together still occupy a very tiny point of space), the decay of these unstable atoms over time produces a sphere of damage around the radio-centers.

As mentioned before, uranium decays to lead through a series of intermediate steps, each of which has its own characteristic energy level upon decay. If

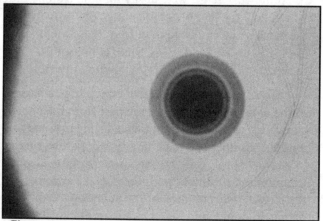

Characteristic set of halos for Uranium-238. Photo by Dave McQueen.

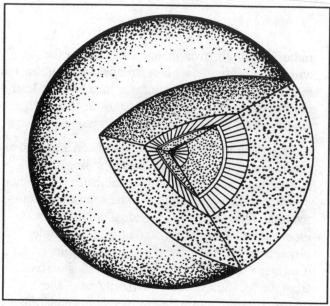

A radioactive inclusion produces damage in the form of concentric spheres, with each diameter recognizable as the decay of a particular isotope.

the inclusion resides in a well-formed crystalline structure, as is common in the mineral biotite (a form of mica frequently found in granitic rocks), the damage will form a series of concentric spheres around the inclusion or a series of concentric circles when one views a slice of the sphere through a microscope. These circles have come to be known as "pleochroic halos," or radio halos. Each element has its own characteristic halo. By observing the particular array of halos, one can deduce the make-up of the original inclusion (or the type of parent element present when the mineral formed).

Several of these intermediate decay steps have extremely short half-lives. For instance, when radon-222 (half-life of 3.82 days) changes into polonium-218 (half-life of 3.05 minutes), it rapidly changes once again into lead-214. Likewise, when bismuth-214 (half-life of 29.7 minutes) changes into polonium-214 (half-life of 1.6×10^{-4} seconds), it rapidly changes once again into lead-210. Obviously, the atom does not linger very long in either polonium state before it decays into the next isotope in the decay chain.

Amazingly, the set of halos characteristic of polonium isotopes is sometimes found without the more slowly forming uranium halos, showing no evidence of a parent cluster of uranium—just polonium. Apparently, there never was a uranium

---

24 Dr. Gentry's book, *Creation's Tiny Mystery*, 2nd Edition, 1988, is published by Earth Science Associates, Knoxville, Tennessee, and is available from Master Books.

cluster present at this location, and the original cluster must have been only polonium.

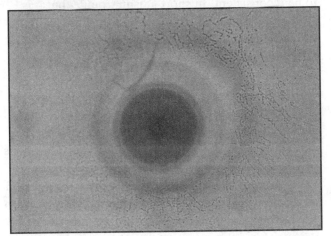

Characteristic set of halos for short-lived Polonium-218. Photo by Mike Armitage.

Granite is thought to require many years to cool from an original melted condition in order for its several types of mineral crystals to form, although the individual minerals, especially when concentrated, can rather quickly solidify once the temperature drops to the crucial point. Even pegmatite, a coarser-grained version of a granite, frequently occurring as veins within a granite, requires an appreciable length of time to harden. Since polonium isotopes have such a very short half-life, it would be incredibly unlikely for the polonium halo to occur by itself with no evidence of its parent material. This has led Gentry to speculate that the granites were instantaneously created in a hardened condition with polonium inclusions present, which subsequently decayed.

It is contended by Gentry that polonium occlusions by themselves could not occur in a slowly cooling granite, nor could they migrate to a central location all the while decaying rapidly. The granite would have to be in a rather fluid state so that polonium could concentrate in one location in the first place, then must be solid when the polonium decayed, in order for the zone of damage to be preserved. But the granite cools too slowly, and the polonium decays too rapidly to accomplish this in any scenario other than instantaneous creation, or so it apparently seems. Evolutionists have come to call this a "tiny mystery."

Gentry feels that the evidence only fits the idea that God created polonium, with its short half-life, and allowed it to decay instantly during creation week as His signature of creation. An alternative view is that after Adam sinned, and God declared "cursed is the *earth* for [Adam's] sake" (Genesis 3:17), certain elements became unstable and began to decay. Obviously, we can't know for sure. God hasn't given us all the details. But the polonium halos do exist, and must be explained. The only hope for a true interpretation necessitates going back to Genesis for our basic model.

Gentry's proposal is not without critics, even among creationists. Sticky points include the fact that all of these "orphan" halos are of elements included in the decay chain of naturally occurring uranium and thorium atoms. Why have no halos of other possible elements, which are truly independent, ever been discovered? Another problem is that some of Gentry's halos, which while discovered in association with granites, were found in "pegmatite dikes," and pegmatites are suspected to form much more rapidly than the host granite, although not instantaneously. Furthermore, granites are sometimes found within Flood deposits, demonstrating conclusively that granites are not all Creation rocks. Also, how could fully formed uranium halos be found in the same rocks as the polonium halos? The

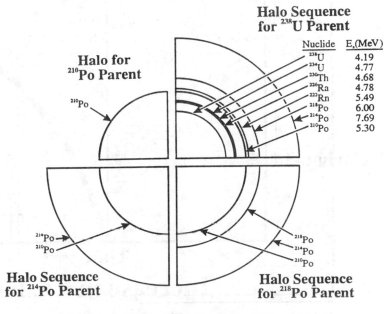

Characteristic ring configurations for different parent elements.

uranium halos, which consist of numerous rings reflecting the longer decay chain, would seem to take a much longer time to form. Gentry proposes a short but intense burst of radioactivity, with altered decay rates for most radioactive isotopes, to account for these halos.

Gentry's proposal of more rapid decay rates at times in the past has some merit. In fact, several creationist theorists, for a number of reasons and with good observational data and Biblical hints to focus their research, have speculated on such changing of decay rates, most likely associated with the "stretching out of the heavens," mentioned often in Scripture, as occurring during Creation week, and possibly during the Flood. These projects are as yet incomplete, but are leading in some interesting directions.

Several critiques of Gentry's concept have been advanced,[25] and as yet, some questions remain. I present this evidence here because I feel it is quite compelling, and I suspect that out of this exercise will come a strong and persuasive argument for the Biblical model of earth history.

As encouraging as these findings are, let me not leave the impression that radioisotope dating has been disproved. It has been called into question, flaws in its foundation exposed, and its results shown to be inconsistent. In short, it is in trouble, but it is still a very formidable concept in the minds of many. Much research needs to be done, and *is* being done at ICR and elsewhere.

Carbon-14

Many people have the mistaken notion that the carbon-14 dating technique places the age of the earth at billions of years and various rocks at millions of years. But, in reality, the carbon-14 method is valid only for "recent" times. Even the most devoted advocate would not claim that it has anything at all to say beyond about 60,000 years before the present time, and its inaccuracies are well-known.

On the other hand, the carbon-14 technique *does* have some application in the most recent few thousand years. If the standard assumptions are valid, i.e., that the rate of carbon-14 decay is constant, that there have been no additions or deletions of parent or daughter materials in a specimen, and that the amount of the daughter material present at the start is known, then the method can perhaps tell us

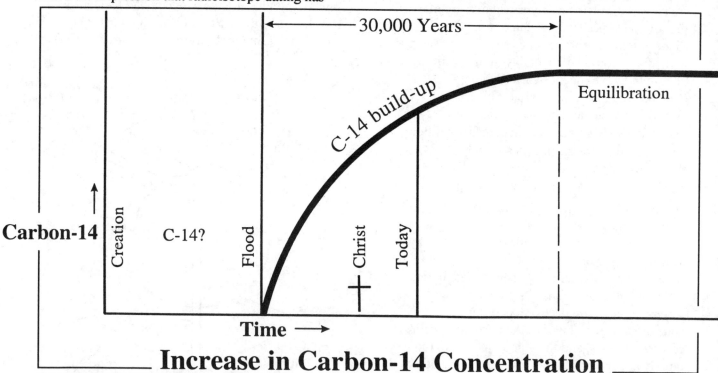

Increase in Carbon-14 Concentration

25 See in particular a review of Gentry's book by R. H. Brown, et al., "Examining Radiohalos," *Origins*, Vol. 15, No. 1, 1988, pp. 32–38. Gentry has attempted to answer these issues in the appendix of his book, 2nd Edition, pp. 313–321.

something about the specific dates of *historical* artifacts.

Keep in mind that carbon-14 is not thought to be helpful in dating inorganic rocks, but, rather, materials that contain carbon and were once living, such as bone, plant material, or fleshy parts. For instance, a tree buried by a lava flow can be dated, but the hardened lava itself cannot be dated by this method.

First, a short description of the concept. Carbon-14 is formed when nitrogen-14 is altered in the outer atmosphere by cosmic-ray bombardment. This radioactive isotope of carbon comprises only a minor percentage of total carbon. This ratio of radioactive carbon (C-14) to stable carbon (C-12) can be measured, even though C-14 is continually being formed from and decaying back into nitrogen-14. Both forms of carbon are found distributed throughout the atmosphere, oceans, and earth. Once the plant or animal dies, it ceases to interact with the environment by breathing, eating, and/or absorbing. Thus, it ceases to take in the normal ratio of C-12 to C-14 atoms, and the unstable C-14 atoms begin to decay back into N-14, thus changing the C-12/C-14 ratio over time. By measuring this ratio at any time after death, one can get an idea of when the plant or animal ceased taking in C-14 from the outside, and thus derive a time for its death.

Many processes can occur, such as ground-water leaching, bacterial action, etc., which can alter the concentrations of the parent or daughter material, and so care must be taken, and usually is taken, to date only those specimens which give no appearance of having been contaminated or leached. Carbon-14 decays at a rather stable rate, as shown from precise measurements, but the assumption of the original concentration is once again the technique's Achilles' heel.

It would take only 30,000 years or so to produce an equilibrium state between C-14 formation and decay, starting from an atmosphere with no C-14. Normally, the assumption is made that such an equilibrium has existed throughout the past, since most think the earth's atmosphere is much older than 30,000 years. This assumption of equilibrium provided a value for the concentration of C-14 at death; however, it has now been disproved. It is now admitted by all investigators that equilibrium does not exist—that the C-14 concentration is constantly increasing. Thus, the carbon-14 "age" must be adjusted, using a calibration curve derived by dating objects of "known" age. There are many such objects of known historical date which can be used to check and calibrate the C-14 method.

Unfortunately, many times C-14 dates on objects don't agree with historically derived ages. I remember talking once with a famous archaeologist from the University of Pennsylvania doing an excavation in the country of Turkey. He had discovered an ancient tomb with wooden timbers. I asked if he had sent timber samples off for dating through the carbon-14 method. His reply shocked me and all those standing around. He had, of course, sent samples off for dating, but claimed he would *never* believe anything that came back from a carbon-14 lab. Nor was he aware of any archaeologist in the world who would accept such dates. If the date agreed with what he knew it should be *historically*, then the data would be published; if not, it would be ignored. He was obliged to carbon-date artifacts to keep his grant money coming in, and so he always did so, but, he did *not* trust the method or its results.

On another occasion, I was debating an evolutionist at the national convention of the American Archaeological Society when dating processes came up. I chided the archaeologists present by insisting that they should be honest and admit that they never trust carbon-14 dates. There was nervous laughter throughout the audience, but no one even attempted to contradict me.

This distrust of the method is, of course, an overstatement. There are many who do take the results from carbon-14 dating seriously. But only on very rare occasions does anyone take it as *definitive,* particularly when the date cannot be verified by another technique, usually a historical dating method.

The salvation of the carbon-14 technique has supposedly come through calibration by dendrochronology (tree-ring dating). By comparing the C-14/C-12 ratios in tree rings stretching back into the past, a "calibration curve" can be drawn. This is believed to give the researcher information on the precise carbon inventory in the atmosphere at the time the tree-ring formed, and therefore makes possible the dating of other objects which died that year and presumably possessed the same C-14/C-12 ratio at death.

The technique is very precise and persuasive, but it has a serious weakness, one which hasn't been resolved, involving the reliability of dendrochronological methods as developed by researchers. The oldest living tree is thought to be on the order of 4500 years old. Yet the tree-ring chronology extends roughly twice that. Obviously, since no single tree lived throughout the entire time, dendrochronologists must match up tree-ring patterns from trees whose life spans are thought to have overlapped in order to extend the series far back into the past. This, of course, is fraught with difficulty and subjective analyses. Even trees living today don't always show the same tree-ring patterns. Variations are seen from tree to tree, others are due to distance from water source, prevailing sunlight direction, nutrients in the soil, etc. Investigations look for shorter sequences within the pattern thought to be unique, and thus can be used for correlation. Much care is taken, but problems still exist.

> Among the pines, [the bristlecone] is, if anything, even more undependable than the Junipers.... We have many cores from bristlecones growing in the White Mountains of California, east of the Sierra Nevadas, at altitudes of 10,000 feet, where the rainfall is low and erratic. There are also a number of cores from bristlecones growing at high altitudes in south-western Utah and on the San Francisco Peaks at Flagstaff, Arizona. Comparison of charts of measured rings show no similarity whatever.
>
> Harold S. Gladwin, "Dendrochronology, Radiocarbon and Bristlecones," *Anthropological Journal of Canada*, Vol. 14, No. 4, 1976, p. 5.

Both the dendrochronology and the C-14 scales depend very much on at least pseudo-uniformity in the environment throughout the time spans covered. This, of course, would be impossible, given the Biblical Flood. If the Flood really occurred the way the Bible says, no tree could have survived. Furthermore, the Flood would have drastically altered the carbon inventory in the world, certainly as it laid down the vast limestone deposits (calcium *carbon*ate), coal deposits, and oil shales. At the time of the Flood, great amounts of carbon were removed from the atmosphere and oceans and were no longer available for ingestion or absorption into animals or plants, thus destroying any semblance of uniformity in nature and also any hope of a calibration curve going back *before* the Flood. Nor would such a calibration be possible for the first few centuries following the Flood, during which things re-stabilized.

We don't know all that happened to the available carbon at the time of the Flood and the years soon after. Nor do we know what happened to the environment, with any precision. In all likelihood, there were intense weather patterns and numerous volcanic events for hundreds of years. It would not surprise me a bit if unstable weather conditions, particularly during the Ice Age which followed Noah's Flood, would have caused numerous tree rings to develop in any one year, but this is something that is not yet known. It needs to be subjected to careful scrutiny.

Dr. Larry Vardiman of ICR is researching a similar problem with ice cores, formed by snowfall, taken from the glaciers of Greenland and Antarctica. Uniformitarian researchers claim the accumulation represents many "winter/summer" patterns, extending back for tens of thousands of years. But Dr. Vardiman's research indicates that the evidence better points to a time of intense volcanism and snowfall for hundreds of years, with many pseudo "winter/summer" patterns each year. This, of course, would be the Ice Age, caused by the Genesis Flood. Evidently, the earth's processes were so destabilized by this global cataclysm, that it took several hundred years to restabilize. The "Ice Age" occurred during this time. What would this environmental crisis do to trees and their tree rings?[26]

Dr. Gerald Aardsma of ICR has investigated the tree-ring and carbon-14 problems and has concluded[27] that even if one accepts the standard tree-ring chronology, the only way to make sense out of the C-14 data is to accept a world-restructuring event no longer ago than about 12,000 B.C. While that

---

26 See his monograph *Ice Cores and the Age of the Earth*, by Dr. Larry Vardiman, ICR, 1993.
27 Aardsma, Dr. Gerald, *Carbon-14 and the Age of the Earth*, ICR, 1991.

date may be high, note that the C-14 data is not compatible with *any* sort of an old-earth model. We don't have all the answers yet, but the evidence is strongly in favor of the overall young-earth/Flood model. Research needs to continue, particularly on the tree-rings. Of all the radioisotope dating methods, carbon-14 is one of a very few which could potentially tell us something about *true* history. The rest have essentially little or no sensitivity below several million years.

Research is continuing, and progress is being made. In fact, ICR has on premises a C-14 lab, not for dating specimens, but for research on the basic method.

Again, please don't get the impression that radioisotope dating techniques have been disproven, because they sometimes do yield results which are consistent. The make-up of the early earth and the dynamics of the Flood and the centuries following are still not completely known, and until more is known, we cannot fully understand what these isotope ratios are telling us.

However, as we have seen, there is much that indicates that the radioisotope dating methods are not as accurate as we are told, and need not be intimidating to the advocate of the young earth. This is especially true as we recognize the basic assumptions of all such techniques, which in essence involve denial of the Biblical facts of Creation and Flood. Our distrust of these methods even increases when we recognize that the methods frequently give discrepant, discordant, or fictitious dates, and are frequently, if not usually, discarded.

The troubles of the radiocarbon dating method are undeniably deep and serious. Despite 35 years of technological refinement and better understanding, the underlying *assumptions* have been strongly challenged, and warnings are out that radiocarbon may soon find itself in a crisis situation. Continuing use of the method depends on a "fix-it-as-we-go" approach, allowing for contamination here, fractionation there, and calibration whenever possible. It should be no surprise, then, that fully half of the dates are rejected. The wonder is, surely, that the remaining half come to be *accepted*.

No matter how "useful" it is, though, the radiocarbon method is still not capable of yielding accurate and reliable results. There are gross discrepancies, the chronology is uneven and relative, and the accepted dates are actually selected dates.

Lee, Robert E. "Radiocarbon, Ages in Error," *Anthropological Journal of Canada*, Vol. 19, No. 3, 1981, pp. 9, 29 (Assistant Editor).

Chapter 6
Human History and the Young Earth

O f all the dating techniques available to us, only a few tend to give ages on the order of millions or billions of years, namely, those radioisotope dating techniques (with the exception of carbon-14) discussed above and a few others which I have not included. There are, however, many other techniques available to date the earth and its various systems, many of them based on much sounder science than radioisotope dating. The vast majority of these dating methods give *maximum* "ages" for the earth which are much too low to have allowed for evolution to occur.

Each dating technique is based on careful measurements and sound theory, but they share a common weakness in that they all employ the same uniformitarian, naturalistic assumptions inherent in radioisotope schemes, and therefore give questionable results. However, many such methods are more reliable than radioisotope schemes, even though not necessarily absolutely correct. I am convinced that rocks and other earth systems are not at all reliable for dating the earth, whether individual rocks or physical systems, simply because dating methods rely on unprovable assumptions which are in some instances Biblically incorrect. But the methods I'll explain in this chapter and the next involve less objectionable *applications* of these assumptions than radioisotope dating. They rely to a greater degree on *true* history—written and observed history—and these more reliable examples each give ages for the earth much too low for evolution.

A very effective debating technique is to show that the assumptions used by one's opposition lead to illogical conclusions, conclusions that even *they* don't like. In that spirit, we can use the set of assumptions employed by old-earth advocates, and demonstrate internal inconsistencies in that way of thinking. When we do that, the weight of the evidence, even using *their* assumptions, points toward a young earth. Most of the evidence implies that the earth is far too young to be compatible with the evolutionary world view.

That is the key. Since the rocks themselves are not definitive as to age, the most we can hope for is to show that rocks and systems are not compatible with a particular world view. Having said that, we must acknowledge that, to some degree, the radioisotope techniques are loosely compatible with the view that the earth and its systems are millions or billions of years old, all the while recognizing that questions regarding them give us reason to distrust their conclusions. But there exists a large body of evidence which does not fit at all with old-earth ideas, although derived by using old-earth techniques. We can't disprove old-earth ideas, but we can show internal inconsistencies within that model.

Some of these alternative dating techniques point to an age of only thousands of years, while others give ages in the low millions. Remember that all these techniques involve assumptions which largely exclude the possibility of Creation or Noah's Flood. But even given those invalid assumptions, still the weight of the evidence is much more compatible with the young-earth position than with the old-earth position. The data can't specifically tell us one way or the other, but the young-earth position appears to be favored. Let me, in this and the following chapter, give several of these specific chronometers which point toward the young earth—an earth too young to have allowed for evolution. We'll first look at some involving human civilization.

Recent Dating of Civilization

Several writers have advocated various dating methods, which, even if not definitive, are compelling.[1] One involves the fact that civilization dates to only five thousand or so years ago, at the beginning of written history. Evolutionary ideas, however, would insist that humans diverged from ape-like ancestors some three million years ago and through a gradual increase in culture developed into "stone age" people and then "bronze age," "iron age," and up into the modern era. This gradual

---

1 See for example, Morris, Henry M., *Biblical Basis for Modern Science*, Baker Books, 1984, pp. 414–426.

increase in technology and cultural levels should be reflected in archaeological discoveries.

In reality, this is not borne out. Archaeologists have shown that in a variety of places around the world, very advanced, modern cultures sprang up suddenly, almost simultaneously. These were complete civilizations, possessing a complex language, sophisticated culture, agricultural knowledge, rather impressive technology, and many times a written language. These cultures were able to devise elaborate calendars, and build pyramids, impressive buildings, and sea-going vessels. Most, eventually lost their advanced technology, and only in the last few hundred years has mankind begun to regain it. This early technology, even more advanced in some cases than modern technology, is not what would be expected if humans had recently been heavy-browed, stoop-shouldered, long-armed knuckle-walkers, hunting and gathering food.

Yet, *true* history, that is *written* history, relying on human observation and authentication, agrees remarkably with that suggested by Biblical history. Human culture from its very start was advanced, and humans have always been intelligent. The only claims which disagree with this perspective are those derived from the illegitimate use of dating techniques as described before, as well as from the evolutionary assumption of human development. But evidence for primitive cultures can be more easily understood in terms of isolated language groups of intelligent people, migrating away from the Tower of Babel, having been separated linguistically, and no longer having access to the broad array of technology available to other groups. "Primitive" people groups were those which totally lost their technology from misuse or hardship, and who didn't compete well against larger, better-situated, and advanced language groups.

Population Statistics

Observation of earth's population and population growth likewise supports the young earth. Given the total number of people on earth today, now approaching 6 billion, and its present rate of population growth of about 2% per year, it would take only about 1100 years to reach the present population from an original pair, which is of the same order of magnitude as the time since Noah's Flood—at least it's within the right ballpark.

But suppose man has been around for one million years, as evolutionists teach. If present growth rates are typical, there should be about 10^{8600} people alive today! That's 10 with 8600 zeros following it. This number is obviously absurd, and no evolutionist would claim it to be accurate. But it is an example of uniformitarian thinking in action.

Of course, the assumption of stable population growth throughout the past might seem unreasonable because of famines and plagues and wars. However, the last few centuries, which have seen

---

The Fossil Record

- 95% of all fossils are marine invertebrates, particularly shellfish.

- Of the remaining 5%, 95% are algae and plant fossils (4.75%).

- 95% of the remaining 0.25% consists of the other invertebrates, including insects (0.2375%).

- The remaining 0.0125% includes all vertebrates, mostly fish. 95% of the few land vertebrates consist of less than one bone. (For example, only about 1,200 dinosaur skeletons have been found.) 95% of the mammal fossils were deposited during the Ice Age.

- The fossil record is best understood as the result of a marine cataclysm that utterly annihilated the continents and land dwellers (Genesis 7:18-24; II Peter 3:6).

interdependent societies, mass weaponry, and crowded cities develop, have also seen the most brutal genocide, rampant abortion rates, the worst wars, the worst famines, and the worst plagues, in which multiplied millions have died. And yet the population growth rate hasn't changed much.

But let's assume man has been here for one million years. We can calculate the population growth rate necessary to produce today's population in that length of time from an original pair, and we find it to be only 0.002%, quite different from known measured rates throughout recorded history.

Even so, starting one million years ago, with a growth rate of 0.002%, and a present population of 6 billion, can you guess how many people would have lived and died throughout history? The number is so large, it is meaningless, and it's approximately the number which could just fit inside the volume of the entire earth! If all these people lived and died, where are their bones? Why are human bones so scarce?

The numbers don't get any better when we consider only the Stone Age, in which the evolutionists tell us that Neanderthal and Cro-Magnon civilizations dominated.[2] These people groups even buried their dead, increasing the chances that bones and teeth would be preserved. If the Stone Age really lasted 100,000 years and supported a population of between 1 and 10 million individuals, they should have buried about 4 billion bodies in the uppermost soil layer! We find only a very few.

This argument applies even more so for all the other plants and animals which have comprised a much greater volume over a much longer period of time. I recognize that plant and animal, as well as human, remains decompose, are eaten, are recycled, and take unusual conditions to be preserved, but surely such conditions would *sometimes* occur. Actually, fossil remains are abundant, especially for marine organisms buried catastrophically in sedimentary rock units. But these trillions of fossils do not compare to the *trillions* of trillions which should have lived throughout the supposed billions of years. The present fossil array (consisting almost entirely of marine fossils) is more compatible with the idea that the world at one time contained abundant life, which was buried essentially simultaneously by a cataclysmic flood. Where is the fossil evidence of billions of years?

These calculations don't allow any firm conclusions. Too many conditions are subjective. But we *can* say that the earth and its fossil contents are quite compatible with the Flood and young earth, and not at all compatible with an old earth. Population calculations and volumetric quantities can only be made compatible with the old earth by adopting unusual conditions and unrealistic assumptions about the past.

Why Are Human Bones So Scarce?

- Fossils are formed when buried in sediment beneath moving water.

- Land vertebrates, especially mammals, bloat when dead, and float in water.

- Land vertebrates dismember easily, and fairly quickly disintegrate or are scavenged in a water environment.

- The processes acting during the Flood would tend to destroy soft-bodied organisms, and preserve those with hard outer shells.

- The destruction of *mankind* was the primary goal of the Genesis Flood.

- Human bodies have a low fossilization potential.

- Of all living things, humans are among the least in number. (Some estimate that about 350 million people died in the Flood of Noah's day.)

- Even if all were preserved, and evenly distributed throughout the world's 350 cubic miles of Flood sediments, the chance of exposure, discovery, recognition, and reporting of even *one* human fossil would be extremely remote.

---

2   See Dritt, J.O., "Man's Earliest Beginnings: Discrepancies in the Evolutionary Timetable," *Proceedings of the Second International Conference on Creationism*, Vol. 1, 1991, pp. 73–78.

Cutaway View of Grand Canyon

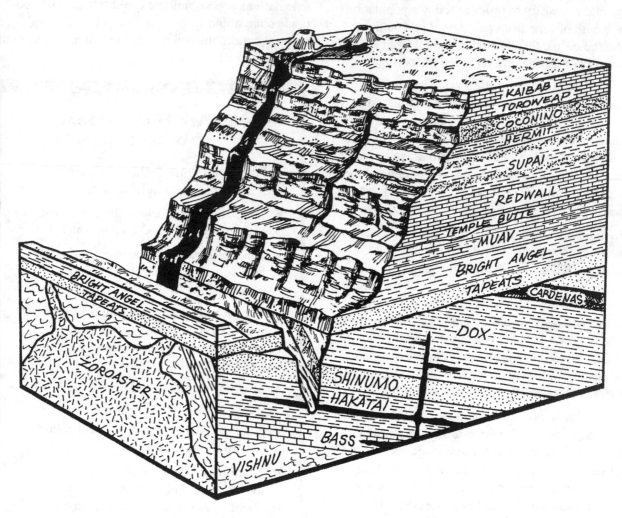

How Old Are These Rocks?

- Only igneous rocks can be dated by radioisotope dating techniques.
- Fossil-bearing rocks are dated by the fossils they contain.
- Fossils are dated by the false assumption of evolution.
- The igneous rocks on the rim date "older" than the igneous rocks at the bottom, according to radioisotope dating.

Chapter 7
Worldwide Physical Processes

As already mentioned, radioisotope schemes are not the only ways we can "date" the earth or its systems. In fact, there are hundreds of "clocks." Studies of many of these physical processes or systems give ages far too young to allow for evolution. These "clocks" are evaluated in exactly the same conceptual way as radioisotope clocks, but are quite different in scope. In radioisotope techniques, an individual rock or set of rocks is examined and dated. But a rock can, of course, be contaminated and altered in its mineral and chemical make-up. In the other techniques to which I will be calling your attention, the entire world will be the sample. Since it is nearly impossible to alter the entire world's chemical make-up to any significant degree, these processes should be given more weighty consideration.

One of these worldwide processes has already been mentioned—the global build-up of radioactive carbon. Remember that C-14 is extremely rare compared to C-12. Given the present rate of cosmic-ray influx (which causes C-14 to form), the equilibrium amount of C-14 globally should be about 75 tons. Calculations show that at present production rates it can grow no higher than this since it is continually decaying back into nitrogen. At present only about 62 tons exists, but the total *is* climbing.

Recognizing that the C-14/C-12 ratio hasn't yet reached equilibrium, but is still building up, we can calculate backwards to the time when *no* carbon-14 should have been present. This calculation has some uncertainty, but it yields a maximum age for the earth's present surface layers (including oceans, atmosphere, and land surface) approximately 10,000–15,000 years, and they might be much younger. If the earth's surface is any older than that, some environmental crises must have severely depleted the environment of C-14. Now, evolutionists might claim that the present rate of C-14 production reflects a temporary fluctuation in cosmic-ray influx, but certainly this is little more than *ad hoc* wishful thinking. As far as we know from scientific observation, the rate of cosmic-ray incidence and C-14 production is constant.

The word "maximum" needs a little explaining. The assumptions employed in any dating technique make it impossible to derive a truly accurate age. In this case, the calculation assumes that there was no carbon-14 present when the present atmosphere formed. This, of course, is reasonable only if an event stripped the earth of all or almost all of its oceanic and atmospheric C-14. I suspect the intense and prolonged rain during the break-up of the pre-Flood canopy, coupled with deposition of limestone and other carbon-bearing deposits by ocean waters would have done just that. But in all likelihood there *were* still some C-14 molecules at the end of the Flood that would tend to bring the maximum age of the present atmosphere down somewhat further.

As an interesting sidelight, only about one carbon atom in a trillion is of the C-14 isotope. The various carbon isotopes are equally likely to combine with other atoms to form larger molecules, such as CO_2. From studying certain chemicals and minerals in sedimentary rocks, it has been determined that much higher concentrations of CO_2 existed throughout the past, when the partial pressure[1] of CO_2 was up to 16 times higher than at present![2] Since CO_2 in the atmosphere seeks equilibrium with CO_2 in the oceans, and since animals emit CO_2 and plants assimilate it, a much larger concentration of CO_2 would imply that a much larger biomass could likely be sustained in the past than in the present. This supports the impression we get from Scripture that the pre-Flood world was a well-designed place which could support abundant life, an idea equally well supported by studies of the fossil record.

For purposes of our discussion, let us assume that the concentration of atmospheric nitrogen and the

---

1   Partial pressure is the contribution any single gas in a mixture of gases makes to the total pressure of the mixture.

2   Yapp, Crayton J., and Harold Poths "Ancient Atmospheric CO_2 Pressures Inferred from Natural Goethites," *Nature,* 23 January, 1992, pp. 342–344.

rate of cosmic ray influx was the same before the Flood as it is today, and thus the maximum amount of C-14 would be the same as today (i.e., about 75 tons). But in the pre-Flood case, only one carbon atom in 16 trillion would be of the C-14 variety, due to the greater presence of carbon in the atmosphere as CO_2. The same amount of C-14 and more C-12—thus, an unnaturally low (by today's standards) C-14/C-12 ratio would result, both before the Flood and in the centuries following. This would tend to give older C-14 "dates" than otherwise suspected, if we assume uniformity throughout the past. Again we see that the Biblical model adequately handles the C-14 data, while the old-earth model doesn't handle it nearly as well.

Many similar chronometers could be discussed, using the entire world as a specimen, and tending to give "young" ages, but let me give you just a few of my favorites.

Decay and Reversals of Earth's Magnetic Field

Dr. Thomas Barnes, formerly Dean of the ICR Graduate School and Emeritus Professor of Physics at the University of Texas, El Paso, has done the pioneering work on this classic geochronometer, as originally published in the ICR Technical Monograph # 4, *Origin and Destiny of the Earth's Magnetic Field* (2nd edition, 1983). More-recent studies have extended Barnes' pioneering work, to deal with the large amount of new data gathered since Barnes proposed his straightforward concept.

As we know, the earth has a dipolar magnetic field with North and South poles. The earth is not

permanently magnetized like a metallic magnet (permanent magnetism is destroyed by heat, and the earth has an extremely hot interior), but, rather, its field is due to an *electromagnet*, produced by currents in the earth's interior.

Observations have shown that the earth's magnetic field has been measurably decaying over the last century and a half. Precise measurements of the field's intensity, or strength, have been made on a worldwide basis since 1829 that determine the state of the field at any point in time. The intensity represents that force which attracts ferromagnetic particles, including those in a compass needle, turning it northward.

Measurements of Magnetic Field Over Time	
Year	Magnetic Moment in amp-meter^2 x10^{22}
1835	8.558
1845	8.488
1880	8.363
1880	8.336
1885	8.347
1885	8.375
1905	8.291
1915	8.225
1922	8.165
1925	8.149
1935	8.088
1942.5	8.009
1945	8.065
1945	8.010
1945	8.066
1945	8.090
1955	8.035
1955	8.067
1958.5	8.038
1959	8.086
1960	8.053
1960	8.037
1960	8.025
1965	8.013
1965	8.017

Earth with Magnetic Field

From these measurements, we can ascertain that the field's overall strength has declined by about 7% since 1829. These measured data-points plot along a curved line, which best fits that of exponential decay, as do many natural processes.[3] From this, it can be calculated that the half-life of the magnetic field's strength is approximately 1,400 years. If this half-life doesn't change with time, the field must have been much larger in the past, and will be much smaller in the future.

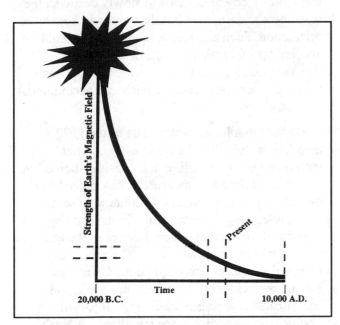

If we apply the same sort of uniformitarian assumptions used in radioisotope dating to the magnetic field, the consequences of its decay in the future are significant. The measured half-life of 1,400 years implies that 1,400 years from today, the magnetic field will be one half the strength that it is now. It will continue to decay at this rate, with half of its strength decaying every 1,400 years until sometime in the future, say 10,000 A.D, when it will, for all practical purposes, cease to exist.

But a robust magnetic field is important for life as we know it, because the field forms a protective shield around the earth, which deflects back into space much of the harmful cosmic radiation continually bombarding the earth, preventing it from impacting the earth's atmosphere and surface. Without a magnetic shield surrounding the earth, life would be rather harsh.

There are also consequences of the decay in the past. If the earth's magnetic-field intensity had been twice as strong every 1,400 years as you go back in time, that would mean that only 100 thousand years ago, the magnetic field would have been incredibly strong, comparable to that of a neutron star. The heat generated by resistance to the electrical currents in the molten core, sufficiently strong to produce such a large magnetic field, would have dire consequences. Barnes speculated that in the not-too-distant past, life would have been nearly impossible and some 20,000 years ago, the earth's internal structure would have been disrupted by the heat produced. This may be an over simplification, but you get the picture.

Furthermore, since cosmic-ray bombardment generates carbon-14 in the outer atmosphere, a stronger field, which would deflect more cosmic energy, would dramatically decrease the carbon-14 inventory in the past, and, therefore, the results from that dating process are even more uncertain.

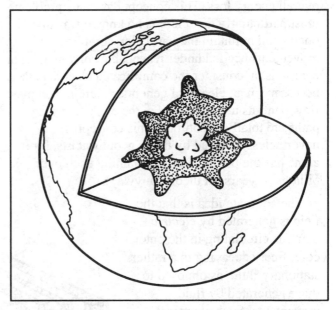

From seismic studies, scientists are fairly certain of the makeup of the globe. It appears that the earth possesses a very thin (about 20 miles thick on average) outer "crust" on its surface, which, while thin, has never been completely penetrated by drilling. Below the crust is the very thick (about 1,760 miles thick) "mantle" of the earth consisting primarily of solid materials. The very center portion

---

3   By exponential decay, it is meant that the quantity lessens by a certain fixed percentage each year, and that this yearly decay percentage stays the same over time.

of the earth is called the "core," which is divided into the outer and inner portions. The "outer core" (1,400 miles thick) is in a fluid state, and thought to consist primarily of molten iron and nickel. The "inner core" (780 miles in radius) is solid once again. (Near the boundaries of these zones, subdivisions are proposed, but for our purposes here, only the main divisions are considered.)

What Causes the Magnetic Field?

There are only two models (with variations of each) that have been proposed to account for the magnetic field as it exists. Uniformitarian scientists have proposed a self-exciting "dynamo" in the core, with slowly circulating *fluid* flows of molten iron and nickel in the earth's outer core, capable of generating electric currents which sustain and add to the magnetic field for billions of years. The energy fueling this movement is thought to be from the earth's rotation and its internal heat. Somehow, this energy is converted into magnetic energy without an overall energy loss. This concept has many problems, most particularly that there is no known way to obtain and maintain the particular, complex movements needed under reasonable conditions. (For comparison, consider the complicated electric path necessary in an electrical generator. Similar complex flow patterns are necessary in the earth, and such paths are totally unnatural.) This concept is, nevertheless, favored by many geophysicists, for it alone has the potential of maintaining itself over billions of years (in theory, anyway).

The alternate idea is that the field is generated by *electric* currents circulating in the outer core, freely decaying in a rather stationary fluid, as opposed to those generated by fluid movements. Such electrical currents are known to exist, and would decay in a manner consistent with the known field decay rate, due primarily to electrical resistance. Thus, the freely decaying electric-current theory fits modern observations of the decay rate quite well.

Next, consider the fact that much evidence exists that the

earth's field has reversed its polarity many times in the past, as inferred from measurements and samples taken from archaeological sites, sedimentary rocks, lava flows, etc. The most important reversal data come from measurements of reversely magnetized rock on land, and to a lesser degree from mid-ocean ridges. More on this later.

The self-starting and self-exciting dynamo theory proposes that reversals occur when the fluid motions cause the electrical currents to slowly decay all the way down to zero, then build up again in a reversed orientation. Such a dynamo, theoretically, could account for reversals more easily than freely decaying electrical currents. As mentioned, this theory has serious problems, but it can accommodate reversals.

On the other hand, creationists of the 1970's theorized a smoothly decaying magnetic field without reversals, insisting that consideration of the overall field decay, as measured, took precedence over the measured reversed orientation in some rocks, relegating them to local effects. But ongoing research developed much confidence in the idea that whole-field reversals *did* occur. Thus, the early creationist concept was deemed inadequate to explain the evidence. As it turns out, rapid and complicated reversals are an essential part of the free-decay theory also, once the effects of Noah's Flood are considered.

The reversal concept derives from the measured orientation of magnetic particles in rock, called

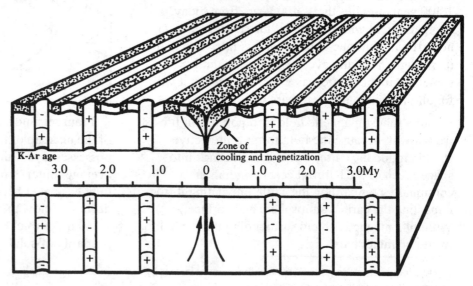

remnant magnetism. This can be measured in a laboratory for an individual specimen, or it can be recorded, using a magnetic sensor towed along the ocean bottom, measuring the magnetic field recorded in basaltic rocks along mid-ocean ridges. Here it appears that large sections of the earth's crust (called plates) have spread outward from the ridges, being formed as emerging lavas cool into basaltic rock, which acquires the magnetic signature of the magnetic field at the time and place they cool. These rocks sometimes show alternating positive and negative magnetized bands, roughly paralleling the ridge, and are interpreted as showing many reversals throughout the past. This evidence of spreading has been considered the "proof" of the idea of continental separation.

There are many problems associated with this evidence. To start with, the gathering of the data is done by those who "know what they are looking for," and those measurements which don't seem to fit preconceived notions are frequently discarded. One of my former colleagues on the faculty at the University of Oklahoma had been a researcher aboard a scientific vessel in the mid-Atlantic. Although he was a devoted advocate of plate tectonics, he grew skeptical of the sea-floor magnetic evidence, because he saw the selective manner in which it was being gathered. Likewise, a former graduate student of mine acquired a laboratory job at the University, measuring the remnant magnetism in individual specimens. He had never thought to question the theory, but he was puzzled to find how often discrepant readings were discarded by the scientist in charge. If the readings matched the theory's predictions, they were kept. Abnormal readings were thrown out. Once he and I discussed the scientific problems with the theory, he understood better.

To make matters worse, there are seven different types of remnant magnetism, only one of which is associated with the earth's magnetic field, and there are four theoretical types of self-reversal possible. When analyzing specimens, investigators attempt to erase or estimate the improper signals by subjecting the specimen to a series of heating cycles below the melting temperature, thus isolating the true paleomagnetic signal related to the earth's field at time of formation. Researchers have, in recent years, developed good techniques for dealing with signals,

and have determined that self-reversal would be extremely rare, but you can imagine the difficulties and possibility for error, especially in the early, formative days of this theory, during which many of the ideas of plate tectonics and paleomagnetic reversals were developed, ideas still popular today.

Another problem stems from the fact that in the lab, an individual rock is studied to deduce the field for the entire earth. Measurements from many specimens are averaged to minimize the effect of variant readings, but small errors in measurement yield large errors in the estimation of overall field strength and orientation.

The JOIDES Resolution — the deep-sea drilling project research vessel.

This is *not* to say that the theory and measurements are without merit. Far from it. I feel that both are quite valuable, now that many of the problems (such as those alluded to above) have been solved. I recently toured the Deep-Sea Drilling Project research vessel, the *JOIDES Resolution*, when it was being refitted in San Diego. One must be impressed with the sophisticated equipment on board and the professionalism of its staff. Make no mistake, reversals did occur. But I am convinced that the rocks have recorded events which are much more complex than is frequently admitted, and that the data's complexity is sometimes obscured or denied in order to support the standard dynamo theory.

Plate Tectonics

Let me divert briefly here to discuss plate tectonics. While no one observed the proposed separation of the world's land mass into the present-day continents after they were once together, the evidence which supports this is strong. Not only does the rather amazing fit of the continents support the idea, but also, once the continents are placed back together, mountain chains on both continents line up, as do major fault zones. Other evidences could be cited. It does appear that continental separation, in some form, did happen in the past, and if it did, we have to include it in the Biblical model.

I am convinced that continental separation was part of the overall restructuring of the earth's surface at the time of Noah's Flood. The continents probably separated in the later stages of the Flood, after much of the strata had been deposited as muds, and after mountain chains and fault systems had developed, and in all likelihood this separation was instrumental in bringing about an end to the Flood. Let me explain.

There is plenty of water available to cover the earth. If the earth were completely smooth, the water would stand over a mile and a half deep.

Evidently, before the Flood and during the early stages of the Flood, the world's topography was much less pronounced—the oceans weren't so deep and the mountains weren't so high, allowing the waters to cover the entire earth for a time. But how did the Flood end? Where is the water now? Obviously, the water is now in the ocean basins, which are much deeper than the continents are high, and cover over two-thirds of the globe. Such deep and wide ocean basins couldn't have existed *during* the Flood, because then it would have been impossible to cover the continents with water for a period of time, as the Bible implies. Somehow, the oceans must have been deepened and widened, allowing the water to drain into them, thus ending the Flood on the continents. Continental separation may have been one of the physical mechanisms involved. This partially explains why *no* oceanic crust has been discovered dating from the early earth. It was all formed late in the Flood.

Nevertheless, we should keep in mind that plate-tectonic theory has never been observed, and thus not "proven" in any real sense. True enough, the earth's surface is divided up into "plates," whose boundaries are identified by plotting the observed epicenters of modern earthquakes. And there is evidence for some plates sinking below an adjacent plate, and others moving laterally related to the adjacent plate. But the idea that the continents were once connected and have moved to their present separate locations is a subjective reconstruction of history, but it is fairly well supported by a lot of data.

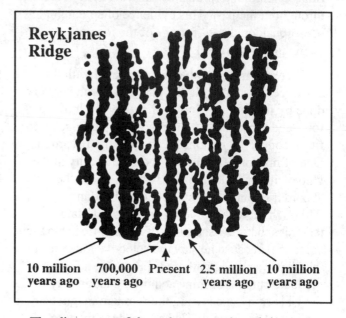

Reykjanes Ridge

| 10 million years ago | 700,000 years ago | Present | 2.5 million years ago | 10 million years ago |

The discovery of the paleomagnetic striping patterns parallel to the spreading mid-ocean ridges has been recognized as an important "proof" of the theory of plate tectonics. Every textbook on geology reflects this, and most reproduce the same paleomagnetic trace as measured on the Reykjanes Ridge near Iceland. As you can see, it looks convincing, but it is hardly typical. Almost nowhere else does such a clear mirror-image pattern exist. In other places, the striping is perpendicular to the ridge, not parallel, and in others there is no clear pattern at all. The data are extremely complex.

Problems in the theory of spreading along the rift zones are compounded by studies showing that reversals are not only found in parallel zones perpendicular to the mid-ocean rifts, but vertically in *each* rock zone, as drill cores have displayed for years, a fact seldom admitted by my uniformitarian colleagues. In my opinion, these zones are best understood as resulting from rapid reversals coupled with rapid spreading, and go hard against the slow-and-steady spreading hypothesis. This will be discussed in the next section.[4]

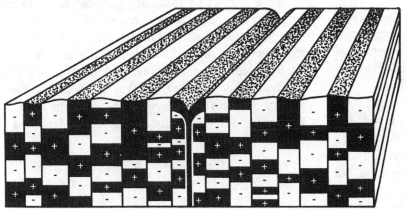

Cores drilled into the positively and negatively polarized zones show a very chaotic paleomagnetic pattern. This provides strong evidence for rapid spreading along the rift coupled with rapid magnetic field reversals.

There are yet other data which seem to contradict the standard theory. Precise measurements of distances across the Atlantic and at other places don't observe the predicted movement.[5] In some cases, there is *no* movement occurring today, and in others the movement is *opposite* to that expected.[6] The theory's main weakness is that there is no way to move a continent without relying on unnatural conditions. It appears that major plate movements may have occurred in the past, but that they have come (or are coming) to a halt today.

A minority of scientists have always held out against continental separation. A recent proposal entitled "Surge Tectonics" claims to account for all known data in a much more straightforward manner than plate tectonics.[7] This theory of rapid, episodic movement even claims to account for the observed magnetic "striping," by movements of lava *along* the oceanic rifts (not perpendicular to it), without field reversals. I make no claim for this rival theory. I mention it only because it illustrates the difficulty which exists in reconstructing the past, and the fact that there is always more than one valid interpretation of scientific data, especially as it relates to history.

Incidentally, one of the originators of the "Surge Tectonics" concept recently attended one of my seminars. I talked to him before the lecture, and he admitted he was there only as a favor to a friend (who had been witnessing to him). Obviously, he is open to "different" ideas, but young-earth creationism? He left at the end of the seminar, visibly affected, claiming he didn't want to accept my ideas, but that he couldn't find anything wrong with them, particularly given my presuppositions. He could see that the young-earth model worked well in science.

Reconstructing history from partial evidence is risky business. I feel we must do so in submission to true history as given in Scripture, and even then the job is difficult, for Scripture doesn't give us all the details. Without Scripture, we have no chance. And, as a matter of fact, the only proposed scenario for continental separation which provides an adequate mechanism for plate movement involves "runaway subduction of oceanic crust," initiated by a cataclysmic event, perhaps asteroid impact into the ocean. While there is admittedly no direct Scriptural basis for this idea, it incorporates the geologic and geophysical evidence into the overall Scriptural framework. This model, well received in both the creationist and non-creationist camps, was developed by creationist geophysicist and ICR Adjunct Professor, Dr. John Baumgardner, with the Flood of Noah's day in mind.[8] He feels that this "event" destroyed all pre-Flood oceanic crust, sinking it

4 Hall, J. M., and Robinson, P.T. "Deep Crustal Drilling in the North Atlantic Ocean," *Science*, 204, May 11, 1979, pp. 573–586.
5 Thomsen, D. E. "Mark III Interferometer Measures Earth, Sky, and Gravity's Lens," *Science News*, Vol. 123, Jan. 8, 1983, pp. 20–21.
6 Carter, W. E., and Robertson, D. S. "Studying the Earth by Very-long Baseline Interferometry," *Scientific American*, Vol. 255 (5), 1986, pp. 44–52.
7 Meyerhoff, A.A., et. al., "Surge Tectonics: A New Hypothesis of Earth Dynamics," *New Concepts in Global Tectonics*, edited by Chatterjee, S. and Hutton, N., Texas Tech University Press, 1992, pp. 309–411. This compendium of articles contains much in the way of new proposals. Reconstructing the past provides fertile ground for innovative ideas.
8 Dr. Baumgardner's model is best developed in a series of technical papers presented at the International Conference on Creationism, 1986, 1990, 1994. His two papers in 1994, "Runaway Subduction as the Driving Mechanism for the Genesis Flood"; and "Computer Modeling of the Large-Scale Tectonics Associated with the Genesis Flood," are well worth the study.

beneath the continents, moving the continents, and forming new oceanic crust between them. While contributing to the horror of the Flood, these movements eventually led to its end.

To sum up, plate tectonics is an observable fact. The plates do exist and some do move with respect to one another. Furthermore, the idea of the separation of a prior super-continent in the past is well supported by the evidence. But, in my opinion, large-scale movements are made possible only by the rapid and dynamic events surrounding the Flood. At the very least, the Flood provides us with the energies and circumstances capable of moving a continent. Certainly, more research must be done, but imagine the depth of frustration experienced by my uniformitarian colleagues who are trying to move the continents around with only present-day energy levels and process rates.

Rapid Reversals Coupled With Decay

Back to magnetic-field decay. If the magnetic stripes formed slowly, over long periods of slow separation as proposed by evolutionists, what do we make of the fact that the most recent reversal is dated at 700,000 years ago? (Some have proposed possible reversal events at 20,000 years ago and greater, but these are not well accepted). Life would have been impossible had the earth's magnetic field decayed along its present trend for 700,000 years, or even 20,000 years. Furthermore, during a slow reversal event, the magnetic field would be quite weak for long periods of time, with harmful effects on life. On the other hand, how do young-earth advocates handle the fact that the earth's crust *does* contain rocks with reversed magnetic orientation, particularly those along the active mid-ocean ridges?

Dr. Russell Humphreys,[9] a physicist at the Sandia National Laboratories in New Mexico, and Adjunct Professor of Physics at ICR, has attempted to solve this problem. He has adopted as fact, as I have in this book, that the Flood of Noah's day *did* occur only a few thousand years ago. With this as his starting point, he has proposed a very ingenious solution—one that explains the true data, including reversals, in an elegant and straightforward theory.

In the early years following publication of Barnes' original concept of freely decaying electrical currents, creationists had little way to handle the fact that *much* data support the idea of field reversals. As we have seen, these reversals, and the data indicating them, are very complex, but they *did* occur. Literally thousands of reversely polarized specimens have been studied from ancient rocks, both on land and sea.

Another category of specimens comes from archaeological sites—from bricks, kilns, campfire stones, pottery, etc., the dates of which can be discerned. Iron minerals in these artifacts were able to orient themselves with the earth's field when heated. This orientation was preserved when the object cooled, and can be measured today. Archaeomagnetic measurements indicate that the earth's magnetic field was about 40% greater in 1000 A.D. It has declined ever since, and is still declining today. Thus, both paleomagnetic and archaeomagnetic measurements contradict the concept of a magnetic field whose intensity is freely decaying due to simple electrical resistance. Briefly listed below are several lines of reasoning and discoveries. Weaving them together, Humphreys has been able to develop his model.

It has been recently shown that our sun's magnetic field regularly reverses itself, in connection with its sunspot cycle, every eleven years. Evolutionists had considered the sun's field to have been generated by a dynamo in some regards similar to earth's, but now recognize a big problem. How can the field frequently reverse, each time using up significant energy, yet maintaining itself for billions of years? The dynamo concept is on shakier ground than ever.

The main character of the earth's field seems to be due to electrical currents in the rather motionless core, not electrical currents maintained by a dynamo.

---

9 Humphreys has published his ideas in numerous papers. Two summary papers have appeared in *Acts & Facts, Impact* articles Numbers 188 and 242. These contain many references for further study, and a synopsis of the theory is included. Other papers include "The Creation of the Earth's Magnetic Field," *Creation Research Society Quarterly*,. Vol .20 (2), 1983, pp. 89–94. *'The Creation of Planetary Magnetic Fields,"* CRSQ, 1984, Vol. 21 (3), pp. 140–149; "Reversals of the Earth's Magnetic Field During the Genesis Flood," *International Conference on Creationism*, 1986, Vol. 2, pp. 113–126. "Has the Earth's Magnetic Field Ever Flipped," *CRSQ*, 1988, Vol. 25 (3), pp. 130–137; and "Physical Mechanism for Reversals of the Earth's Magnetic Field During the Flood," *ICC*, 1990, Vol. 2, pp. 129–142.

The presently observed decay is quite consistent with that predicted by a simple model of electrical resistance. This is assumed to be data from the creation of the earth, complete with a "very good" magnetic field caused by electrical currents which are now decaying. It makes sense that God would furnish the earth with such a protective shield. The decay probably dates back to the curse on the earth in Genesis 3:17, because of Adam's rebellion.

Dr. Humphreys has developed a corollary theory for the likely strength at creation of other planetary magnetic fields as well, the predictions of which have been supported by space-probe measurements.[10] This provides a possible original strength for the earth's field.

Another startling discovery involved firm evidence of a very rapid reversal event on earth, taking only about 15 days,[11] the time estimated for a pool of molten lava to cool. Evidence of a reversal was observed *within* a now-hardened basalt rock. Evidently, a complete reversal occurred during the short time the lava pool was cooling (a maximum of 15 days for this volume of lava).

Still another discovery involves fluid motions in the outer core. They do exist, and have now been measured by geophysical techniques, but they are not at all what was expected from the hypothesized dynamo.[12] They are, however, compatible with the revised free-decay model.

Dr. Humphreys proposes that at the onset of the Flood, very likely associated with plate movements and the breaking up of the "fountains of the *great deep*" (Genesis 7:11), a very powerful event initiated fluid convection in the outer core. The movement of molten metallic material in the presence of the existing magnetic field would produce a magnetic flux. A strong-enough flux of magnetic energy would cause the entire earth's magnetic field to eventually reverse—a natural consequence of rapid convection flows. Continuing movement would cause continual rapid field reversals, which would be recorded in rocks being continually extruded or deposited on the earth's surface. Note that these reversals do not add

to the field's energy. Instead, rapid reversals within a decaying field use up its energy, contributing to and hastening its overall decay.

As the Flood year ended, the energy for massive fluid movements was no longer present, and the magnetic flux waned. Today, we measure only a relic convection current. The earth's field gradually returned to its original configuration and decay rate.

A look at the field's total change in *energy* is more enlightening, at this point, than its change in *intensity*. The intensity reflects the effect of the field on the earth, from orienting a compass needle to polarizing the magnetic particles in a molten lava. The *intensity* can go to zero, and reverse in the complex scenario above. But the total *energy* in the system can not increase unless outside energy is added to it. If it drops to zero there is nothing left to start it up again. It can only decay, as does every energy system; and the more it is perturbed, the faster it decays.

Based on the measured intensity of the earth's field, scientists can calculate its total energy. As the intensity declines, so does the total energy. The half-life of the *intensity* was seen to be 1,400 years, but the half-life of the field *energy* is only 700 years! The types of trauma experienced by the field during the Flood, as briefly outlined in the preceding paragraphs, would serve to temporarily *increase* the decay rate of the field. Instead of a *free* decay of the magnetic field, we should, instead, consider a *dynamic* decay model.

Dr. Humphreys has produced two graphs which illustrate these points. The first, which is qualitative only, portraying the general idea, shows how the field's surface *intensity* varies with time, and demonstrates the measured decay at present. This is preceded by a series of numerous rapid reversals at the time of the Flood, followed by a lengthy period of fluctuation during which the earth's field settled back down. Before the Flood, the field was presumably much stronger than today but still decaying at the present half-life.

10 See Humphreys' article "Beyond Neptune: Voyager II Supports Creation," *Acts & Facts, Impact* No. 203, May 1990.

11 Coe, R.S., and Prevot, M. "Evidence suggesting extremely rapid field variation during a geomagnetic reversal." *Earth and Planetary Science Letters*, Vol. 92, 1989, pp. 292–298.

12 Lanzerott, L.J., et al. "Measurements of the large-scale direct-current earth potential and possible implications for the geomagnetic dynamo," *Science,* Vol. 229, 5 July 1985, pp. 47–49.

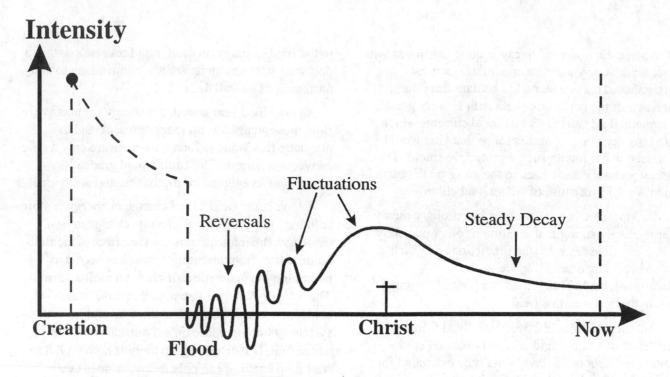

Magnetic field intensity at the earth's surface, from Creation to now.

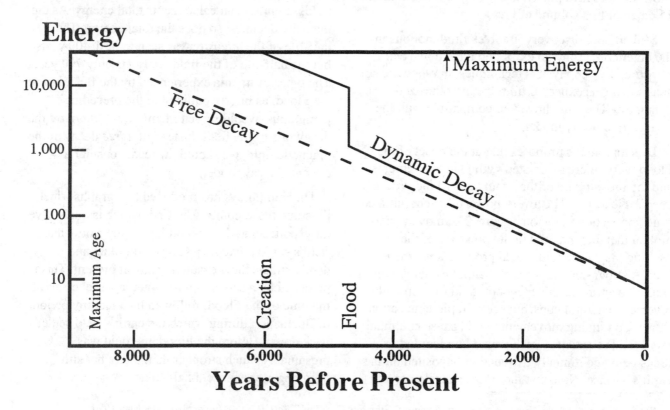

Total energy (in trillions of kilowatt-hours) stored in the earth's magnetic field. Free decay theory gives maximum age of 8700 years.

The second graph, which is numerically accurate, plots the field's total *energy* versus time. Again it shows the measured decay rate, but a time of almost instantaneous energy loss due to the rapid reversals during the Flood. The half-life before the Flood would be the same as now, but with the rapid step-decrease of energy due to the Flood.

Humphreys postulates a maximum possible energy for the earth magnetic field at Creation, consistent with his now substantially verified planetary model. He finds that the known decay would project back to this maximum in a time remarkably consistent with the Biblical date for Creation.

Old-earth advocates maintain hope that somehow the dynamo theory can still be salvaged. At present, it conflicts with observations of rapid reversals in modern lava flows, sun-spot cycles, minor convection currents in the core, and it has no support in physical theory.

The only existing model for the magnetic field which handles *all* the data specifies a young earth and a recent Creation. It is based on sound physics, and its predictions have been substantially verified.

To summarize, unless the earth's magnetic field has been altered or energized by an unusual magnetic event in the past, about which we know nothing, the present decay rate yields an upper limit of 20,000 years or so for the age of the earth.

I must stress, however, that the earth's age is not necessarily that high, because this number was derived using uniformitarian assumptions of decay (which, in this case, have a better chance of being valid). But even using the standard dating assumptions, the age calculated is "young," not "old." Furthermore, the evidence of magnetic reversals is quite compatible with predictions based on the Biblical Flood.

And note this! Since this chronometer is based on worldwide measurements, monitored for a long time, and showing a dramatic trend, it perhaps represents the very best application of uniformitarian principles. The weight of the evidence is on the side of the young earth, not on the side of the old earth.

Helium in the Atmosphere

One of my favorite young earth arguments involves the helium found in our atmosphere. Helium, of course, is a very lightweight gas because the helium atom contains less mass than any other atom except hydrogen. Helium is found in the atmosphere in measurable quantities, and based on the volume of the atmosphere and the percentage of helium, the actual number of atoms of helium in the atmosphere can be estimated.

Helium is produced beneath the earth's surface by the process of radioactive decay. When certain of the radioactive isotopes undergo an *alpha* decay episode, they give off an *alpha* particle. This particle consists of two protons and two neutrons, and is equivalent to the nucleus of a helium atom. This atom, because it is very small, lightweight, and mobile, migrates through the pores in the rock and eventually makes its way to the surface of the earth, where it joins the other gases in the atmosphere. Obviously, if we know how fast the helium is being added to the atmosphere and how much helium is in the atmosphere, then we can estimate how long it would have taken for all the helium to accumulate, providing us with a maximum age of the atmosphere.

Dr. Larry Vardiman, Chairman of the Physics Department at ICR, has done most of the work through the years on this very important chronometer. He continues to refine his and our understanding of it. His work presents an "air-tight" argument.[13]

Sensors have measured the rate of introduction of helium into the atmosphere. Believe it or not, the measured rate stands *at thirteen million helium atoms per square inch each second!* This phenomenal rate compares to the theoretical rate of helium escape into outer space of a maximum of about 0.3 million helium atoms per square inch each second. Therefore, helium in the atmosphere is accumulating at a very rapid rate. Dividing the known amount of helium in the atmosphere by the rate of accumulation shows that all of the helium in the atmosphere today would have accumulated in no more than *two million years!*

Please keep in mind, I *don't* conclude that the atmosphere is two million years old. Instead, this

---

13 See Dr. Larry Vardiman's monograph *The Age of the Earth's Atmosphere*, Institute for Creation Research, 1990.

teaches us that, using the uniformitarian assumptions inherent in every dating process, the atmosphere couldn't possibly be any older than two million years. I'm convinced it's much younger.

These assumptions include the notion that the rate of accumulation has never been any different throughout the past. But I suspect that during Noah's Flood, the rate was much more rapid, because the earth's crust was in such turmoil that the helium would have been able to escape more easily. This would bring the maximum age down.

The Age of the Atmosphere

Outer Space

Atmosphere

Earth's Crust

^{232}Th

^{238}U ^{235}U

Earth's Mantle and Core

All of the helium now in the atmosphere would accumulate in a maximum of 2 million years!

This argument also assumes that at the time the atmosphere formed, there were absolutely no helium atoms present, and that all of the helium atoms there now have come about by this process. But I suspect that at the time of Creation there *were* some helium atoms in the atmosphere, once again making the age much less. Helium is a very useful, "very good" element, and I suspect that the wise Creator would have included some in the original atmosphere.

This also assumes that nothing has happened to add or take away any helium from the atmosphere. Can we assume that no comet has come by and sucked all the helium off? I think so. Can we assume

that no asteroid has blasted into the earth bringing helium with it? Perhaps.

Another fact presents itself, however, that of the recent discovery of large volumes of helium in the earth's crust which don't appear to be of radiogenic origin.[14] If non-radiogenic helium (identical to radiogenic helium) is added to the earth's atmosphere from time to time, then the age decreases even more.

Next, can we assume that since helium does have some finite weight, it does not continue to rise and escape the earth's gravitational pull? Again, I think so. In order for the helium to escape, it has to overcome earth's gravitational pull by achieving "escape velocity," as does any object, which is many times faster than the speed of sound. Certainly, some atoms would reach such outwardly directed velocities when in an excited state in the outer atmosphere, but this would be, at best, a relatively rare occurrence. As we have seen, the maximum loss is significantly lower than the rate of helium influx from the crust. If the atmosphere is as old as evolutionists say, there ought to be a lot more helium here!

We can conclude from all this that the earth's atmosphere is quite young, much too young to have allowed evolution to take place. But keep in mind that with this method or any method, we can't accurately date things. The only thing we can do is put a maximum age on them.

You might ask how the evolutionists answer this problem, and the fact is they don't have an adequate answer. Many scientists have, over the years, tried to propose mechanisms by which helium might more readily escape into outer space, overcoming the earth's gravitational pull, but none have been successful. This is not to say that there is no such mechanism, only that science hasn't yet discovered it.

There is another point we can make here. We have seen that helium is lightweight, inert, and mobile, and rises in any fluid medium. This includes both gas and liquid. The rocks of the earth's crust contain both gas and liquid in the tiny spaces between grains and

14 See, for example, Craig, H., and Lupton, J. E. "Primordial Neon, Helium, and Hydrogen in Oceanic Basalts," *Earth and Planetary Science Letters*, Vol. 31, 1976, pp. 369–385.

in cracks. They *must* be filled with some fluid, and if any helium is present, it would rise, eventually reaching the surface.

But the fact is, the crustal rocks presently contain much helium! How long would it take for a helium atom at any depth to percolate through the rocks and reach the surface? This is a function of the rock's permeability, a measure of the ease with which fluids can migrate through it, and the driving force, in this case the difference in density between the helium and the other fluids (usually a salt-water brine). Different rock types have different permeabilities, but no rock provides a helium-proof seal. Helium would move through the rocks faster than any element other than hydrogen. And yet it is still there.

Radioactive decay in the rocks continually replenishes the helium, so the presence of it there is no surprise. But if this production has continued throughout billions of years, and the helium rushes to the surface, there should be much more in the atmosphere! The fact that it's in the rocks in abundance, but *not* in the atmosphere is a puzzle.

Thus, the lack of helium in the atmosphere provides a "young" date for the atmosphere itself, while the presence of helium in the crust (both radiogenic and non-radiogenic) implies a young date for the crustal rocks.

Salt in the Ocean

Another worldwide chronometer which speaks to this issue regards the amount of sodium (Na)—(best known as a component of salt, NaCl) in the ocean. We all know that the ocean is salty to the taste, and it stands to reason that it is getting more and more salty each year as rivers dump dissolved salts from the continents into the ocean. Evolutionists have traditionally assumed that life evolved in a salty sea, some 3 to 4 billion years ago. If the ocean is so old, and must have been salty long ago, wouldn't it be *too* salty by now?

Actually, there are quite a number of possible ways in which the ocean can be enriched in sodium. There are also many possible mechanisms by which the salt might be removed from the ocean. Discovering the present and historically possible values of both input and output processes would provide insight into the ocean's history.

Drs. Steve Austin and Russell Humphreys have formalized this argument.[15] They have attempted to identify rates of addition and removal of salt for each mechanism, both in the present and throughout the past. Furthermore, to arrive at the absolute *maximum* age, they have taken the *minimum* input rates that they can justify, both in the present and throughout the past, and have taken the *maximum* output rates that can be justified. Their analysis provides a strong evidence for a young ocean.

For decades investigators have attempted to monitor sodium input and output, and have identified numerous mechanisms. The processes are well known and accepted, and are briefly discussed below:

Input Processes

1. **Rivers: Silicate-Weathering Component**. Chemical weathering of continental silicate minerals (especially feldspars and clays) produces dissolved sodium, which finds its way into rivers and, eventually, the ocean.

2. **Rivers: Chloride-Solution Component**. Some deposits on land consist of chloride and sulfate minerals which easily dissolve and are transported to rivers.

3. **Rivers: Sea-Spray Component**. Spray from ocean waves gets transported to land, where it falls as rain or snow. Eventually it is picked up by rivers and transported back into the ocean. Obviously, this will also be considered later as output.

4. **Ocean-Floor Sediments**. Some ocean-floor sediments contain sodium that is released into the ocean.

5. **Pulverized Sediments in Glacial Ice**. Fine particles of rock flour produced by glacial movement are added directly to the ocean. They contain significant amounts of sodium.

6. **Atmospheric and Volcanic Dust**. Wind-blown dust from land sources may drop into the sea.

7. **Coastal Erosion**. Waves pounding the shoreline erode considerable amounts of land.

15 Austin, Steven A., and Humphreys, Russell D. "The Sea's Missing Salt: A Dilemma for Evolutionists," *Proceedings of the Second International Conference on Creationism*, Vol. 2, 1991, pp. 17–33.

8   **Glacier Ice**. The melting of glacial ice and snow directly into the sea adds small quantities of sodium to the sea.

9. **Volcanic Aerosols**. Volcanic steam contains some sodium, much of which falls into the ocean.

10. **Ground-Water Seepage**. Fresh ground water from the continent seeps toward the ocean. It contains dissolved solids, including significant amounts of sodium.

11. **Sea-Floor Hydrothermal Vents**. Hot springs located on the ocean floor contain a high concentration of dissolved solids, including sodium.

Output Processes

1. **Sea Spray**. As discussed above, waves produce spray, which contains sodium. Some evaporates, and winds carry the sodium inland.

2. **Ion Exchange**. River-borne clays exchange calcium ions for sodium, thus removing sodium from the seawater.

3. **Burial of Pore Water**. Accumulating sediments on the sea floor are sea-water saturated. This water, which contains salt, is thus removed from the ocean.

4. **Halite Deposition**. Most halite (rock salt) deposits are the result of *river-water* evaporation, not sea water. Actually, the ocean would need to be 20 times more concentrated in salt for deposition to occur. This happens infrequently in trapped pools, but such deposits redissolve easily. This output is trivial. The volume of salt water evaporated in trapped lagoons and not redissolved is not significant.

5. **Alteration of Sea-Floor Basalt**. Weathering of cold basalt under water produces certain clays which absorb sodium.

6. **Albite Formation**. It had earlier been proposed that hot basalts exchange calcium for sodium, thereby removing sodium from the ocean. However, more-recent studies show that this would not result in a net removal of sodium.

7. **Zeolite Formation**. Alteration of volcanic ash produces minor amounts of zeolites, which absorb sodium.

In order to calculate the appropriate minimum input rates and maximum output rates for such a possible mechanism, one must impose a concept of earth history on the data. For instance, during the Ice Age, both weather patterns and glacial processes were far different in intensity from those of today. Also, by examining the fossil record, it is obvious that throughout most of earth history the climate was generally warmer and supported lush vegetation. This would affect climate pattern, erosion, etc. Austin and Humphreys selected the most extreme of any reasonable conditions in each case to determine the minimum input and maximum output. Their conclusions, and the model they used are included in the accompanying table.

	Sodium-Input Process	Modern	Minimum
1.	Rivers: Silicate Weathering	6.2	6.2
2.	Rivers: Chloride Solution	7.5	7.5
3.	Rivers: Sea Spray	5.5	5.0
4.	Ocean-Floor Sediments	11.5	6.21
5.	Pulverized Sediments/Glacial Ice	3.9	0.0
6.	Atmospheric and Volcanic Dust	0.14	0.14
7.	Coastal Erosion	0.077	0.074
8.	Glacier Ice	0.12	0.0
9.	Volcanic Aerosols	0.093	0.093
10.	Ground Water Seepage	9.6	9.3
11.	Sea Floor Hydrothermal Vents	1.1	1.1

	Sodium-Output Process	Modern	Maximum
1.	Sea Spray	6.0	6.7
2.	Ion Exchange	3.5	5.2
3.	Burial of Pore Water	2.2	3.9
4.	Halite Deposition	<0.004	4.0
5.	Alteration of Sea Floor Basalt	0.44	0.62
6.	Albite Formation	0.0	0.0
7.	Zeolite Formation	0.08	0.2

Simply using modern measurements, the ocean's present salt content would accumulate in only 32 million years. In other words, at present rates of input and output, the imbalance is so great that all of the salt in the oceans would accumulate in 32 million years.

Using the extreme minimum and maximum values, the *maximum* age which results is only 62 million years! The ocean could simply not be any older than this. As far as science knows, there is no process which did or could remove the excess salt.

At the very least, we can surely say that the ocean is today not nearly salty enough to be more than 3 billion years old, the age required by the evolutionary tale of life's evolution and history.

This kind of calculation could be repeated for

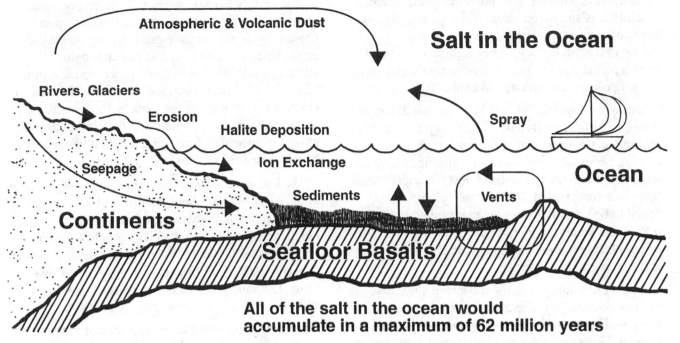

Salt in the Ocean

Atmospheric & Volcanic Dust

Rivers, Glaciers

Erosion

Halite Deposition

Spray

Seepage

Ion Exchange

Ocean

Sediments

Vents

Continents

Seafloor Basalts

All of the salt in the ocean would accumulate in a maximum of 62 million years

Again, I am not claiming that the ocean is 62 million years old, but that it *couldn't possibly be any older than that*. As with all dating attempts, there are assumptions involved. This number assumes that there have been no large, unaccounted-for additions or deletions of salt, but, of course, at the time of the Flood, erosion was occurring on a much greater scale! No doubt, much of the ocean's present salt was added then, thus drastically reducing the maximum age. This method also assumes that at the start, the ocean was fresh water, but this does not seem likely. Whatever salts were present at Creation would lower the maximum age even more. Reasonable assumptions would bring that age quite a bit further down, but again, not derive a precise age. The values used are extremely generous to the old-earth concept, in order to arrive at the maximum age. They are uniformitarian assumptions, generously applied. But even the best use of uniformity results in a figure incompatible with the old earth as presently understood.

scores of processes. Ocean water contains many dissolved elements and compounds, and most of them yield maximum ages for the ocean far too young to be compatible with old-earth ideas.[16]

Meteoric Dust from Space

In college, I was a co-op student—go to school for a quarter, then work for a quarter at industrial jobs. One spring, I worked for the Army Corp of Engineers, but roomed with a government engineer working on the space program. This was in the days before NASA had landed a spacecraft on the moon.

My roommate, indeed all of NASA, was quite worried about what would happen to a spacecraft landing on the moon. Their problem was this: We know that dust from outer space continually impinges on earth. We assume it strikes the moon at a proportionate rate, given its size and gravity. Measurements back in the fifties and sixties indicated that meteoric dust, made up primarily of iron, nickel, and other recognizable compounds, was coming onto the earth at 14 million tons per year.

---

16 See *What is Creation Science?* by H. Morris and Gary Parker, pp. 288–293, for a list of geochronometers and their implications.

It was inferred that if the earth has been here for 5 billion years, then there should be enough such material here on earth to form a layer over 150 feet thick. No one expected to find such a layer, of course, since the earth's surface is continually mixed by rain, wind, erosion, etc., but it *did* bother scientists that nickel is so rare on earth. If the earth is old, and the rate of accumulation has been the same throughout earth history, there ought to be more! The earth's nickel content is much more compatible with a young earth than with an old earth.

But what about the moon? With no rain, wind, or water, what falls on its surface stays right there. My roommate's design team spent much time concocting landing pedestals to minimize the distance the vessel would sink into unconsolidated dust. Of course, their fears were unfounded, for only an inch or so was found to be present. Given the measured rate of influx, this small volume of dust could easily accumulate in a few thousand years, but if the moon is old, something is wrong.

This young-moon argument became a real favorite of creationists everywhere, both because it was so clear, and because it was easy to understand and explain. However, more and better-quality data were obtained over the years, and questions began to be raised.

One of our adjunct faculty here at ICR, geologist Andrew Snelling, with an ICR physics graduate student, Dave Rush, recently did a careful literature survey and analytical study on this subject.[17] What once seemed to be a strong argument for the young earth/moon is not quite so clear now. Since the sixties, several measurements of dust influx have been made, and they all disagree, sometimes varying by a factor of 1000. The point is, we just don't know, at the present time, how much dust is coming in, and, therefore, can't make any clear statements about the earth's/moon's age on this basis.

It appears that the influx rate varies quite a bit, and we need more observation time to get a reasonable average. But it seems to me, that if meteoric dust comes in at alternating high and low rates, there would have been many such cycles in 5 billion years, and a relatively large quantity of dust would have accumulated. Once more is known, this argument may again be a good one. But it's not definitive right now, and we should stick to better arguments.

Rocks on the Earth's Surface

The earth's crust, both continental and oceanic, consists of rock similar in chemical make-up and potentially derived from materials deep inside the earth. Volcanic activity spews material onto the surface, while other activity emplaces great volumes of material below the surface, but still in the crust. Once in the crust or on the surface, the igneous material can weather, erode, and metamorphose, changing into other forms, but the total volume must be accounted for.

We know the total volume of sediment of all kinds in the earth's crust (about 5 billion cubic kilometers), and can estimate the volume of new material (i.e., not recycled) added, to be on the order of 4 cubic kilometers each year.[18] When we do, the time needed to accumulate the entire crust is only 1.25 billion years. Obviously, that is only a ballpark figure, but still far too young for evolutionary tastes.

Again this assumes there was none of the present crust here at the beginning, either continental or oceanic. It assumes that the rates of emplacement have been constant, but what about the Flood? the number 1.25 billion years has no direct meaning, except as a critique of uniformitarian assumptions.

Erosion of the Continents

Our modern continents are thought by uniformitarians to have existed for about 3.5 billion years, and to have been in recognizable configuration for tens of millions of years, at least since the postulated break-up of Pangea some 200 million years ago. In their model, continents have been crumpled into mountain chains, upthrust into elevated plateaus, sometimes underwater, but never static.

In Western North America, the Laramide Orogeny some 70 million years ago (as dated by uniformitarian geologists) thrust up the Rocky Mountains, and along with them elevated areas like the Colorado Plateau. The rocks which typically cap

17 Snelling, Andrew, and Rush, Dave. "Moon Dust and the Age of the Solar System," *Creation Ex Nihilo Technical Journal*, Vol. 7, No. 1, 1993, pp. 2–42.

18 Decker, R., and Decker, B. Eds. *Volcanoes and the Earth's Interior*, Freeman, 1982.

this plateau are thought to be 100 million years old, and have never been underwater since. Thus, erosion supposedly has been cutting them down for 70 million years.

Colorado Plateau—showing flat, featureless, uplifted area through which the Canyon has been eroded. Was this uplifted 70 million years ago and basically untouched by erosion ever since?

Once eroded, the sediments are carried away by streams and rivers, eventually entering the ocean. The sediment load in these rivers can, of course, be measured, and the average yearly amount of sediments carried into the sea from the continents stands at 27.5 billion tons per year.[19,20]

By now, you know what comes next. The volume of the continents above sea level has been measured at 383 million billion tons. At present erosion rates, all the continents would be reduced to sea level in 14 million years!

But they are thought to be many times that old already. Were they many times greater in bulk when they uplifted? No, because rocks thought to be on the surface at the time of uplift are *still* on the surface, and have hardly been eroded at all!

Let's go back to the Colorado Plateau. There has been significant erosion—just look at Grand Canyon. But much of the Colorado River drainage basin is virtually untouched—a flat, featureless, uplifted plateau, bearing no evidence of 70 million years of erosion. Was erosion occurring at a slow rate in times past, only now to pick up to a rate where all the continents of the world will be gone in 14 million years? Such rapid erosion can't be blamed on human activity, for it would have increased erosion only by about a factor of 2½,[21] at the most, and then only for the most recent few thousand years.

This line of reasoning might not be a method of dating the earth or its continents. Rather, it is a devastating critique of the story uniformitarians tell. That story has no internal consistency.

The uniformitarian may try to take solace in the proposal that the continents are still rising, and volcanoes are continually erupting, thereby replacing the volume being displaced, and keeping pace with erosion. But that doesn't address the problem that the surface at the time of uplift is still the surface, and erosion has hardly touched it. Nor does it account for the present-day existence of so much ancient (hundreds of millions of years old, so it is thought) sedimentary

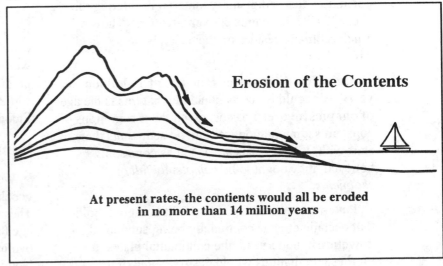

Erosion of the Contents

At present rates, the contients would all be eroded in no more than 14 million years

19 Nevins, S.E. "Evolution: The Oceans Say No!" *Acts & Facts*, 1973, *Impact* Article No. 8.
20 Roth, Ariel A. "Some Questions About Geochronology," *Origins*, Vol. 13, No. 2, 1986, pp. 64–85.
21 Judson, S. "Erosion of the Land—or What's Happening to our Continents?" *American Scientist*, Vol. 56, 1968, pp. 356–374.

rock. If the uplift and erosion had been continuing for even two or three times the 14 million years, all the sedimentary rock would be gone! This fact is made more disconcerting if one realizes that mountain chains (as opposed to continents in general) are rising several times faster than erosion, yet contain much "ancient" sedimentary rock. Much of this rock is dated at hundreds of millions of years old, some even up to 3 billion years. This is enough time to completely erode the continents many times over, yet the continents are nearly everywhere covered with sediments. The uniformitarian story doesn't make sense!

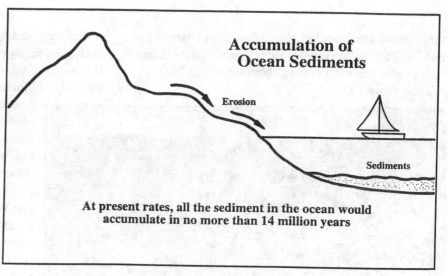

Accumulation of Ocean Sediments

Erosion

Sediments

At present rates, all the sediment in the ocean would accumulate in no more than 14 million years

Again, don't get hung up on the 14-million-year figure. I think the crustal sedimentary rock was, in most cases, deposited by the Flood of Noah's day. Then the continents and mountains were upraised toward the end of the Flood, and erosion rates have varied since then. The 14 million years represents only a critique of uniformitarian, old-earth ideas.

Sediments in the Ocean

A corollary to the erosion problem has to do with the volume of sediments in the ocean. We've already noted how fast sedimentary material is entering the ocean, 27.5 billion tons per year. Now note how much sediment resides on the ocean bottom, 410 million billion tons.

Simple division arrives at an age of 15 million years. We could properly conclude that this is the age of our present ocean basins, given the assumptions of constant sedimentation rate and no sediments there to start with. If the oceans are as old as commonly believed, they ought to be *completely full of sediments*.

Plate-tectonics theory, one might point out, holds that oceanic crust is continually being subducted, or downthrust, underneath the continental plates. It might seem that this would destroy some of the sediments, thereby solving the apparent problem.

But two factors argue against this. At the trenches where subduction is supposed to occur, most of the sediments are thought to be scraped off and piled up. (They are mostly still there, have been measured, and are included in the total figure above.) But even if the sediment is being subducted, subduction rates are still only between 10–20% of the rates of erosion and accumulation. Furthermore, most river deltas, where the bulk of sedimentation occurs, are not near subduction zones. Thus, the amount of sediment subducted and recycled does not significantly change the calculated "age."[22] It seems that both the measurements of sediment carried *into* the ocean and the rate of sediment accumulation *in* the ocean don't square with the long-age scenario. Again, the flood would increase the rate of deposition, thus lowering the time required to accumulate the sediments. But what can be said for Christians who hold to the old earth concept? They must deny the history of the worldwide Flood, for even a *tranquil* flood would produce much sedimentation. Thus, old-earth Christians must believe in a local Flood or in no Flood, an untenable position for Bible-believers.

Summary

We have studied only a few of the many geochronometers which can be used to date the earth. These and many others not discussed here point to an age for the earth much too young to have allowed for evolution. As we've seen, the Flood is the key. Nothing on the surface of the earth could have escaped its devastation. Uniformitarianism, by its

22 See papers by both Nevins and Roth, op cite.

very nature, assumes that processes haven't changed much in their intensity throughout the history of the earth, and thus adherents mistake certain devastated features for age.

Remember each "clock" relies on the same basic assumptions as for radioisotope dating, (1) constant process rate; (2) relative isolation of the system, so no loss or gain of quantities has occurred; (3) knowledge of the initial state of the system; (4) the earth is at least old enough to have produced the present state through the observed process.

Since all these assumptions are questionable at best, and very likely wrong altogether given the historical facts of Creation, Fall, and Flood, we don't expect any such geochronometer to give a valid age. However, it is reasonable to conclude that those geochronometers which make use of worldwide observations and systems (like magnetic field decay, helium in the atmosphere, and salt in the ocean), would be better, all things being equal, than those employing the dating of a single rock or local system. Such a worldwide scope minimizes the possibility of loss or gain of the materials being measured. As far as its mass is concerned, the earth is very nearly a closed system.

It would also be better for a system to have a long-enough history of measurement behind it (like the magnetic-field decay) to identify and smooth out any temporary fluctuations in the process rate.

And, if the history of measurement of a particular system represents a significant portion of a half-life, it also lends credence to the method. Note that the half-life of the magnetic field's energy is 700 years, and its history of measurement covers almost 25% of the half-life. The half-life of Uranium-238, on the other hand, is 4.5 billion years, and has only been accurately measured for several decades (about 0.000002% of a half-life). Surely the *better* dating schemes point to a young earth.

It might even be reasonable to assume that the larger the "date" derived by a particular system, the more opportunity there has been for contamination or alteration, which would yield an incorrect date. Therefore, those that tend to give young ages are probably more likely to be accurate than those that give old ages.

It seems reasonable to conclude that while any chronometer, whether limiting or actual, would be untrustworthy, for each employs questionable assumptions about the unobserved past based on uniformitarianism, the weight of the evidence does point towards a young earth, rather than an old earth. The only way we could know for sure how old things are would be if someone (or Someone) who saw these processes occurring made careful observations and recorded them for us. Then and only then would we have true empirical evidence.

And that is exactly what we do have in Scripture. An Observer (in fact a Participant in these events) did record for us what went on. We can read that Scientist's "lab book" and conclude the age of things. Any other way of dating is fraught with error-prone assumptions. How much better to trust the Accurate Record of the Capable Observer.

Grand Canyon—the Canyon is thought to have eroded rapidly in very recent times. Why has the uplifted plateau been untouched by erosion?

Polystrate Trees
Incompatible with Long Ages

Chapter 8
Geologic Evidence for a Young Earth

The publication of the book *The Genesis Flood*, by Whitcomb and Morris in 1961, is generally recognized as starting the whole modern Creation movement. Not that it discussed creation very much; rather, it explained the nature and power of the Flood. And the Flood *is* the key. Such a Flood could account for the fossils and the strata which have traditionally been misinterpreted as evidence of long ages of uniformity. For the first time, Biblical inerrancy could be considered a credible, scholarly position. The Flood really happened, and the evidence for catastrophism in geology abounds. The young-earth position directly follows from the global Flood, just as belief in an old earth by otherwise Bible-believing Christians necessitates a belief in the local-flood idea.

But things have changed in the years since. My evolutionary colleagues would probably not admit it, but the Creation movement has even caused a revolution in secular geologic thinking. At the very least, secular geology has adopted many of the "radical" positions espoused in *The Genesis Flood*, for now we find the entire discipline of geology moving back toward catastrophism. Many leading geologists now even identify themselves as "neo-catastrophists," and have begun to invoke large-scale, dynamic processes for the production of geologic layers and earth features.

Consider for a moment the perspective of Dr. Derek Ager, former President of the British Geologist's Association. While attempting to distance himself from creationist geologists who believe in Noah's Flood, he has spearheaded a revival in geology back toward flood processes. "The hurricane, the flood or tsunami may do more in an hour or a day than the ordinary processes of nature have achieved in a thousand years. . . . In other words, the history of any one part of the earth, like the life of a soldier, consists of long periods of boredom and short periods of terror."[1]

Ager insists, as do numerous leading geologists of today, that many (and perhaps nearly all) of the geologic deposits are actually a sequence of rapid catastrophic deposits, usually water related. For instance, many would argue that each horizontally bedded layer of fossil-bearing strata in Grand Canyon was laid down by a catastrophe of one sort or another. The growing number of "neo-catastrophist" geologists who advocate this position feel that the series of catastrophes which laid down the Tapeats Sandstone were not the same catastrophe or catastrophes that laid down the overlying layers up to the rim of the Canyon. They would claim that each sequence of catastrophes was separated by millions and millions of years. By doing

Tsunamis are incredibly destructive.

so, they recognize catastrophism in geology, but still hang on to the concept of the old earth, and retain the time necessary for evolution, presumably, to occur.

I hope you can grasp clearly what they are advocating. They would say that nearly all of the rock material was laid down rapidly, as sediments, by catastrophic processes. These events were separated by great lengths of time. But while the evidence points toward rapid catastrophic deposition which took very little time, great amounts of time supposedly passed between the layers *where there is*

1 Ager, Derek, *The Nature of the Stratigraphical Record*, 1981, pp. 54, 106.

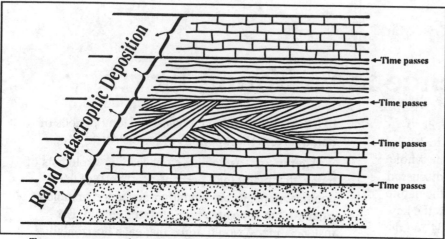

To a neo-catastrophist, the rocks show evidence of rapid catastrophic processes, requiring little time for deposition. Time passes between the layers were there is no evidence.

no evidence! The "evidence" for time is the *lack* of physical evidence. All the evidence points toward rapid, catastrophic flood processes.

Back in the early days of modern creationism, particularly with the publication of *The Genesis Flood* in 1961, the duty of the creationist geologist was to prove catastrophism as opposed to strict uniformitarianism (the idea that each geological layer accumulated slowly and gradually by processes and process rates similar to those occurring today).[2] Now, with the acceptance of rapid, catastrophic processes by many leading geologists, the creationist's duty has somewhat changed. Now we must also strive to tie these layers together into *one* catastrophe, and show that the length of time which passed between the deposition of any two adjacent layers was not long at all.

Discussed below are several ways which demonstrate how the layers can be "tied" together into a rather short period of time. I will not be advocating that we can date the earth by using these methods. Rather, what I intend to show is that the evidence speaks of a single, rapid geologic event, responsible for the

majority of the world's fossiliferous sedimentary rock, which continued throughout the geologic column, leaving no time for evolution.

Surface Features

One way to show that only a short time elapsed between the deposition of one bed and the deposition of an overlying bed is to show that the various surface features present on the top surface of the lower bed would not last very long if exposed. Therefore, these features had to be covered rather quickly, before they had a chance to erode or be destroyed.

One very common feature, seen in many rock layers in many locations, is the presence of "ripple marks," formed as water moves over a surface. These can frequently be seen on a beach after the tide has receded, and can also be seen on the ocean bottom where a particular current direction dominates. In many other situations we see what have been called "raindrop impressions," although these "raindrop marks" may actually be blisters formed as air bubbles escaped from rapidly deposited sediments under water. Animal tracks are also common. In any case, these features, which had to be formed in soft sediment, are very fragile, and if present on any surface, unconsolidated material or hard rock, will not last very long.

---

2   The book *The Genesis Flood*, by John Whitcomb and Henry Morris, 1961, is considered the catalyst for the modern creationism movement. For the first time, a systematic and scientifically credible defense of Biblical world history was possible. It is still a highly valuable work.

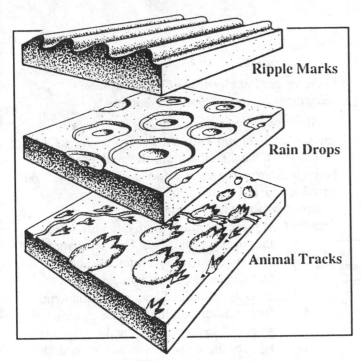

Ripple Marks

Rain Drops

Animal Tracks

Surface features are easily destroyed. They must be quickly protected in oreder to be preserved.

Keep in mind that almost every sedimentary rock layer was deposited under water. Every geologist agrees with this. Unless erosion dominates locally, sediments accumulate on an ocean bottom, lake bottom, delta, beach, lagoon, stream bank, etc., in the presence of water currents. If subsequent events lift the deposit up out of water, erosion and/or non-deposition will result. But if a zone stays under water, it will continue to be subjected to water action and will likely receive more sediments. In such an active environment, ripple marks can be preserved

Dinosaur tracks in central Texas. Animal tracks, in mud or in solid rock, would not last long if exposed on the surface.

only if they are quickly buried by overlying materials, so that they are protected and have time to turn into rock.

In many places around the world, these ocean-floor sediments have been solidified into rock, and are now uplifted onto continental surfaces. Ripple marks and similar features are readily seen in many locations, "frozen" in solid rock.

One example sticks in my mind. In a stream bed I once studied, numerous limestone layers were present, each only a few inches thick. Each one displayed obvious ripple marks about one inch high. Interestingly, the ripple marks in different layers were in different directions, indicating the water current responsible for deposition shifted rapidly and erratically while deposition continued. How could they all be preserved?

Ripple marks in dislodged block of Hakatai shale, Grand Canyon.

If such a mark is exposed on any surface, under water or above water, it will soon erode and disappear. Even on a hard rock surface, markings will erode in a few decades. There is no possibility that fragile features will last for millions of years, waiting to be re-submerged and buried, and thus protected from destructive forces. We can't determine exactly how much time passed between the deposition of two layers simply by looking at ripple marks, raindrop impressions, animal footprints, etc., but we can conclude that much less time passed than it takes for surface features to be eroded and disappear.

Since almost every layer gives demonstrable evidence of having been laid down rapidly and catastrophically, and since nearly all such catastrophic layers have surface features which were not eroded, one can reasonably conclude that the whole sequence of rocks was deposited by a rapid, possibly continuous, event.

Bioturbation

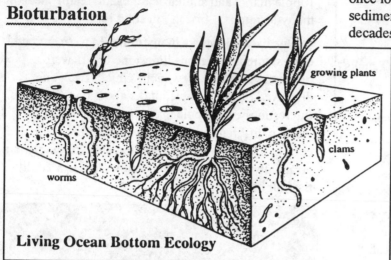

Living Ocean Bottom Ecology

A similar line of reasoning can be used by observing the deficiency of evidence of living communities within a layer of rock. By this I refer to the fact that on and below any surface, whether it be on land or in the sea, life is present which will leave its mark. In the ocean bottom or near the shore, worms, clams, fish, and all sorts of plants and animals live and disturb the sediments. Many actually ingest the mud, utilizing the nutrients present.

On land, tree roots, gophers, and numerous other animals, will alter the surface layers in fairly short order. Weathering will further hasten deterioration.

Consider a recent example. In 1961, Hurricane Carla devastated the central Texas coast. As it retreated, it laid down a recognizable layer of sediments on the shore and far out into the Gulf of Mexico. These graded sediments contained within them many "sedimentary structures," such as buried ripple marks and cross-bedding. These internal sedimentary structures were well studied

in the years after Hurricane Carla, and were recognized as rapid deposition features.[3]

About twenty years later, others went back to study what had happened to the stratum. Due to bioturbation, the disturbance of the geologic zone by biologic activity, the layer could hardly be found, and once located, it retained almost no evidence of sedimentary structure. Within just a couple of decades (and probably much more quickly), life at the surface of this bed, both on shore and off, had destroyed its internal character that had been formed by catastrophic processes.[4] Indeed, in any environment, from a desert sanddune to the shallow marine, life is abundant, and continually agitates the sediments within several feet of the surface. Particularly in shallow water, where most of the sedimentation occurs, living communities of plants and animals are especially active.

Compare the layer from Hurricane Carla to sedimentary layers of rock around the world, almost all of which are full of sedimentary structure. While individual exceptions could be cited, they are exceptions. The broad trend is for each stratum to contain abundant

Graded bedding—typical in sedimentary rocks, but destroyed by bioturbation.

---

3   Hayes, M.O. "Hurricanes as Geological Agents: Case Studies of Hurricanes Carla, 1961, and Cindy, 1963," *University of Texas, Bureau of Economic Geology, Report of Investigation No. 61*, p. 56.

4   As reported in Dott, Robert H. "1982 SEPM Presidential Address: Episodic Sedimentation—How Normal is Average? How Rare is Rare? Does it Matter?" *Journal of Sedimentary Petrology*, Vol. 53, No. 1, March 1983, p. 12.

internal structure. Evidently, the sediments were not exposed to an environment of biologic activity for any length of time before they were buried out of reach of plant and animal activity and subsequently hardened. Perhaps the sediments continued to build up so rapidly that the structure was out of reach of burrowing animals, but this implies continual catastrophic deposition. Where fossilized bioturbation does exist, it usually looks quite different from modern habitats. It better resembles that left by burrowing animals as they escape from deepening sediments, having been buried there against their will. These "escape burrows" are frequently oriented upward only, not in the variety of directions employed in living communities. It's as if the organisms were digging out of a continually growing supply of sediments.

Again, we can't tell how long the lower layer existed before the overlying layer was deposited, but we *can* say that it was less than the time for bioturbation to destroy sedimentary structures within the lower zone.

In this manner we can march up the geologic column, "tying" the layers together, and conclude with a relatively short time for the entire sequence.

Lack of Soil Layers

Exactly the same logic can be applied to another obvious feature, the almost complete lack of recognizable soil layers anywhere in the geologic column.

Within the standard, old-earth thinking, the continents now exposed have on numerous occasions been underwater, as evidenced by the fact that nearly all of the rocks themselves were deposited by ocean water, perhaps by off-shore wave action, in deltas, in lagoons, or by major storms or mud slides. While on land, they presumably supported soil, wherein plants and animals could live. Even in near shore environments, underwater "soils" are needed.

Soils today, consist primarily of weathered rock, broken up by the cycle of freezing and thawing water, by chemical deterioration of rock minerals, by wind and water erosion, and due to the action of rooting plants and burrowing animals. To this is added organic debris, mostly decaying plants and animal carcasses and droppings. Without a soil, abundant life is impossible, but we know from the

fossil record that abundant life has existed throughout much of this planet's history. It takes a while for soil to form, but once present, it tends to remain, barring erosion.

Each rock stratum usually immediately overlies another, with no soil between, even though vast lengths of time are presumed to have passed between the two.

What happens to the soil as the land surface submerges beneath the sea? Whether the land is covered rapidly by a catastrophic process, or slowly by transgression of the sea, certainly some of the soil would be preserved.

So what do we make of the fact that soil layers, or even soil materials, are seldom found in the geologic record? A possible soil sometimes mentioned is "underclays," typically found under a coal seam and thought by *some* to represent a leached soil layer; but the make-up of an underclay is not what one would expect of a soil layer capable of supporting a lush swamp. And even this attempt at identifying a fossil soil is rare. The geologic record is one of rocks, with few exceptions, not soils or "paleosols." And these rocks are not thought to consist of materials which have ever been soils.

Standard geology tells us that land surfaces supporting lush life have been here continuously for

Coal layer near Tuba City, Arizona— no soil layer beneath. Photo by Steve Austin.

hundreds of millions of years. Where, then, are the soils?

A better explanation is that only *one* soil existed before the depositional episode which resulted in the majority of the geologic record. The soils which are "missing" never existed. The time to produce many soils never happened.

Undisturbed Bedding Planes

Much the same logic can be brought to bear on the nature of the bedding contacts themselves. Frequently, one will find two formations of totally different rock types, lying one on top of the other, with a "knife-edge" bedding plane between them.

Note the picture of a contact seen in Grand Canyon between two such rock units. Here the dark-colored Hermit shale lies below the Coconino sandstone, as it does throughout much of the area.

The Hermit shale is thought to have accumulated as silt and mud in an off-shore environment. It's found in a geologic context and contains index fossils by which evolutionists date it at about 280 million years of age.

The overlying Coconino sandstone, dated at about 270 million years, tells a different story, although its history is in dispute. Most uniformitarian geologists interpret it as a desert sand-dune deposit, now solidified into hard rock. They base this interpretation on the presence throughout the rock of inclined planes, called cross-bedding (i.e., sedimentary structure) found at an angle to the general horizontal bedding of the rock unit as a whole. These are thought to be the "rippled" sand-dune surfaces in an otherwise "flat" desert.

Other geologists interpret these as giant "ripple marks" from an *underwater* sand-dune deposit. They base their contention on certain features more representative of wet sand than dry sand, such as the angle of the cross-beds, presence of amphibian tracks fossilized in the sand, source of the original sand, features of the sand grains, etc. The underwater case would probably be convincing to all, if it weren't for certain implications which necessarily follow.

We know that moving water can transport sand grains, and we can measure the average sand-grain size present in the Coconino. It turns out that the Coconino is made of "fine" sand grains ranging in size from ⅛ mm to ¼ mm in diameter. Obviously, a measurable velocity of water at the sand-water interface is required to move "fine" sand grains. As it turns out, a velocity of three to five feet per second is necessary.

The Coconino sandstone immediately overlies the Hermit shale— no evidence of erosion.

Measurements of the sand-dune geometry coupled with experimental results show that those giant sand dunes (or in this case, long, underwater ripples) were made in a water depth of over 100 feet.[5]

Crossbedding in Coconino sandstone (note person for scale).

Now we know from observation that water moves much more rapidly on the surface than it does at depth. In order for water at a 100-foot depth to move at three to five feet per second, it must be moving at a *much greater* velocity on the surface.

Actually, at a depth of 100 feet in the open ocean, sustained water velocities of three feet per second have *never* been observed. Clearly, it would take a storm of *intense* magnitude. Such a catastrophe is far beyond that which most uniformitarians dare to consider. Of course, most creationists favor the underwater model, since they are not intimidated by the thought of catastrophic water events, and also, since this sandstone unit is best understood as having been deposited during the height of the Flood of Noah's day, and it's hard to imagine how a desert deposit would develop then. But it's more than just an interpretation of necessity. The evidence clearly favors the underwater model. Those who advocate the desert interpretation, illustrate the maxim *"I wouldn't have seen it if I hadn't believed it."*

But let's return our thoughts to the bedding plane between the Hermit Shale and the Coconino sandstone. Regardless of how the Coconino was deposited, it originated in a completely different environment than the Hermit, and according to evolution, was separated in time by about 10 million years. If the Coconino represents a desert (one which covered over 100,000 square miles, by the way), then the ocean bottom which accumulated the Hermit material had to be uplifted, out of water, to an elevation high enough and dry enough to be a desert. Can you imagine the erosion which would take place over this gigantic area, particularly as it was near sea level, both above and below? And yet, the upper surface of the Hermit is exceptionally flat, with *no evidence of normal erosion*. It is not possible, as far as has been observed, for these kinds of erosional processes to scour off all possible overlying sediment and leave behind a completely flat Hermit surface on which the Coconino desert could form. Or if no other sediments were ever present, how could it remain stagnant with no erosion, leaving a flat, featureless Hermit surface on which sand began to collect 10 million years later? No surface on earth remains stagnant, with no erosion and no deposition. It certainly wouldn't sit there with nothing at all happening for 10 million years! Especially for *this* 10 million years! According to the evolutionary old-earth scenario, the earth was, at that time, enjoying an extended period of wet climate. A huge desert near a warm ocean with little rainfall—that's a contradiction in terms. Even if the Coconino was formed underwater, no surface such as the top of the Hermit would remain there with no changes for a long time.

The point is, the existence of the sharp, knife-edge contact between those two beds argues *against* the passage of long periods of time between their depositions, regardless of their index fossils. If it weren't for the *assumption* of evolution, these two beds would speak either of continuous, rapid

5 For an explanation of this, see *Grand Canyon, Monument to Catastrophe*, 1994, the Guidebook for the ICR Grand Canyon Tours, edited by Steve Austin, published by ICR.

deposition with perhaps a near-instantaneous shift in current direction and sediment load, or of rapid deposition of the Coconino after an episode of "sheet erosion," due to massive volumes of water flowing rapidly at equal depth over a wide area. In both cases, we're talking about a flood on the scale of the Genesis Flood.

The Toroweap limestone directly overlies the Coconino, with no evidence of erosion, even though the two are presumed to have originated in very different environments and to be separated by a long time period.

Contacts between rock units in every area exhibit the same feature. Not between every two consecutive layers, but between at least some layers in each locality. The rocks simply do not support vast ages passing between the deposition of adjacent layers.

Polystrate Fossils

Underground coal mines have always been an extremely dangerous place to work, particularly in times past, before mechanization revised coal-mining methods. Miners are continually in danger. One of the most dangerous aspects of a coal mine is the presence of features known as "kettles." Seen as rather circular shapes in the mine's roof, kettles are the bottoms of cylindrical bodies of rock which can easily detach and fall, crushing the miners beneath.

As it turns out, these circular features are the bottoms of upright tree trunks. The lower portions, including the roots, are frequently mined away along with the rest of the coal, leaving only the trunk penetrating up through the roof into the strata above.

If not stabilized and secured by bracing, roof bolts, screws, or some other device, these cylindrical tree trunks can prove deadly.

The popular explanation for the origin of coal suggests that peat (an organic deposit thought to be the precursor of coal) accumulated in a peat swamp. As the swamp trees and bushes lived and died, the organic material would accumulate as peat in the stagnant water of the swamp. Great thicknesses of peat are thought to have accumulated over the years as the swamp slowly submerged beneath the sea.

Once the peat swamp was completely submerged by the ocean, it was buried by slowly accumulating mud on the ocean floor. This overlying mud is thought to have slowly turned into rock (usually shale or limestone), while the peat, deeply buried for millions of years, gradually altered into coal through the action of heat and pressure. This process involves driving the water and other volatile materials out of the peat, leaving behind mostly carbon.

Furthermore, ocean-bottom mud accumulates very slowly, usually at about one millimeter to one inch per year near the continental margins or in a shallow sea. In the deep ocean, sediments accumulate at about one millimeter per 1000 years. At this rate, deep burial and alteration of peat into coal, and mud into rock, requires millions of years. But in some eastern U.S. coal regions, up to fifty different coal seams are stacked on top of each other, separated by limestone and shale layers. Theoretically, in evolutionary terms, each layer took a vast time for accumulation, making the total time for deposition lengthy, indeed, as the area slowly bobbed up and down like a yo-yo—under the ocean, out of the ocean.

But fossil trees, such as mentioned above, give us additional information that helps us date the entire sequence and tie at least some of the layers together. If the trees grew in the place in which they are now found (in other words, were trees growing in the swamp), then after the peat had accumulated and the whole area eventually slowly submerged, their dead trunks would have extended up into the ocean water overhead, sometimes as much as thirty to forty feet.

Polystrate tree extending from coal to overlying shale.

Consider an exposed tree trunk extending thirty feet up from the bottom of an ocean. No woody tree can long survive under sea water. Some may grow with their roots in salt water, but when any tree is covered by sea water, it will die. How long would it take that dead tree trunk to rot and fall over? Could it remain upright for millions or for even hundreds of years, while the mud slowly accumulated around it? Obviously not. Some polystrate trees even intersect more than one coal layer! Did it ride the strata down and up again and then down again for millions of years? From studying these trees, we can conclude that the length of time for accumulation of the peat (which later turned into coal) and the overlying sediments was less time than it takes for wood to decay. Obviously, wood decays in only a few decades at most, whether in an active ocean environment, standing in air, or buried in sediments.

Polystrate trees which extend through more than one layer (hence the name "poly-strate"— meaning "many strata") in effect "tie the layers together" into a short period of time. This period of time can't be explicitly determined from the data, but it is *wholly incompatible* with the long-age model normally taught.

One polystrate tree might be understood as having been deposited in a freakish scenario, but the fact is, the world contains many polystrate trees. In coal mines, they are quite common. I have personally been in many underground coal mines and with one exception, saw polystrate trees or kettles in each of them. Dramatic examples are sometimes found in areas where the coal cross-section is exposed by erosion or by open pit-mining.

The argument is not limited to large tree trunks. In one location in Oklahoma, I studied an area where thinly bedded limestones were present in a road cut, scores of three-inch-thick limestone layers, piled on top of one another like pancakes. My evolutionary companions interpreted the limestone layers as the results of lengthy, slow accumulation processes. But throughout the entire outcrop, evidence of rapid, continuous accumulation could be seen. Everywhere we looked, we found polystrate fossils protruding up through several limestone layers each. These were not large trees, but fossilized reed-like creatures called Calamities, in some cases up to six inches in diameter, but usually just an inch or so. These segmented "stems" were evidently quite fragile once dead, for they are usually found in tiny fragments. Obviously, the limestones couldn't have accumulated slowly and gradually around a still-growing organism, but must have been quite rapidly deposited in a series of underwater events.

Polystrate tree spanning two narrow coal seams and the intervening shale. Photo by Andrew Snelling.

Other types of fossils likewise testify to the same conclusion. Sometimes, an *animal's* fossilized body will intersect more than one layer or lamination within a rock, and the same argument applies.

One of the standard examples cited for long ages involves the Green River Formation in Wyoming. Here extensive shale deposits consist of millions of millimeter-thick laminations, interpreted by uniformitarians as representing winter/summer sequences of sedimentation in calm lake environments. Yet fossils exist here in abundance!

By the way, how do fossils form? Do animals or plants sink to the bottom of a lake or an ocean and remain while minuscule yearly amounts of sediment cover them up and fossilize them? No, of course not. They usually float to the surface, although sometimes they sink to the bottom, where, in either case, they are eaten by scavengers or decomposed by bacterial or mechanical action. In no case do they remain for long. Often, fossils are even found in "fresh" condition, sometimes giving evidence of having been buried alive. While specific mechanisms vary, suffice it to say that in order to be preserved, they must be buried *quickly*, out of reach of destructive agents.

And this is how it is at the Green River Formation. Fossilized catfish are found in abundance, some up to ten inches long, having the skin and soft parts preserved in some cases, obviously buried rapidly.[6] The catfish fossils are found in many orientations, transgressing numerous millimeter-thick laminations. They did not die and lie for hundreds of years on the lake bottom while being slowly covered. Other types of fossils, including "enormous concentrations" of bird fossils[7] are found in these "lake-bottom" sediments. Surely the time has come to recognize that this formation, a classic "proof" that the Bible is wrong, *actually supports rapid catastrophism instead*.

Coal

While we are talking about the origin of coal, it might be well to mention the fact that the metamorphosis of peat into coal has never been observed under natural conditions. We have all grades of coal, lignite, and peat, but any changes seem to have ceased. Perhaps, the old peat-bog theory should be abandoned. Research has shown that coal does *not* take millions and millions of years of heat and pressure to form as is commonly asserted. In recent years, several laboratory schemes have been devised whereby coal or coal-like substances can be made rapidly, in hours or at the most days.[8,9] It doesn't even require pressure, but mainly higher temperature (ideally, perhaps, very hot water[10]). It must be heated in a way in which the organic material is isolated from oxygen so that it can not ignite. The process needs heat to get it started, but produces its own heat and pressure once it starts.

This chemical reaction needs a catalyst, the presence of which causes the reaction to occur relatively rapidly. That catalyst is a certain type of clay, usually a derivative of volcanic ash. Interestingly enough, almost all coal beds are underlain by such a clay layer, usually called the "underclay." Thin, volcanic clay layers, called "partings," are also found throughout the coal, and frequently volcanically derived material is disbursed throughout the organic material itself, and forms "clinkers" when the coal is burned.

The clay partings themselves are quite interesting. Many times these thin, flat, layers cover hundreds of square miles in area. In contrast, extensive, flat layers *don't* exist in modern peat swamps, where the surface is quite undulating, with many stream channels and local high places throughout. There is no such thing as one flat plane in a peat bog. It appears that peat must accumulate rather rapidly under the right

6 Buchheim, H. Paul and Surdem, Ronald C. "Fossil Catfish and the Depositional Environment of the Green River Formation, Wyoming," *Geology*, Vol. 5, April 1979, p. 196.

7 Feduccia, Alan "*Presbyornis* and the Evolution of Ducks and Flamingos," *American Scientist*, Vol. 66, May/June 1978, p. 298.

8 See for example Davis, A., and Spackman, W. "The Role of Cellulosic and Lignitic Components in Articulate Coalification," *Fuel*, Vol. 43, 1964, pp. 215–224. See also Hill, George R. *Chemical Technology*, May 1972, p. 296, and Larson, John "From Lignin to Coal in a Year," *Nature* 31, March 28, 1985, p. 16.

9 Hayatsu, R., et al. "Artificial Coalification Study: Preparation and Characterization of Synthetic Macerals," *Organic Geochemistry*, Vol. 6, 1984, pp. 463–471.

10 Pennisi, E. "Water, Water Everywhere: Surreptitiously Converting Dead Matter into Oil and Coal," *Science News*, Feb. 20, 1993, pp. 121–125.

conditions, and that the right conditions don't occur in peat swamps. Likewise, it appears that the clay partings require a flat depositional plane, not an active, growing peat swamp.[11] Some other model of coal formation is obviously needed.

The May 18, 1980, eruption of Mount St. Helens devastated 150 square miles of forest north of the mountain. Within minutes, over a million logs were floating on Spirit Lake, surrounded by great volumes of organic material and volcanic ash. Within just a few years, an organic deposit consisting mostly of tree bark and decayed woody materials, and containing volcanic ash, had accumulated at the bottom of the lake. This "peat" has much the same make-up and geometry as coal. Many sheets of bark are piled on top of each other, having been abraded off the floating trees and sunk to the bottom. Since it is known that the hard, black shiny bands in coal are actually "mummified bark," the Spirit Lake peat looks very much as if it would make good coal.

To make matters more interesting, many of the floating tree trunks are becoming water-logged, and as they do they typically sink to the bottom, root end first, and ground themselves in the organic muck and bark sheets at the bottom of the lake. As the organic material continues to accumulate, and as volcanic and erosive activity continues, adding volcanic ash and other sediments to the lake, these upright trees are being buried on the lake bottom. If further sediment accumulation occurs, these tree trunks will be buried in an upright "polystrate" position.[12]

The peat not only resembles modern coal beds in character and geometry, but volcanically derived clay abounds throughout. If the mountain were to erupt again, depositing a layer of hot material on top of the peat deposit, it would likely be quickly turned into coal, probably looking just like the bituminous coal beds found today. And this coal layer would be penetrated by polystrate trees.

Regional Evidence for Continual Deposition

So far in this chapter, we have discussed evidence that a *local* set of strata was deposited rather continuously, with no significant time gap between any two consecutive layers. A similar line of reasoning can be applied to geologic layers on a *regional* scale.[13]

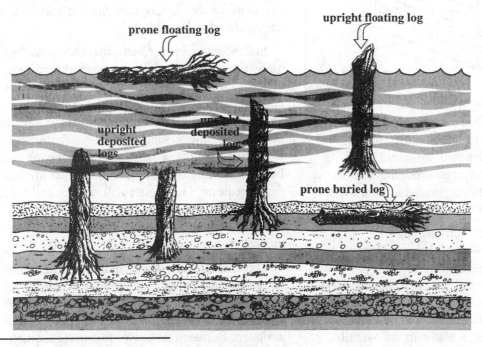

prone floating log

upright floating log

upright deposited logs

upright deposited logs

prone buried log

Trees floating on Spirit Lake, Mount St. Helens, frequently sink in an upright orientation as they waterlog.

---

11 Austin, S.A. "Evidence for Marine Origin of Widespread Carbonaceous Shale Partings in the Kentucky No 12 Coal," *Geological Society of America Abstracts*, Vol. 11, 1979, pp. 381, 382.

12 For a good overview of the evidence of Mount St. Helens, see, Dr. Steve Austin's "Mount St. Helens and Catastrophism," ICR *Impact* Article 175, 1986. The Institute for Creation Research has begun leading tours to Mount St. Helens every other August.

13 For a fuller discussion of this concept, see the book by Drs. Henry Morris and Gary Parker, *What is Creation Science?* Master Books, 1982.

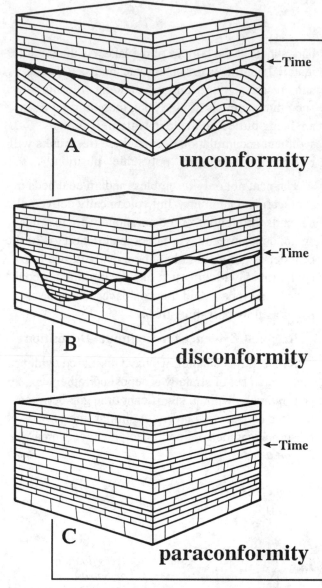

A   **unconformity** ← Time

B   **disconformity** ← Time

C   **paraconformity** ← Time

deposition interspersed with rapid erosional episodes. In this model, erosion was as *rapid and catastrophic* as deposition, neither taking much time. But in the old-earth model, while deposition can be considered as either rapid or slow, erosion usually takes long periods of time.

Erosional episodes are normally easy to recognize in the rock record. In general, they are represented by a zone where the adjacent rocks are not in a *conformable* sequence, which is the term applied when one layer overlies the other in a parallel, undisturbed manner. Conformity indicates continual deposition, with no erosional break. If strata are not in *conformity*, they are described as an *unconformity* or a *disconformity*. The cross-sections shown pictorially define those concepts, and identify the various types of erosional expressions.

In a conformity, each rock layer (itself laid down rapidly) is conformable with those above and below it. As discussed earlier in this chapter, reasoning from the presence of surface features, lack of bioturbation, lack of soil layers, or presence of polystrate fossils, we can conclude that, as a rule, no significant time passed between the deposition of any two conformable layers, and thus the entire sequence accumulated rather rapidly.

Individual layers (or beds, members, etc.) are many times combined into a group of similar layers called a *formation*. A formation would typically contain the same index fossils, i.e., groupings of fossils arranged by evolutionary ideas to have lived at the same time. Usually, each layer within a formation is of the same rock type (for example, limestone), although an individual layer might vary from the norm. Geologists will seldom call for an erosional episode within a formation, which is considered to be a period of continual deposition, fast or slow, over a short or long time period.

The change from one formation to another might be represented by a change in rock type (perhaps from limestone to sandstone), or a change in fossil content, and a corresponding change in the age assigned. Between these two formations, erosion may have occurred, as represented by *a lack of conformity* between formations.

In a *disconformity*, the rock layers remained parallel, no tilting or faulting occurred. But as seen in illustration B, an erosional sequence which reminds

We've already noted that many leading geologists have become committed to "neo-catastrophism," claiming that nearly all deposits were laid down rapidly, by catastrophic processes, but that the catastrophes were episodic, separated in time by perhaps millions of years.

With few exceptions, the environment of deposition is underwater—that's where *deposition* takes place. When a deposit is uplifted, out of water, and exposed to rainfall, wind, and river action, that's when *erosion*—not deposition—takes place. To modern old-earth advocates, an erosional event marks the passage of time, a hiatus in the overall rapid, depositional sequence. We're interested in just how much time did elapse.

In the young-earth/Flood model, nearly the entire sequence of fossil-bearing rocks was deposited in short periods of time during the Flood, with

one of river or stream erosion, forming an uneven land surface, appears. Obviously, this takes time, but how *much* time?

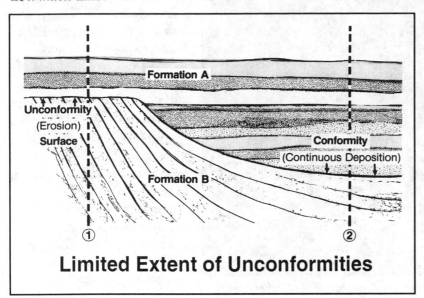

Limited Extent of Unconformities

In an *unconformity*, the lower rock layers have been tilted and then eroded, as seen in illustration A, and at a later time, the upper layers were deposited horizontally on top of the tilted eroded surface. The edges of the tilted beds of the lower formation would even have been exposed on the erosional surface for a while. Again, how much time elapsed?

The answer can't always be obtained in the local setting. But, the erosional episode, either the disconformity or the unconformity, can usually be traced laterally through the use of information from oil wells or other outcrops. This may take a lot of work, but as the layers and formations, which themselves may cover vast areas, are traced laterally, they will either pinch out into a zone where they were not deposited at all, or to an area where they were not tilted or eroded. In such cases, an erosional sequence can eventually be resolved into a conformable, continuous depositional sequence.

This might be more easily understood, and certainly more easily demonstrated, by considering the various geologic periods in a hypothetical sense. For example, the Devonian Period is thought to have extended from about 345 million years ago to 405 million years ago. The next older period, the Silurian, extended back to 425 million years ago. One might not be surprised to discover that formations designated as within the Devonian and Silurian formations were each deposited as continuous series.

Frequently, the Devonian rests conformably on top of the Silurian, and by application of the principles discussed above, one might conclude that no great time gap occurred between the end of the Silurian and the beginning of the Devonian.

But sometimes an erosional sequence can be found between the two, indicating a time gap. The question is, how long?

Even though the question might not be answered locally, and resolving it regionally might be difficult or impossible, the fact remains that in numerous other locations, no time gap is observed between the two systems. In fact, many locations can be cited where an entire series of layers, including the Ordovician (resting beneath the Silurian) and the Mississippian (lying *above* the Devonian) are conformably present with the Silurian and Devonian. Thus, the majority of the fossiferous column resolves into a single, continuous depositional sequence.

Therefore, any local erosional episode, while it may represent more time than a normal conformable surface, still *does not represent a significant time lapse*. The entire column of flood formations represents a single series of depositional episodes, interrupted locally by limited erosion, but continuing elsewhere.

In many cases, an individual formation may be overlain conformably by another formation, but *the fossil content* of the two demands that their times of deposition be separated by many millions of years! This is called a *para-conformity* (illustration C) or *pseudo-conformity*. A "surface of non-deposition and non-erosion" is implied, a surface that remained absolutely stagnant for millions of years. Obviously, there is *no* such stagnant surface on land today, with nothing happening on it, no erosion, no rooting by plants or burrowing by animals, anywhere on earth. Nor can a surface be stagnant underwater, with no bioturbation or deposition. This is a totally hypothetical concept representing the lengths to which old-earth advocates will go to salvage their millions-of-years' theory.

Paraconformities in Grand Canyon—layers rest conformably on each other. Only an evolutionary view of fossils would call for a time gap in between. Photo by Steve Austin.

Soft Sediment Deformation

My favorite way of "tying the layers together" is to use "soft-sediment deformation." Evidently, many sediments were deformed (that is, bent or broken) while they were still in a soft, unconsolidated condition (i.e., soft, muddy sediments as opposed to hard rock.)

In old-earth thinking, conformable layers of sediments were deposited consecutively, but separated in time, perhaps by millions of years. Subsequent to deposition, the strata sequence was deformed (i.e., bent or broken). This may have occurred at a time much later than the time of deposition. If already quite old, one would suppose that the sediments would have already hardened into solid rock, and should give evidence of having been in a hard, "brittle" condition when deformed.

The young-earth model, however, predicts a much different situation. If Creation/Flood thinking is correct, then great thicknesses of sediments were laid down during the year of the Flood and perhaps the first few centuries following. The lowest of these flood sediments were laid down early in the Flood, and those nearer the top were laid down late in the Flood, only months later. Much deformation would have taken place late in the Flood as the oceans were deepened and widened, and the continents were

uplifted. In many cases, these uplifts and the concurrent deformation would have taken place when the sediments were less than a few years old. We would expect that some of them would give evidence of having been deformed when still in a soft, muddy condition, not hard rock as they are today.

The first question which must be answered is this: How long does it take for sediments to turn to solid rock? Unfortunately, there can be no specific answer to this question, for each situation is different. In general, the presence of elevated temperature, the presence of an adequate cement to bind the grains or minerals together, and deep burial, forcing the pore water out and bringing the individual grains into contact with one another, all speed up the hardening process.

It must be recognized that even now, some of the sedimentary layers in the geologic column are softer than others. Some have not yet turned into solid rock for one reason or another. The conditions for hardening just weren't satisfied in all areas. But most of the layers are, of course, solid rock.

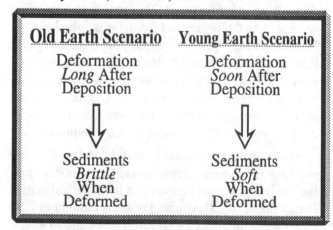

Old Earth Scenario	Young Earth Scenario
Deformation *Long* After Deposition	Deformation *Soon* After Deposition
⇓	⇓
Sediments *Brittle* When Deformed	Sediments *Soft* When Deformed

Under normal conditions, sediments harden into rock in a matter of years, at the *most* perhaps as much as *a hundred years*. It does not take millions and millions of years to form rock from sediments. Under ideal conditions, it can happen within *days*.

For instance, modern-day concrete is very much analogous to a rock, albeit a man-made rock. Chemicals are present which cement the grains together, and as the water in the mixture is incorporated into the mineral structure, or squeezed out and evaporated, the concrete turns quite hard. This happens in hours to days. Many rocks are formed in much the same fashion.

Consider the sediments deposited by mud slides associated with the recent eruptions of Mount St. Helens, caused as the mountain's glacier rapidly melted and descended, incorporating mud, boulders, trees, and animals along the way. One mud slide after another covered the area like a stack of pancakes, resulting in a sediment pile up to 600 feet thick in places. These units, deposited by catastrophic water action, look essentially the same as rock layers frequently seen elsewhere. Even though these materials were not subjected to optimum conditions for hardening, within five years the sediments were hard enough to stand in a near-vertical slope. It doesn't take long to form rock from sediments; it just takes the right conditions.

Once a rock does become hard, it is extremely difficult to bend it without breaking it. Rocks would be expected to behave in what engineers call a hard, "brittle" fashion, and not in a soft, "plastic" or pliable fashion. Usually, the rock's state when it deformed can be determined by examination, especially under a microscope.

Many times a rock will appear to have deformed while in a soft, unconsolidated condition, and yet the timing of deposition and bending raises concern. According to the old-earth scenario, rocks would often have been laid down millions of years before they were deformed. Since they had plenty of time during which to harden, they should have behaved in a brittle fashion, and yet, frequently, they seem to have deformed as would an unconsolidated mud.

Let me illustrate this concept from Grand Canyon. When you stand at the 7000-foot-high south rim of Grand Canyon and look over the edge, you will see horizontally bedded sedimentary layers totaling thousands of feet thick. The Canyon is carved through an elevated plateau called the Kaibab Upwarp. The very same rocks which can be seen at Grand Canyon Village are also present 250 miles away in eastern Arizona, but there they are a mile or

so *lower* in elevation. The plateau was pushed up into its current elevated position some seventy million years ago, according to uniformitarian geologists, at the time the Rocky Mountains were being formed, and the Canyon was *later* carved through this uplifted plateau.

The strata are flat at Grand Canyon Village, and flat in eastern Arizona, 250 miles away. Most people don't know that on the edge of the plateau, where a "monocline" has developed, the rocks are, in places, standing in a near-vertical orientation.

Canyon wall at Mount St. Helens, showing several layers of strata deposited during and since 1980. Within five years, the strata had hardened into rock (note person for scale).

As can be seen in the accompanying cross section, the lowest sedimentary layer in most locations, the Tapeats sandstone, is thought by uniformitarian geologists to be on the order of 550 million years old. The Kaibab limestone on the rim is thought to be 250 million years old. But upwarp occurred only 70 million years ago. This means that the Tapeats sandstone was already about 480 million years old at the time of upwarp!

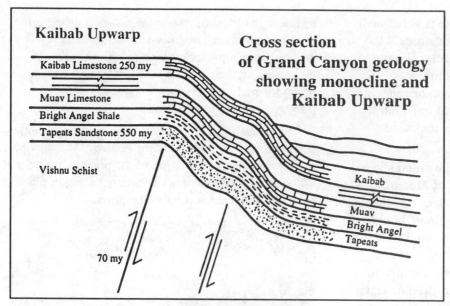

Kaibab Upwarp

Kaibab Limestone 250 my

Muav Limestone

Bright Angel Shale

Tapeats Sandstone 550 my

Vishnu Schist

70 my

**Cross section
of Grand Canyon geology
showing monocline and
Kaibab Upwarp**

Kaibab

Muav

Bright Angel

Tapeats

As we study the nature of bending at the hinge point, we will see that the sandstone appears to have been in a soft, unconsolidated condition when bending occurred. Nowhere are found elongated sand grains, or the cement which bound the grains together broken and recrystallized. It appears that the rocks, while they had somewhat hardened due to the weight of the overlying sediments, were still rather soft and "fresh." They were not in a rock-hard, brittle condition at the time of bending. Evidently, they had not been there very long.[14]

Evolutionists will say, however, that if a rock is deeply buried and confined on all sides by surrounding pressure, bending can occur on an otherwise brittle rock. This is, of course, quite true, especially for certain rocks which can "flow," like rock salt. But in a hard rock like the Tapeats sandstone, that sort of bending always results in elongated sand grains or broken cement crystals, neither of which have been found in these deformed Grand Canyon rocks.

As can be seen on the accompanying stress-strain diagram, there is a limit to how far any substance can strain (or deform) under a given stress condition. Deformation will occur with the application of stress, but if the stress is maintained at a constant level, the material will continue to deform, or "creep."

Any rock can be loaded to failure by the addition of stress. If the stress is maintained at a constant level

below the rupture point, deformation will continue in most rocks to a terminal value, at which time it will either become stable, or it will fracture. Most rock types will not continue to undergo unlimited deformation. There is a limit to the amount of creep which will occur over time, as shown on the graph.

As can be seen from the photographs of the point of greatest bending, these rocks bent at a 90° angle within a distance of 100 feet or so. This would place the rock in the outer half of the fold in tension. Hard rock is notoriously weak in tension, and yet this material stretched quite a bit. At places along the monocline, the entire layer visibly thinned as it bent. It's hard to imagine how hard rock could have withstood that much stretching, even if confined. Hard rock simply doesn't behave this way! From all we can gather,

The Tapeats sandstone in Carbon Canyon, showing vertical orientation.

14 For a similar study, see Austin, S., and Morris, J. "Tight Folds and Clastic Dikes as Evidence for Rapid Deposition of Two Very Thick Stratigraphic Sequences," *Proceedings of the First International Conference on Creationism*, Pittsburgh, PA, 1986, pp. 3–15.

both visually and under the microscope, the rocks were still in a soft unconsolidated condition at the time of bending.

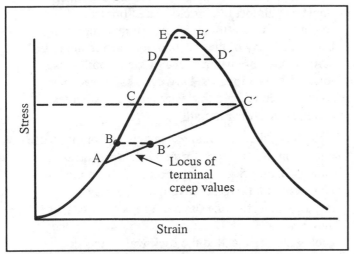

Adapted from Goodman, R. E., Introduction to Rock Mechanics, 1980 (John Wiley and Sons), p. 74.

The 5,000 feet of uplift produced different reactions by different rocks. The Tapeats sandstone and overlying sedimentary rocks merely draped over the fold. They bent and stretched and accommodated the movement. More recent faulting such as along the Bright Angel fault, broke the sedimentary layers which had by then hardened into solid rock, even though movement along the fault was much less.

Beneath the Tapeats in most locations lies the Vishnu Shist, an extremely hard metamorphic rock. This formation is the basement rock in this area and is correlated laterally with rocks across the continent. In the creationist model, it normally is assumed to date from creation itself, part of God's original creation of the earth. Perhaps it was metamorphosed and altered by the Flood, but it was already hard and brittle by the time of the Flood. Uniformitarians date it as over a billion years old.

The Vishnu behaved as brittle rocks should during the uplift of the plateau. It broke! Seismic studies have located the faults, and have concluded that one side moved upward at least 5,000 feet relative to the other side.

Thus, the hard metamorphic rocks broke. The sedimentary rocks, which are now quite hard and break when faulted, merely draped

over the fault at the time of the uplift. It appears that they were recently deposited muds, and had not yet turned to stone, as they have since the Flood.

This does not prove the young earth or the Flood or any other Biblical doctrine. All we can say from this observation is that the Tapeats sandstone had not yet had enough time to turn to solid rock at the time it was deformed. The currently accepted dates of the deposition and deformation are incompatible with the nature of the rocks themselves. This observation, in effect, wipes out 480 million years of supposed earth history.

The situation at the Grand Canyon is far from unique. There are many, many other places where rocks have deformed while in a soft, unconsolidated condition. The Rocky Mountains are full of such occurrences. The Appalachian Mountains likewise. One such occurrence might be passed off as an anomaly, but the world is full of examples of soft sediment deformation, just as it should be if the earth is young and the Flood really is responsible for most of the world's geologic features.

Clastic Dikes

A similar argument can be made from the observance of features called *clastic dikes*. A *clastic rock* is made up of pieces of a previously existing rock. A sandstone, for instance, is made up of sand grains, and sand grains are actually pieces of quartz, usually derived from the erosion of a previously

The Tapeats sandstone was evidently deformed while still in a soft, plastic condition. Photo by Steve Austin.

existing granite. Thus, sandstone is a clastic rock. A dike is a vertical, wall-like feature, buried underground. Many *igneous* dikes can be seen surrounding volcanoes, but our interest turns to clastic dikes.

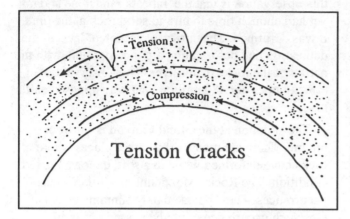

Tension Cracks

Once I was asked to investigate some very interesting sandstone dikes in Central Texas. These dikes were found in Rockwall County, east of Dallas. The capitol city of the county of Rockwall, is Rockwall, Texas. Both are named after some very unusual "rock walls" which are found throughout the county. Farmers frequently curse these dikes because their plows are broken as they encounter stone "walls" hidden just below the ground surface.

On occasion, the rock walls have been excavated to see what they look like. From the side, they appear to be man-made rock walls consisting of broken flagstone, almost like bricks. The "bricks" sometimes appear to be beveled, with a mortar in between. Many of the local citizens are absolutely certain that a prehistoric race of giants built these rock walls as a fortress. However, every geologic study had concluded that they were clastic dikes, and not a fortress after all.

Some of the local real estate agents, hoping to use interest in the ancient "fortress" as a means to increase land prices asked geologists from the University of Texas at Austin, and others from Baylor University, to come and see evidence that they had gathered. But much to their disgust, the geologists again called the rock walls "clastic dikes," and gave a purely natural cause.

Next, they called the Institute for Creation Research for help. Since they wanted to promote their area as the site of a prehistoric race of giants, and knew the Institute for Creation Research didn't agree with the commonly held geologic time table, they thought ICR might be sympathetic. I was on the faculty at the University of Oklahoma at the time, and since I had long been affiliated with ICR, I was asked to go down and investigate.

Tight folding of rocks at Split Mountain, California.

As much as I might have liked to conclude that these walls were made by a pre-Flood race of giants, I had to inform my frustrated hosts that the walls were in reality clastic dikes. There's a perfectly good geologic explanation for them. But, there's also a wonderful lesson to be learned from these clastic dikes.

Most of the dikes are sandstone, and are of significant size, varying from ¼ inch to 18 inches in thickness, getting slightly thicker with depth. Dimensions vary, but some are several miles long, and are up to 150 feet in height. There is no discernible change in sand-grain size or lithology, either vertically or horizontally. Sometimes a smaller dike branches off a larger one, occasionally to rejoin it. A few other dikes consist of limestone or marcasite.

Apparently, the swarm of dikes stems from a series of related events, but all are found in cracks within limestone layers, common in Central Texas, which, according to the standard dating scales, are on the order of 80 million years old. Some have interpreted the dikes to be due to infilling of submarine cracks by material from above,[15] but this is not likely, at least not for the larger dikes made of sandstone. No horizontal layer of sandstone more than a few inches thick is present stratigraphically above the dikes which could serve as a source, and in no case would pure sand settle out in cracks in the sea bottom without abundant impurities present. Only the limestone dikes show a hint of horizontal deposition, as would be expected if they settled out from above, but this would also occur if injection took place laterally. The sandstone

Two clastic dikes (rock walls) excavated and supported by timber.

Close-up of clastic dike. This was understandably mistaken for a constructed "rock wall."

dikes show no compelling evidence of being formed by shallow or deep marine sand settling out from above.

Examination of the sandstone dike material indicates that it is essentially the same as that of a sandstone bed buried beneath the dikes.[16] They are made of the same chemical constituents, and the same array of sand-grain sizes. The only difference between the dikes and the mother sandstone bed is that the sand grains in the dike appear to be similarly oriented, with their long axes tending to point in the same direction. This would result if the material were squeezed upward from below (as with grit in a toothpaste), but would not result from deposition or settling out of moving water. No deformed sand grains are seen, and there is no hint of broken and recrystallized cement. The material in the dikes appears to have still been a saturated and unconsolidated sandy mud at the time it was squeezed up into the overlying limestone.

---

15 Monroe, John Napier. "The Origin of the Clastic Dikes of Northern Texas," M.S. Thesis, Southern Methodist University, 1949.

16 Kelsey, Martin, and Harold Denton. "Sandstone Dikes Near Rockwall, Texas," *University of Texas Bulletin*, No. 3201, 1932, pp. 138–148. Very little interest has been shown in the dikes in recent decades. Dr. T. J. Gholy, geologist at East Texas State University, has, however, investigated them over the years. His conclusion, which agrees with the article above and with my conclusion based on my own field work, is that the main dikes were injected from below (personal communication).

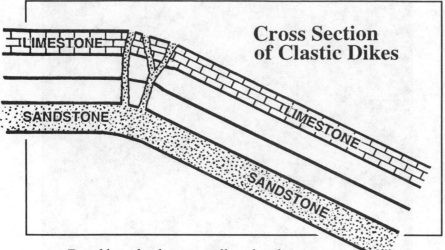

Cross Section of Clastic Dikes

LIMESTONE

SANDSTONE

LIMESTONE

SANDSTONE

But old-earth advocates tell us that the source sandstone bed was already millions of years old at the time of squeezing. Something is genuinely wrong here. Evidently, the source bed had not yet had time to turn hard before deformation occurred. Again, this does not prove the young earth, but it does "take a bite out of" supposed earth history.

As with the case of soft sediment bending, the clastic-dike argument can be applied in many places around the world. For instance, the mountain-building episode which formed the Rocky Mountains uplifted sediments over 20,000 feet in some places. The time of uplift, as we have already mentioned, was approximately 70 million years ago, so they say. Thus, many of the rocks were already hundreds of millions of years old at the time of uplift, and should have been quite hard. But it appears that this uplift episode injected soft material which has now hardened into clastic dikes. These dikes, which are identical to the Sawatch sandstone (470 million years old), were injected into uplifted Pike's Peak granite. If, as is apparently true, the uplift is the same as the

Laramide Orogeny which formed the Rocky Mountains, then this scenario wipes out over 400 million years of earth history.[17]

Another fascinating study could be cited from Kodachrome Basin State Park in Utah.[18] Here, dikes are found in association with pipes, rather cylindrical features sometimes reaching 170 feet in height and 50 feet in diameter. The same problem crops up again. The time of deposition of the source bed is thought to be about 150 million years before the time of injection.

These are not isolated examples. The world contains quite a few examples of clastic dikes (and pipes), just as it should if the Biblical account of the Flood and the young earth are correct.

Clastic dike of Sawatch sandstone injected into Pikes Peak granite. Photo by Steve Austin.

Re-evaluation of a Classic Old-Earth Argument

Many people have the mistaken impression that geology has proved that the earth is billions of years old. As we have seen, nothing could be further from the truth!

One of the classic arguments used in favor of the old earth comes from the Petrified Forest of

17 One of our graduate students at ICR, Mr. Bill Hoesch, conducted a comprehensive field study of this area. His thesis, "The Timing of Clastic Dike Emplacement Along Red Creek Fault, Fremont County, Colorado," was published in 1994.

18 Roth, Ariel, A. "Clastic Pipes and Dikes in Kodachrome Basin," *Origins*, Vol. 19, No. 1, 1992, pp. 44–48.

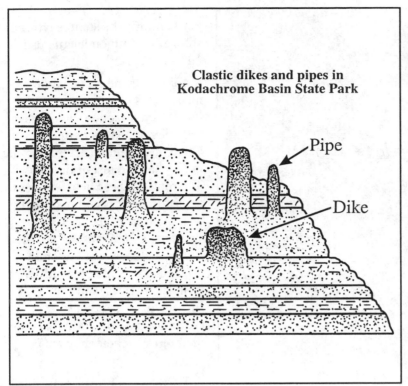

Clastic dikes and pipes in
Kodachrome Basin State Park

Pipe

Dike

Adapted from Ariel Roth, 1992

Yellowstone Park, where beautifully preserved petrified tree stumps are found in great numbers. At Specimen Ridge, a hillside now gouged by erosion, reveals some 27 or more horizontal layers of consolidated volcanic material, each of which contains abundant petrified wood, including many tree trunks in a vertical position with the root ends down and the trunk up. Many other trunks are horizontal. Similar exposures at nearby Specimen Creek consist of over 50 layers.

The upright trees have traditionally been interpreted as having been buried and petrified in their place of growth, as explained on the geologic marker present there. The series of pancake-like layers are interpreted as containing successive, in-place forests, each of which was buried by volcanic ash. It is claimed that after each volcanic eruption the upper surface of the volcanic-ash layer slowly weathered into a suitable topsoil in which seeds and sprouts could take root. Within a few hundred years, a second forest grew to maturity, which in turn was also buried by a second volcanic-ash eruption. This repeating pattern

occurred at least 27 times, so it is thought. Each forest required at least several hundred years to develop, because petrified trees containing up to 400 or so tree rings are typically present in each layer. The whole sequence of events is assumed to have taken many thousands of years at a minimum, perhaps much longer. At any rate, more time elapsed than can be easily fitted into Biblical chronology.

This might be a good time to point out that petrified wood does *not* take millions of years to form. Wood can, under certain conditions, be petrified rapidly, as several laboratory experiments have shown.[19] During one field experiment, researchers placed a block of wood on the end of a rope down inside an alkaline spring in Yellowstone Park. They dangled it in the silica-rich, hot waters to see if such an environment would petrify the wood. When they came back *one year later* and pulled the log out of the hole, they found that substantial petrifaction had occurred.[20] Furthermore, artificially petrified wood is even being produced commercially these days for true "hard

Geologic Evidence for the Young Earth

1. Surface features

2. Deficiency of bioturbation

3. Lack of soil layers

4. Undisturbed bedding planes

5. Polystrate fossils

6. Limited extent of unconformities

7. Soft-sediment deformation

19 Refer to Dr. Austin's *Catastrophes in Earth History*, ICR Technical Monograph No. 13, 1984.
20 Sigleo, A.C. "Organic Geochemistry of Solidified Wood," *Geochimica et Cosmochimica Acta*, Vol. 42, 1978, pp. 1397–1405.

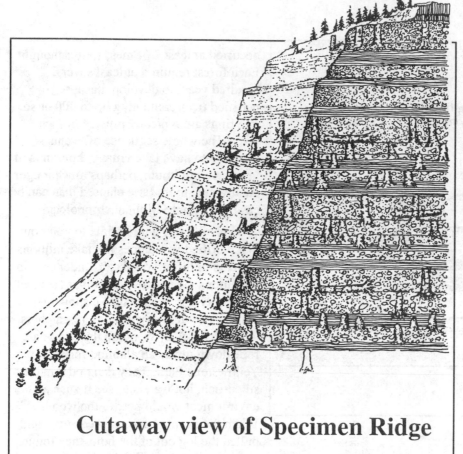

Cutaway view of Specimen Ridge

Furthermore, the stumps typically were of a common length, usually 10 to 12 feet tall.

Likewise, the roots, while many times oriented in a downward direction, didn't have fully developed root systems. Often, in living trees, the roots are larger than the rest of the tree. The roots of these petrified trees appear to have been broken off near the base of the tree. Only "root balls" are present, not the fully developed root system. Thus, the trees are much different from living trees, and we suspected, as had other creationists before us,[21] that they didn't grow where they are now found.

Each layer of trees, embedded as they are in volcanic ash, exhibits other evidence of having grown somewhere else and then having been transported to this location. Each of the layers gives evidence of having flowed as a water-saturated mud primarily made of volcanic ash, but not as a lava flow or a pyroclastic, explosive flow. The consistency of the layers of volcanic mud, and the common height of the stumps suggest that they may have come from a common source.

wood" floors. It does not take long to petrify wood; it just takes the right conditions. Ground water percolating through hot volcanic ash, which typically is full of silica, is thought to be the most suitable natural environment for the rapid petrifaction of wood.

Creationists, over the years, have studied the Petrified Forest in Yellowstone to see whether the evidence allowed any other interpretation. I was there in the mid 70's and observed the many upright trees petrified with their roots down, trunks up. The question was, did they grow there? If so, then the earth is older than a straight-forward reading of Scripture would indicate. Or, could they have been moved into this location quickly, somehow maintaining an upright posture?

We noticed several things about the trees. In each case, they were only stumps; no complete trees were present.

Petrified tree stumps at Specimen Ridge—in growth position, but not growth location.

21 This position was advocated in *The Genesis Flood,* Whitcomb and Morris, 1961, pp. 418–421.

The petrified trees are in growth position, but appear to have been rafted to this location by mud flows.

This is indeed a wonderful time to be a young-earth creationist, because so much information is now available that confirms our understanding of Scripture. A friend of mine, Dr. Mike Arct, recently performed such a study on the nearby Specimen Creek area. In his study, he discovered a "signature" ring pattern in several different layers, demonstrating that the various "forests" grew at the same time and must have been transported to this location on successive mud flows,[23] thus disproving the consecutive-forest model.

Other investigators have noted features about this area which likewise support a "rafting-in" model. Dr. Harold Coffin found that the twigs and branches, as well as horizontal tree trunks, are oriented in a preferred direction. This would be the case if they had been rafted in by moving mud. He also noted a great variety of plant material, seemingly too much variety to have all been growing in one location when covered by volcanic ash. It appeared, then, that the trees may have come from some distant source in a mudflow which picked up a variety of materials along the way.[22]

The petrified trees in Arizona's Petrified Forest National Park are now recognized to be a "petrified log jam."

The recent eruption of Mount St. Helens further reinforces this rafted-in interpretation. As a result of the eruption on May 18th, 1980, an energetic blast cloud raced from the upper mountain and devastated 150 square miles of forest. Likewise, a concurrent avalanche sped from the summit into Spirit Lake, causing a wave almost 900 feet high, which scoured slopes adjacent to the lake.

Many trees from the "blow-down zone" found their way into Spirit Lake, but others sloshed into rivers draining Mount St. Helens, and were carried along in mud flows for scores of miles downstream. As this mud moved along, many of the trees were observed to be floating upright, roots down, moving along at a high rate of speed. Perhaps this was due to the fact that boulders may have been trapped in the truncated roots, or because the wood in the roots is more dense than that in the trunk. For whatever reason, they were floating in moving mud, still in an upright position. When the mud finally came to a halt, they were still upright, and are still upright today.

In 1975, I predicted a way to solve the problem. I suggested that the tree rings in petrified trees from several of the layers should be compared. I predicted that if the layers had come from a common source and the trees had lived at the same time, then tree-ring patterns in different layers would match. But, if they had grown in successive forests, at totally different times, their tree-ring patterns would show no correspondence whatsoever.

22 For a good discussion of this and other subjects, see Coffin's *Origin By Design*, Review and Herald Publishers, 1983.

23 Arct, M.J. "*Dendroecology in the Fossil Forests of the Specimen Creek Area, Yellowstone National Park*," Ph.D Dissertation, Loma Linda University, CA, 1991. See also his M.S. Thesis, "*Dendrochronology in Yellowstone Fossil Forests*," *1985*.

Likewise, on Spirit Lake, as many of the trunks become water-logged, they turn to an upright position and sink. They bury themselves in the ash and peat deposit at the bottom of the lake, a fact which we confirmed both by scuba investigation and side-scanning sonar. Since Mount St. Helens continues to be active, depositing more material in the lake as time goes on, these upright trees will be buried in "separate" geologic layers, even though they came from the same forest. If the lake were to fill up and be excavated by geologists centuries from now, the trees might look as if they represented several separate

The May 18, 1980 eruption of Mount St. Helens devastated 150 square miles of forest. Over one million logs were washed into Spirit Lake.

When the lake was partially drained, some upright trees were found stuck in mud formerly on the lake bottom.

forests. But, of course, they don't, and, furthermore, their tree-ring patterns would certainly match.[24]

So we can see that on Mount St. Helens, two completely separate mechanisms resulted in upright trees being deposited where petrifaction can take place. They are deposited in growth position, but not in growth location. We suspect that similar events occurred at Yellowstone Park.

Interestingly enough, several recent interpretations of the Yellowstone Petrified Forest have included references to the events at Mount St. Helens. Many geologists are now agreeing that the Yellowstone petrified trees were, indeed, from the same standing forest, transported on a series of mud flows. And, wonder of wonders, the roadside evolution lesson has been removed. The classic argument that the Bible is wrong has been shown itself to be wrong. The Bible stands.

Parenthetically, Dr. Arct also found some other intriguing features in the Yellowstone petrified tree rings. Within many of the layers, trees were present with up to 900 tree rings. The rings were large, and showed almost monotonous regularity, indicating excellent growing conditions that seldom changed. No frost patterns were found at all. These older trees

---

24 See Dr. Steve Austin's excellent video presentation, "Mount St. Helens: Explosive Evidence for Creation," produced by ICR, 1992.

Many trees were carried downstream by surging mud flows. Some maintained an upright posture even after the mud stopped.

Flood waters receded? Perhaps they remained on the ground while other trees sprouted from their cones and grew around them. Both would then have been removed by dynamic mud flows associated with post-Flood volcanism, of which there was much.[25]

Conclusion

Thus we have seen, from a variety of different measurements and techniques, that the geologic and physical evidence of the world is quite compatible with the Biblical doctrine of the young earth. We can't prove the Bible from looking at geology, nor do we try to. We accept it by faith, but insist that if the Bible is really true, then the geologic evidence must support it, and indeed it does! It not only supports the Bible, but much geologic evidence can be cited which is quite incompatible with an old-earth scenario.

were of the same family as the various redwood species which today grow to great ages, even in hostile environments, and are essentially immune to fire, insects, and disease.

Furthermore, these large trees typically had their bark removed, as do the floating trees in Mount St. Helen's Spirit Lake.

Couple these finds with the fact that in the same layers, many other stumps were found, equally well petrified, but with only 30–50 tree rings. Many of these still retained their bark (sometimes even in "woody" condition), although their branches had been stripped off. Furthermore, their tree rings showed great variation from year to year.

Next, consider the fact that the time period before the Flood was probably less than 2,000 years. No tree could have grown to the ages of present redwoods, some over 4000 years old and still growing.

Can this series of deposits represent a time of volcanism in the centuries following the Flood? Could the older trees be pre-Flood trees, which had floated through the Flood year in a floating mat, finally to be grounded as the

As the trees water-logged, many assumed an upright posture.

25 For a thorough study of this and related subjects, see Beasley, Greg J. "Long-Lived Trees: Their Possible Testimony to a Global Flood and Recent Creation," *Creation Ex Nihilo Technical Journal*, Vol. 7, Part 1, 1993, pp. 43–67.

Man will go to great lengths to avoid worshiping his Creator-God. He will even bow down before "Mother Earth" and "Father Time."

Chapter 9
What Do the Rocks Mean?

While I have not, and (as I have maintained) indeed couldn't have, proved scientifically that the earth is young, I have given significant evidence that fits much more easily in the young-earth model than in the old-earth model. In fact, some of the evidence doesn't seem to be at all compatible with old-earth ideas. The weight of the evidence comes down on the side of the young earth.

More important, however, is the way of thinking about the unobserved past presented here. My contention throughout has been that *only* Scripture gives *specific* information about the age of the earth and the timing of its unobserved events. Rocks, fossils, isotope arrays, and physical systems do not speak with the same clarity as Scripture. The truth is there in nature, but can we find it? Such systems in many ways are rather generic with respect to age: they can be adequately interpreted within more than one model, depending on one's presuppositions.

In order to properly interpret them, we must first go "Back to Genesis" and get our overall model—get our thinking straight. Then we must interpret the physical evidence in accord with that model. In this Biblical model, fossiliferous rocks were by and large deposited by Noah's Flood. Fossils are the remains of organisms which descended from those created during Creation Week and died in the Flood (with some exceptions). Radioisotope dating methods suffer from wrong assumptions about the past, mainly because physical systems were drastically altered by the global and destructive nature of the Flood and also because the assumptions used deny the possibility of Creation. Scripture doesn't give us all the details, but only as we place our interpretations in agreement with the teachings of Scripture, do we have a chance rightly to understand the past.

Evolutionists follow exactly the same method of thinking, only they bow before a different philosophy, that of naturalism, evolution, and uniformitarianism. These doctrines about the past are, at best, based on *unprovable assumptions*, and are *not* well supported by the data. By definition, they deny the great worldwide events of Genesis. But if Creation and the Flood are facts of history, they must be included in one's view of the past. To deny historical truth before attempting to reconstruct history is forever to embrace error.

Does It Matter?

The questions then arise, "Why are we concerned with something so elusive? Shouldn't we concern ourselves only with knowing the Rock of Ages, and forget abut the ages of rocks? Let's talk about where we're going, not about where we've been."

Comments and questions like these may seem very "spiritual," but they are little more than cop-outs. All too many Christians have chosen not to see or become involved in the battle around us, in effect surrendering to the enemy, and in so doing, abandoning all those who come under the influence of the enemy.

Battlefronts captured by those with views adversarial to Christianity include the news media, television, politics, academia, the judicial system, public education, and, in this case, much of "science," with resulting havoc everywhere. Each of these battles *were* winnable, and some of them still are! The Christian's resources far surpass those of the humanist, and the evidence is very clearly on our side. Losses are avoidable.

Especially in real science. Creation far excels evolution as a scientific model. Evolution survives only by suppression of alternatives. The tactics of evolutionists include ridicule, personal attacks, bureaucratic policies, and court rulings. Mostly, it survives because so few have ever heard a credible case for Creation. All that most people know is what they've been taught.

Few advocates of Creation even recognize the philosophical nature of the question. The discussions usually sink to a "my evidence" versus "your evidence" level, while in reality all evidence must be *interpreted*, and nearly all evidence can be included in either model. The discussions should be "my interpretations based on my assumptions" versus "your interpretations based on your assumptions" and the reasonableness of each set of assumptions and interpretations. And, of course, we must never confuse *circumstantial* evidence for *direct* evidence.

Please don't think I'm claiming that a proper presentation of creation and young-earth thinking guarantees victory in every legislative committee, school administration, and think tank. Most of these arenas are infiltrated by persons who know they are in a battle, and know which side they're on. Often, the rules are set up so that creationists can't even come up to bat, let alone score.

But the battle *is* winnable, at least on a local and individual level, and the battle is worth fighting! In the pages to follow, I've identified several reasons why a follower of Christ *must* join the battle, for the battle is for the minds and hearts of men and women, boys and girls, scientists and lay persons, Christians and non-Christians. The fight must be carried to several battlefronts, and all soldiers of the King can play a vital role. Eternal matters are at stake!

The Scientific Battlefront

Few people, especially Christians, ever stop to think that science has been ordained by God, and that each human has been commanded to take part in this enterprise. As God's week of creating came to an end, He placed Adam in charge. Adam was told to "subdue" the earth, and "have dominion" over it and all of the creatures in it (Genesis 1:28). Theologians call this "The Dominion Mandate," and recognize that it passed through Adam to all his descendants.

> And God blessed them, and God said
> unto them, Be fruitful, and multiply, and
> replenish the earth, and subdue it: and
> have dominion over the fish of the sea,
> and over the fowl of the air, and over
> every living thing that moveth upon the
> earth.

The two verbs are significant. *Subdue* implies the serious study of the earth and its processes, as well as of all living things. We have come to call this understanding process "science." Mankind must fully understand the creation in order to carry out the next part of the mandate.

To *have dominion over* creation would fall into our modern category of "technology," that of the utilization of our knowledge. God has placed mankind in the position of stewards over creation.

We are to care for it, manage it, protect it, and utilize it for our good and God's glory.

Frequently, humanists claim that Christians would spoil the environment and ruin the ecological balance between species. Although some Christians are insensitive, no support can be found in Scripture for abusing the environment.

Actually, the Christian should lead the way in environmental concerns. In recent years, the humanist has laid exclusive claim to this God-commanded activity, and is using it to capture the hearts of young people. Along the way, they have twisted "environmentalism" into *pantheism*, with a host of attendant New-Age evils. Much illegitimate baggage has thus been added to proper, God-commanded concern for the creation. To modern environmentalists, man is the enemy, not the steward. Evolution is the creator, through Mother Nature and Father Time. A Christian must not participate in the pantheistic aspects of the modern environmental movement, but God expects *all* of us, not just *them*, to care wisely for His creation.

Another reason creation understanding is so important is that God deserves praise for His creative majesty, just as He does for His redemptive work. I know my own prayer life would suffer dramatically if I didn't spend time in praising Him for His creative acts and His sovereign care for the Creation. His Word to us includes many references of praise to the God of Creation. How dare we ignore them, and it!

> Thou art worthy, O Lord, to receive glory
> and honor and power: for thou hast
> created all things, and for thy pleasure
> they are and were created.
>
> Revelation 4:11

Furthermore, He validates His Word in time and space, relating many prophecies and historical references in Scripture to specific times and places, things that are in principle, verifiable.

Jesus told Nicodemus:

> If I have told you earthly things, and ye
> believe not, how shall ye believe if I tell
> you of heavenly things?"
>
> John 3:12

If we don't believe Him when He teaches about "earthly things," how can we trust Him when He tells us of "heavenly things." We *can* check the things of science and history, and when we do, we find His Word reliable.

On the other hand, if He is wrong about science and history, He is wrong, and by His own Word, the wrong prophet is a false prophet (See Deuteronomy 18:20–22).

In order to fully appreciate God's creative power and majesty, we must first rightly understand His Creation. This means we must study and comprehend it fully and rightly. Then we can praise Him from knowledge, and bring Him glory as we properly care for Creation and obey His mandate.

This command to understand includes more than Creation, it extends to the young-earth issue as well. The enemy uses evolution as a major weapon in *his* battle, and the old-earth idea undergirds all of evolutionary thinking. In witnessing to others about Christianity, many times you will encounter an unsaved person who will use the young-earth teaching of Scripture to reject Christ as revealed in Scripture. Creationists are tempted to stop with the creation versus evolution issue and ignore the age of the earth, but to many people, the old earth *proves* evolution. It certainly disproves Scripture, and, therefore, the Scriptural doctrine of Creation. Many on both sides consider the age of the earth as the weakest doctrine in Scripture. We must strengthen and defend it.

Creation and New Age

Many secularists today have abandoned strict naturalism in favor of hazy New-Age thinking. Even scientists are leaving Darwinian evolution in droves, recognizing that strictly natural processes, operating at random on inorganic chemicals, could *never* have produced complex living cells. They have grown weary of arguing how random mutations in a highly complex genetic code provide improvements in it.

To avoid the implications of impotent nature, New Agers have chosen to believe that nature is alive and well and doing these things on purpose. Thus, they worship nature (some more openly than others), ascribing to nature qualities and characteristics formerly ascribed to God. They recognize the marvelous design in living things and know that an overriding mind must be behind it. That mind to them is Gaia, or Mother Earth. They would be nearly

as critical of Darwinian evolution as creationists. How can you reach them?

Logical reasoning with one who has chosen absurdity is never easy. Arguing creation versus evolution with a new-age advocates seldom works. But, maybe, the age of the earth can provide an opening. To show firm evidence that the earth may not be so old, might just weaken their commitment to their anti-God philosophy.

The Biblical Battlefront

When I came to work at ICR in 1984, having left my faculty position at the University of Oklahoma, ICR had far outgrown its facility. The only "office" space left was an overflow room for the ICR library, in which were kept thousands of theological books dating from the 1700's and 1800's. They had been donated to ICR by a collector who had been interested in the history of modern Creation and evolution. The books represented the thinking of Christian leaders through the decades during which naturalistic evolution replaced Creation as the norm. Being a confirmed book worm, I read many of these books, and skimmed nearly all of them.

During the 1700's, while exceptions could be cited, most theologians and scientists in western countries were Bible-believing Christians and creationists. But by the late 1800's, most scientists and theologians had abandoned the Creation, Flood and young earth doctrines, and accepted the position that the Bible contains errors and can not be trusted, particularly as it relates to science and history.

Having studied geology in secular settings, I knew that in the late 1700's James Hutton, and in the early 1800's, Charles Lyell had proposed the principle of uniformity and, thus, the old earth. They are canonized by secularists for opening the door for Darwin in 1859 to completely discredit the Bible! Many leading scientists resisted all these ideas, and defended Scripture as both true and scientific. But by the late 1800's, almost all such voices had been silenced. What could have brought such a turn-around?

My "office" reading provided the answer. In many cases, it was *Christians* who led the charge against Scripture. Beginning in the early 1800's, theologians readily adopted first the old earth ideas, then uniformitarianism instead of the Flood. They even toyed with evolutionary ideas long before Darwin. The Bible-believing *scientists* of the day were thus in the difficult position of trying to defend Scripture when *theologians* were against them.

Gradually, belief in a historical view of Genesis waned, and a generation later, when Darwin proposed his mechanism for evolution, even scientists fell into his trap, and few academics, either scientists or theologians, any longer accepted Creation.

Parenthetically, things haven't changed much. The modern Creation revival is led by scientists and laymen, not theologians. By and large, seminary-trained theologians oppose or are indifferent to Biblical and scientific creationism. But it doesn't take a seminary degree to know that the Bible teaches Creation and a young earth. In fact, it probably takes seminary training to accept the various perversions of Scripture, such as the Day-Age concept, the Framework Hypothesis, Theistic Evolution, and the local-Flood theory. Modern evangelicals are hard pressed to find a major seminary that systematically holds to a historical, grammatical view of Genesis. Most prefer to allegorize it and welcome evolution and/or old-earth thinking into their theology.

Today, the hardest pill for liberal and neo-evangelical theologians to swallow is the young-earth doctrine. Even many "fundamental" theologians hold the so-called "Gap Theory" to accommodate the geologic ages. Historically, it was the issue of the age of the earth which was the first doctrine of Scripture to be abandoned, then the Flood, then the Creation. Today, the cycle has reversed. With evolution now exposed as not credible, many Christians are re-adopting Creation, but still hold on to the old-earth and local Flood. How much better it would be to come all the way back to a Biblical world view (one which employs better science, I might add).

Much is at stake, even the issue of Biblical inerrancy. Can God's Word be trusted? When it gives times and places and genealogies, does it contain meaningful information? To Christian old-earth advocates, many Scripture passages must be ignored or allegorized.

Let's look at the Biblical Flood, as a primary example. The Bible teaches that the Flood was a global event, which destroyed the pre-Flood world and all its land-dwelling inhabitants not on Noah's Ark.

Consider, for example, the following passage:

> And the Flood was forty days upon the earth; and the waters increased, and bare up the ark, and it was lifted up above the earth. And the waters prevailed, and were increased greatly upon the earth; and the ark went upon the face of the waters. And the waters prevailed exceedingly upon the earth; and all the high hills, that were under the whole heaven were covered. Fifteen cubits upward did the waters prevail; and the mountains were covered. And all flesh died that moved upon the earth, both of fowl, and of cattle, and of beast, and of every creeping thing that creepeth upon the earth, and every man: All in whose nostrils was the breath of life, of all that was in the dry land, died. And every living substance was destroyed which was upon the face of the ground, both man, and cattle, and the creeping things, and the fowl of the heaven; and they were destroyed from the earth: and Noah only remained alive, and they that were with him in the ark. And the waters prevailed upon the earth an hundred and fifty days.
>
> Genesis 7:17–24

How could words more clearly state the *global* nature of the Flood? But in spite of the obvious intent of Scripture, many Christians have followed evolutionary leads and claim that the Flood, if it occurred at all, was only local, limited perhaps to the Mesopotamian River valley, but not global in extent, and certainly not responsible for the rock and fossil records.

It is true that the Hebrew word translated "all" in this passage can sometimes be taken in a limited sense, just as in English. Such a word must be understood, then, in light of its context, and here, it can only mean all in a *global* sense: "*All* flesh upon the earth; . . . *All* in whose nostrils was the breath of life; . . . *all* that was in the dry land; . . . *every* living substance . . . upon the face of the ground; . . . the fowl of the heaven; . . . destroyed from the earth. . . ." It's just not sufficient to say that "all" is *sometimes* to be understood as limited. To defend the local Flood, it must be demonstrated that "all" is limited to "some" in *this* case in spite of the fact that the *all-inclusive* nature of the Flood is repeated over and over.

Here are some other phrases which could only mean a global flood: ". . . *all flesh* . . . I will destroy *with the earth*" (6:13). (Note that "the earth" means planet Earth, not just the local area.) "I do bring a flood of waters upon *the earth* to destroy *all flesh*, wherein is the breath of life, from *under heaven*; and *everything* that is *in the earth* shall die" (6:17). (Note that the phrase "under heaven" refers to "the atmosphere"—which is worldwide.) The animals "*of every sort*" were to be brought in by twos "to keep them alive" (6:20), a capricious command if the Flood were only local. The list could go on and on. Noah's Flood covered the globe! The entire earth!

This same teaching was echoed by both Christ and Peter in the New Testament:

> But as the days of Noah were, so shall also the coming of the Son of man be. For as in the days that were before the Flood they were eating and drinking, marrying and giving in marriage, until the day that Noah entered into the Ark, and knew not until the Flood came, and took them *all* away, so shall also the coming of the Son of man be.
> Matthew 24:37–39

> The world that then was, being overflowed with water, perished: But the heavens and the earth, which are now, by the same word are kept in store, reserved unto fire against the day of judgment and perdition of ungodly men.
> II Peter 3:6–7

Note that both Christ and Peter based their doctrines of the coming judgment on the *whole* world on the *fact* of the past judgment of the *whole* world in Noah's day. If the Flood had been only local, and much of the earth and at least some people had survived it, what kind of judgment is to come? Will it also be local? Will some sinners be excluded? The local Flood idea produces theological chaos!

Not only did the Flood cover the globe, this mountain-covering, year-long cataclysm accomplished *much* geologic work, operating at rates, scales, and intensities far in excess of modern floods. At the very least, it did what all floods do, eroding some areas and redepositing the eroded material elsewhere as sediments. The sediments would be full of plants and animals that died in the Flood. If Noah's Flood happened the way the Bible says it happened, then modern day sedimentary rocks containing fossils are its result.

The Flood deposits would then give evidence of having been laid down catastrophically, not by calm, uniform processes. They would frequently be of vast regional extent, not local, as uniformitarians propose. Erosion, as well as deposition, would be of catastrophic proportions! As we have seen, these and other features are now recognized and admitted by my evolutionary colleagues, many of whom call themselves "neo-catastrophists." Something radically different was going on in the past—something catastrophic—something global—something like the Flood of Noah's day.

Yet, many evolutionists still wrongly use rocks and fossils as evidence of evolution and the old earth, *misinterpreting* their true history. But if Noah's Flood produced the rocks and fossils, there is hardly any evidence left for evolution and old-earth concepts.

Modern evangelicals who adopt the old-earth concept and/or evolution, *must* deny the Flood as a global, geologically significant event, and all of them who have thought about it in a consistent manner, do. Most claim the Flood was only a *local* Flood. Others propose a non-sensical *tranquil* Flood. Perhaps the majority just look the other way, and ignore the whole issue. In each case, they deny a clear teaching of Scripture, one which forms the basis for much vital teaching in the New Testament. Christians desperately need to return to a consistent belief in *all* of God's Word if we are ever to be effective in reaching the world.

This situation was dramatically illustrated by an event which happened a few years ago to ICR. At the time I was teaching a course in Biblical and scientific apologetics to students at Christian Heritage College (CHC), ICR's sister school. I had been teaching about the Flood, and how those who desired to accommodate the old-earth view into their view of

The Flood
of Noah's Day
<u>The Bottom Line</u>

The world-wide, mountain covering deluge would have deposited most of the world's fossil-bearing rock.

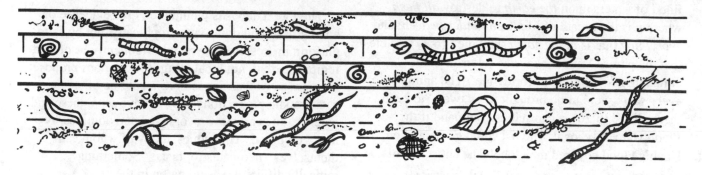

The naturalist—denying the fact of the Flood—misinterprets the rocks and fossils.

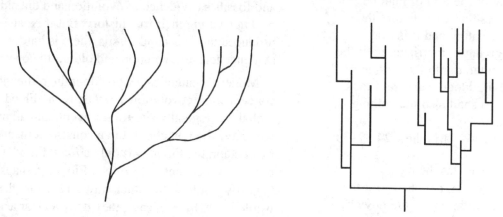

If the Flood was a global event, it laid down the rocks and fossils, and there is no evidence for evolution or for an old Earth.

Scripture always had to modify the clear doctrine of the global Flood (that is, if they are knowledgeable and consistent in their understanding of old-earth thinking). I showed how that both historically and logically, an old earth advocate *cannot* hold to a global, geologically significant Flood, for the evidence for long ages is in the rocks and the fossils. But if Noah's Flood *happened, it* deposited the great majority of the world's fossiliferous rocks. Thus in order to hold to the old-earth idea, one must conclude that the Flood of Noah's day was only local, or tranquil, but not responsible for the rocks and fossils.

One day after class I got word that two Christian scholars were coming to ICR a few days later to discuss our view of the young earth. One of them, astronomer and Big Bang/old-earth advocate, Dr. Hugh Ross, had announced he was coming to ICR for a "Biblical confrontation." He felt it was his Christian duty to "confront" us with our error of teaching the young earth. The other, philosopher/theologian Dr. Norman Geisler, also an advocate of the old earth, was coming in support of Ross, not so much to confront ICR with error, but to take part in the discussion.

Of course, this is serious business, and we took it so. We arranged for all of our scientists as well as interested CHC faculty to be present when they came. If we were in error, we wanted to know it and correct our thinking.

The day before they came, I predicted to my class that these scholars, if they were consistent in their old-earth thinking, would accept either the Local Flood theory or the Tranquil-Flood theory, in order to maintain their belief in the old-earth as well as in Scripture.

The "confrontation" lasted several hours, and continued on a subsequent day. It consisted primarily of Dr. Ross trying to convince us of the Big Bang Theory, radioisotope dating, Einstein's theory of relativity (which many young-earth creationists hold), and plate tectonics (which many young-earth creationists also hold, albeit with a different time frame). Ross even claimed that to a great degree his salvation was based on the Big Bang and old-universe concepts, for as a teenage science buff searching for religious truth, he found that the Genesis account of the Bible was the only religious writing which he could make fit with the Big Bang

and old universe, (which he already "knew" to be true).

Geisler was less committed to any of these specific positions, but adamantly held to the old earth. He even distanced himself from certain of Ross' positions, such as the idea that Neanderthal man was a human-like animal, although with a larger brain than modern man, with the ability to talk, conduct burials with religious significance, etc., but had no eternal spirit. Geisler held that Neanderthal was certainly a descendant of Adam, but Ross insisted that the eternal spirit in man came later, when Adam was created, long *after* the Neanderthals, and based his position on excessively old radioisotope dating of Neanderthal fossils.

But then came the question. What do you think about Noah's Flood? Ross freely admitted that while it was a major flood, it covered only portions of the Middle East. It did not cover Europe, Asia, or Africa, and did not drown the inhabitants of these areas. It certainly couldn't have covered America, nor did it affect the Indians already living here, nor did it cause Grand Canyon. Grand Canyon happened *millions* of years ago, according to secular geologic interpretation and radioisotope dating. To Ross, the Flood must have only *appeared* to Noah to be global, for it covered as far as Noah could see, but certainly was just a *local* Flood. By all means, it didn't deposit the rocks and fossils, for geology has proved they are millions and millions of years old!

At this point, Geisler chimed in to correct Ross. He insisted that the Bible clearly taught a global, world-wide Flood. But, Geisler said, it didn't do the geologic work claimed for it by young-earth creationists. He held that it must have destroyed all the pre-Flood human inhabitants, but *left little geologic trace on the planet*. It rose, covered the world, drowned all of life on land, and then simply drained off. No rocks, no fossils. I asked how he could hold such a position, since even the minor, local floods of today do tremendous geologic work. How could a Flood, which he admitted was much larger and more dynamic, do *no* geologic work? Thus, he proposed a *tranquil* Flood.

The proper way to approach this issue is to accept Scripture at face value, as the Writer of Scripture, God, intended the reader to understand it, and to place our thinking, our research, our interpretation of

The spine labels on the top illustration read (left to right): Care for Creation, Good Science, Government Under God, Right and Wrong, Value of Human Life, Family Values. The base reads "Creation" sitting on "The Word of God".

image and likeness, how can he or she take any action that will harm, deface, or destroy that image?

Note: If man is an animal, promiscuity, homosexuality, racism, treachery, abortion, infanticide, euthanasia, violence, are all understandable as animal traits.

Young-earth ideas likewise influence our thinking. Do we think of God as long ago and far away, or nearby and intimately interested and involved in our lives and in earth history? Did He know what He was doing as He created?

Assume, for the moment, the stance taken by many Christian leaders today, that God created the earth and its systems, but did so over 4½ billion years. I will attempt to show that this view is internally inconsistent in its theology, promoting a view of God totally unlike the God of the Bible.

First, consider God's omniscience. If He knows everything, including His purpose in Creation, why did He take so long, as a seeming afterthought, to recreate His own image in a creature with whom He could communicate, and on whom He could shower His Love and Grace, and from whom He could

data, all in submission to His Truth. We must rethink our presuppositions, allowing God to set our historical world view, not secular scientists. We must judge the opinions of all scientists (including our own opinions) by Scripture. The Bible commands, "Be not conformed to this world: but be transformed by the renewing of your mind" (Romans 12:2). "Prove all things; hold fast to that which is good" (I Thessalonians 5:21). Once we succeed in allowing Him and His Word to direct our study, we will do better science.

The Theological Battlefront

It has been rightly noted that "Ideas have consequences. Ideas have power." The way a person thinks, influences the way he or she relates to society, to self, and to God.

Obviously, evolutionary ideas have great impact on one's self-worth and self-concept. One who considers mankind to be the random by-product of chance events operating on the primeval slime, makes decisions and relates to those around him in a very different way than does one who believes men and women were created in the image and likeness of God. If each human being somehow bears God's

The spine labels on the bottom illustration read (left to right): Worship of Earth, Naturalism and New Age, Socialism, Marxism, Anarchy, Relative Standards, Abortion, Euthanasia, Homosexuality, Promiscuity. The base reads "Evolution" sitting on "The Mind of Man".

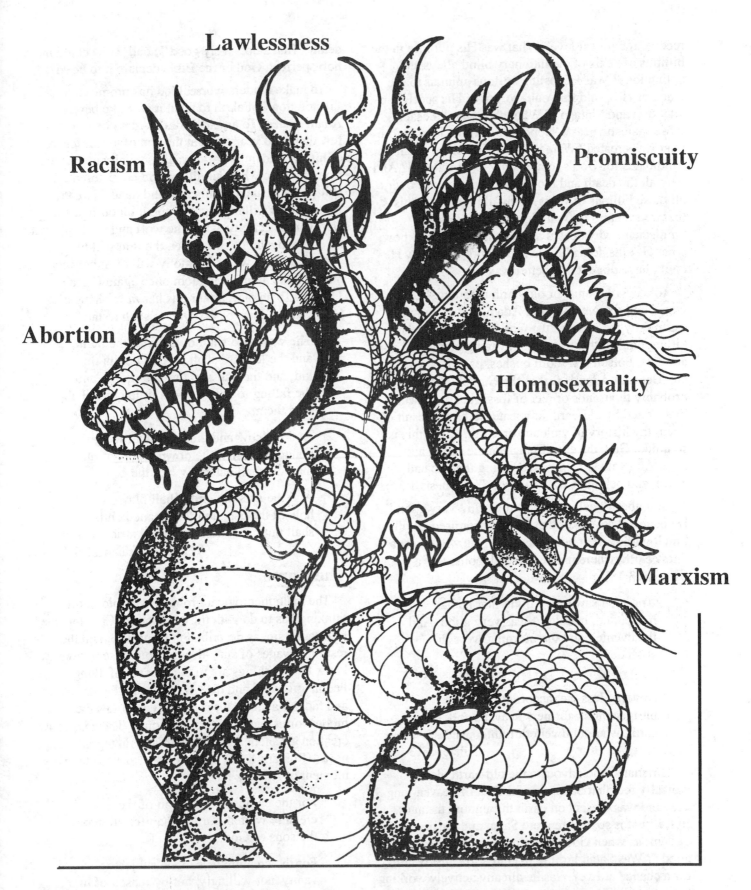

Racism · Lawlessness · Promiscuity · Abortion · Homosexuality · Marxism

Evolutionary Humanism—a Multi-Headed Dragon.

receive reciprocal love? What was His purpose in the billions of years of evolutionary blind alleys and extinctions? Was He testing various animals to see whether He could find one worthy of His special attention and "image"? What about the dinosaurs, those majestic beasts supposedly extinct long before man was created? Were they considered as possible candidates for God's image, only to be rejected? And why all the death and bloodshed and violence over all these billions of years? Why did He set up this bizarre scenario to finally get man? If God is omniscient, why does it appear that He didn't know what He was doing? If He is omnipotent, surely He could have done it in a better way.

To an evolutionist or old-earth creationist, the world both before and after Adam's creation was essentially the same as the world today. Animals killing one another, diseases ravaging plants and animals. Poison ivy, thorn bushes, parasites, viruses, etc. Beneath Adam's feet in the Garden of Eden were probably thousands of feet of fossil-bearing rock, interpreted by old-earth advocates to be the result of a lengthy history of violence on earth. All of this is so unlike God, the ever-living Source of life and love. And yet God "saw everything that He had made, and behold it was *very good*" (Genesis 1:31).

God doesn't call our present world "very good." He deems it so "bad" that He has promised it will "melt with fervent heat," and then He will create a "new earth, wherein dwelleth righteousness" (II Peter 3:13).

> And God saw every thing that he had made, and, behold, it was very good. And the evening and the morning were the sixth day.
>
> Genesis 1:31

> Nevertheless we, according to his promise, look for new heavens and a new earth, wherein dwelleth righteousness.
>
> II Peter 3:13

Christians who advocate the old-earth idea typically feel that Satan was cast out of heaven long ago, and was present on earth throughout the ages. But, if that is so, where were Satan and the myriads of demons when God pronounced everything "very good"? Was Satan lurking behind a tree just waiting for a chance at Eve? Was he already actively working to distort God's creation, causing extinction and

death? That's not "very good" at all. How could the holy, perfect, God of the Bible declare it to be so?

To make matters worse, God has promised a "restoration" of earth to what it was like before Adam sinned. To an old-earther, Adam lived just a few thousand years ago, at the end of 4½ billion years of history. Adam's world was essentially no different from ours. So what will this world be restored to? Billions of years of extinction and death? No, the Bible says it will be a time without bloodshed and carnivorous activity, when the wolf and the lamb will lie down together, where even the lion will be vegetarian, and where harmony will exist between man and the animal kingdom once again (Isaiah 11:6–8). To an old-earther this has *never* happened. How can the earth be *restored* to such a state?

> The wolf also shall dwell with the lamb, and the leopard shall lie down with the kid; and the calf and the young lion and the fatling together; and a little child shall lead them.

> And the cow and the bear shall feed; their young ones shall lie down together: and the lion shall eat straw like the ox.

> And the sucking child shall play on the hole of the asp, and the weaned child shall put his hand on the cockatrice' den.
>
> Isaiah 11:6–8

The Curse

The main theological problem with old-earth thinking has to do with the curse on all Creation due to Adam's sin, as described in Genesis 3, and the resulting wages of sin—death. From observation, we know that all things are in the process of dying. People grow old and die. Animals die. Plants wither and fade. Machines wear. Civilizations die. The moon's orbit decays. Stars burn out. "The *whole* creation groaneth and travaileth in pain together until now" (Romans 8:22) and has done so since the very moment of Adam's fall.

> For the earnest expectation of the creature waiteth for the manifestation of the sons of God.

> For the creature was made subject to vanity, not willingly, but by reason of him who hath subjected the same in hope.

Because the creation itself also shall be delivered from the bondage of corruption into the glorious liberty of the children of God.

For we know that the whole creation groaneth and travaileth in pain together until now.

Romans 8:19–22

This passage, Romans 8:19–26, strikes at the heart of the old-earth concept. Let us look at the words carefully. The words "creature" (vv. 19,20,21) and "creation" (v. 22) are actually the same word. In each case the proper translation is "creation." The "whole creation" (v. 22) is groaning under the effects of the curse, awaiting deliverance such as has already been provided "the children of God" (v. 21) in the spiritual realm. Everything not human is under this "bondage of corruption," including animals, plants, and the very earth itself. The earth's human population (vv. 23–26) likewise suffers in their human bodies, but God's children *will experience* the "redemption of our body" (v. 23). *Everything* suffers under the curse!

The creation has been made "subject to vanity" (v. 20), a state implying failure to achieve the "very good" purpose for which it was created. Because of sin and the resultant curse, it stopped measuring up to God's design as it originally did.

The tense of the verb "was made subject," speaks of a past, completed event at which all of creation was affected. There are only two candidates for this event, Genesis 1:1 and Genesis 3:14–19. If the creation of all things in Genesis 1:1 included the making of all things "subject to vanity," (as Dr. Hugh Ross and other old earth advocates claim), then God is the author of much pain and suffering and death, because that is the state of things. Did God create blood-thirsty animals, poisonous plants, infectious diseases, parasites, etc.? Did He call it all "very good"? Did God design conscious animals, capable of expressing emotions such as loyalty and care for one another, to at times suffer excruciating pain and horrid death?

The situation gets worse when humankind is considered. The world immediately after creation would suffer the same symptoms as our world, both being "subject to vanity." Is this world "very good?" What about miscarried babies, heartbroken widows, lepers, cancer victims, handicapped infants and adults? What about famine, natural disasters, and drought? What about birth defects and tragic mutations? Factor in, human behavior patterns, including genocide, human sacrifice, brutality on unimaginable scales, which, (according to their view of carbon dating) archaeologists tell us have been going on for millennia, long before the Biblical date for Adam. This world *isn't* "very good." This world of ours couldn't be similar to God's created "very-good" earth. If it is, God is responsible for all these things. Where is His holiness in all this? Where is His justice?

If, however, the event which ruined creation is the one recorded in Genesis 3, then it makes sense. Man's rebellion against God brought the curse and death, the "bondage of corruption." God's holy nature and justice shine as He faithfully pronounces the penalty for sin as He had promised (Genesis 2:17), but He also promises in His grace to send a solution to the problem of sin and death (Genesis 3:15), a solution we now recognize as God's only Son, Jesus Christ.

Adam and Eve were created to live forever in fellowship with God. They had had access to the Tree of Life in the Garden. They and the animals were commanded to be vegetarian, and no carnivorous activity was to take place (Genesis 1:29–30):

> And God said, "Behold I have given you every herb bearing seed, which is upon the face of all the earth, and every tree, in the which is the fruit of a tree yielding seed; to you it shall be for meat.

> And to every beast of the earth, and to every fowl of the air, and to every thing that creepeth upon the earth, wherein there is life, I have given every green herb for meat": and it was so.

Genesis 1:29–30

But sin distorts everything. Sin distorted God's original "very good" Creation. God had promised that if they disobeyed and ate of the forbidden tree, "thou shalt surely die" (Genesis 2:17) or, literally, "dying you shall die." They would die spiritually and begin their process of dying physically: " from dust thou art and unto dust shalt thou return" (Genesis 3:19). Everything partook of this curse, the animals (v. 15), the plants (v.18), the ground (v. 17), Adam and Eve (vv. 15–19), etc.—everything is now under this "bondage of corruption" (Romans 8:21).

Note: By way of explanation, plants are *biologically* alive, but have no "breath of life" (Genesis 2:7). Furthermore, "The *life* of the flesh is in the *blood*" (Leviticus 17:11). Plants have no consciousness, no breath, no blood, thus are not "living" in the Biblical sense of living. They were created specifically to nourish "living" things. Their biological "death" (and perhaps also that of many of the "lesser" forms of life technically classed as animals) does not constitute the death of a Biblically living, breathing, blood-filled creature.

The Extent of the Curse

Genesis 3:14–19

All of Creation altered because of Adam and Eve's rebellion

Earth cursed, v. 17

Animals cursed, v.14

Plants cursed, v. 18

Humankind cursed, vv. 16,17,19

Death reigns, v. 19, Romans 8:19–22

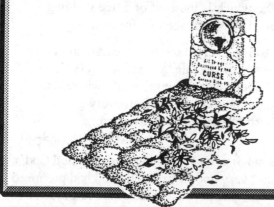

The very first recorded death was that of an animal to provide a covering for Adam and Eve, painfully aware of their sin (Genesis 3:21). Throughout the Old Testament, we see blood sacrifices for sin commanded. "Without the shedding of blood, there is no remission of sin" (Hebrews 9:22). The Biblical teaching of the entrance of death because of sin makes sense *only if the earth is young*.

> Wherefore, as by one man sin entered into the world, and death by sin; and so death passed upon all men, for that all have sinned.
>
> Romans 5:12.

> But now is Christ risen from the dead, and become the first-fruits of them that slept. For since by man came death, by man came also the resurrection of the dead. For as in Adam all die, even so in Christ shall all be made alive.
>
> I Corinthians 15:20–22.

But what if the earth is old? The fossils are then thought to show that the dying of living creatures had already been going on for hundreds of millions of years before Adam sinned. Death, extinction of the less fit as the more fit survive through the process of natural selection, has dominated history. Death is then normal, death is natural, death is just the way things are. If God created *this* kind of world, then what kind of God do we have? Is He sadistic, capricious, and cruel?

But it gets even worse! To an evolutionist, death is the central focus. Death fuels evolution. Death produced man. For instance, it was the extinction of the dinosaurs which gave rise to the mammals, and eventually to man. Carl Sagan, the well-known evolutionary spokesperson of our day says it this way:

> The secrets of evolution are death and time—the deaths of enormous numbers of lifeforms that were imperfectly adapted to the environment; and time for a long succession of small mutations that were by accident adaptive, time for the slow accumulation of patterns of favorable mutations.
>
> Carl Sagan, *Cosmos*, 1980, p. 30.

Charles Darwin recognized the key role of death in evolution by natural selection. The final, climactic paragraph of *Origin of Species* points this out. After describing for several hundred pages the evidence for and effects of natural selection, he concludes: "Thus, from the war of nature, from famine and death, the most exalted object which we are capable of

conceiving, namely, the production of the higher animals (i.e., man, ed.) directly follows." In other words, *from death comes man*.

> Thus, from the war of nature, from famine and death, the most exalted object which we are capable of conceiving, namely, the production of the higher animals, directly follows.
>
> Charles Darwin, *Origin of Species*, last paragraph

Actually, Charles Darwin credited the existence of pain and suffering and death for his commitment to *natural* selection. In response to a plea not to be so atheistic in his writings, Darwin responded: "I had no intention to write atheistically, but I own that I cannot see as plainly as others do, and as I should wish to do, evidence of design and beneficence on all sides of us. I cannot persuade myself that a beneficent and omnipotent God would have designedly created the *ichneumonidae* [a parasite, *ed.*] with the express intention of their feeding within the living bodies of caterpillars, or that a cat should play with mice. Not believing this, I see no necessity in the belief that the eye was expressly designed." (Charles Darwin in a letter to Harvard Professor Asa Gray, May 22, 1860.)

Thus, to an evolutionist, death is the natural state of things, and death produced man. Even to an old-earth creationist, death preceded man (even the death of human-like "animals"), and God used death to prepare the way for man. In either case, a world dominated by death, pain, and suffering was here *before man and certainly before man sinned*.

The Effect of the Curse

Next, notice that death is also the central focus of Christianity. First, death is the penalty for sin. "The wages of sin is death" (Romans 6:23), for that sin separates us from a holy God. But that is not all.

Do you remember what happened in the Garden of Eden after Adam and Eve sinned? What happened when God came down to fellowship with them that evening? Where were they? They were hiding, hiding in the bushes from God. Sin had erected an awful barrier between them and God. Sin does that, doesn't it? Sin had created a gulf between sinful man and his sinless God.

131

God acted from His character of justice as He pronounced the penalty for sin. His holy nature demanded that sin's wages be paid. He was fully just in establishing that penalty. As Creator, He had the authority to set the rules over His Creation, and the penalty for breaking the rules. Adam and Eve had chosen to rebel, and had chosen sin and its penalty. It was God's holy and just nature that demanded the death penalty for sin. Not just physical death, but spiritual death, eternal separation from the Living God.

But more was at work than God's justice. I'm convinced that His Grace was also on display.

Think about it. Adam and Eve were created to live forever. They had access to the Tree of Life. Their newly created bodies contained no genetic defects or diseases. They would have lived forever—hiding in the bushes — separated by their sin from a holy God. Can you think of anything more horrible? There is another name for eternal separation from God because of sin. The Bible calls it "hell." Adam and Eve were not in the physical place called Hell, but their situation was no less ultimate and tragic and hopeless.

Furthermore, think what Adam and Eve would be like *now*, if nothing had changed. They had chosen to rebel, they had refused to repent and even refused to accept the blame for their actions. Their commitment to sin was now well established. They had no access to God, nor did they care to have any. Surely, Satan and their own sinful natures would have led them into ever-deeper debauchery. And, by now, thousands of years later—well, we'd best not even try to imagine.

The death penalty for sin served several purposes. It put a limit on how long a sinner could live, putting a cap on how debased he could become.

It also placed an ever-present reminder before Adam and Eve, of the fact that their choice to rebel had ruined God's perfect creation. Every time they saw an animal kill another, or when their oldest son killed his brother, they must have said, "Oh, this is awful! What have we done?" It would drive them back to God for some solution to the sin-and-death problem.

Most of all, the establishment of death as the penalty for sin made it possible for the penalty to be paid by someone else, someone who did not deserve

the penalty. Now, God, Himself, could come to earth, take upon Himself the form of man whom He had created, live a sinless, penalty-free life, and die in place of condemned man. "The wages of sin is death" (Romans 6:23), but "Christ *died* for our sins" (I Corinthians 15:4). He died so that we would not have to die. And then He rose from the grave, victorious over death, offering *eternal* life to those who believe. Death provides an escape from an eternal sin-plagued life, and serves as the door to a new life, one free from sin and death, made possible by the death and Resurrection of the Creator.

But what if evolution and the old earth are true? What if the fossils were deposited long before Adam lived? What if the dinosaurs had become extinct before sin entered creation? Obviously, if death was

Islamic Mosque

here before Adam's sin, then creation had *already* been spoiled, and death is *not* the penalty for sin. But if death is *not* the penalty for sin, what possible good would have been accomplished by Christ's death?

You see how the two concepts are incompatible? If death was here before sin, then Christ's death was ineffective and meaningless. The central focus of Christianity fails. The old-earth concept *undermines* Christ's work of redemption!

Recently, I had the distinct privilege of giving a lecture to 2,500 public school students, teachers, and university professors in Istanbul, Turkey, a predominantly Moslem Country. My lecture was part of a conference sponsored by a quasi-governmental foundation advocating a return to the Creationist worldview in the Turkish education system.

This was my fourteenth trip to Turkey. All the others had been concerned with my expeditions to Turkey in search of Noah's Ark.[1] Throughout the years, I had studied Islamic thought, to better prepare myself for the work in Turkey, but before *this* trip, I seriously studied the Islamic teaching on Creation and the Flood.

The Koran, the Islamic holy book, restates many Old Testament stories. It teaches Creation in six days, Adam and Eve, the Garden, the original perfect state, eating the forbidden fruit, the expulsion from the Garden, the wicked pre-Flood world, and the world-wide Flood. A few differences occur, but the gist of the stories is the same.

Except, that is, for the Curse, and here the differences may at first seem slight, but they form the basis for their entire view of salvation, and their thinking has something very important to contribute to our discussion here.

In the Koran, when Adam and Eve ate of the forbidden fruit, they incurred God's severe displeasure. The Moslem acknowledges that the penalty for sin is death, and that Adam and Eve were expelled from the Garden to begin a life leading ultimately to physical death. Furthermore, they recognize that each member of the human race chooses to sin and deserves God's sentence of death.

Sounds familiar enough, but Moslems believe that man's sin caused the Creation merely to fall "out of balance," no longer benefiting from its original perfection. They have no comprehension of the Scriptural Curse on all of Creation, nor that Adam's

---

1 See my book for young people, *Noah's Ark and the Ararat Adventure,* for information on the expeditions, adventure, and discoveries on Mt. Ararat.

sin nature was passed on to all of Adam's descendants. Each person's penalty for sin is due to his or her own *personal* sin, and, thus, it is also possible to regain Allah's favor by obedience to Him. In fact, this is the *only* way of salvation. In the Islamic system, obedience involves praying towards Mecca five times a day, giving to the poor, participating in the fast during Ramadan, a pilgrimage to Mecca, and reciting the Moslem creed, i.e., The Five Pillars of Islam. Regular sins must be repented of, but it is up to Allah to grant forgiveness or not. There is *no just basis* on which Allah formally has chosen to forgive.

I submit that the Moslem's low view of the Curse, and his incomplete understanding of man's hopeless condition before God, both because of personal sin *and* the inherited sin nature from Adam, is the reason that they are today in such darkness. They choose, instead, to view sin and its punishment solely as a result of their own *personal* actions, and, thus, their own personal actions must save them. They have no felt need for a Savior. But, the Bible teaches that Christ came to pay the penalty for our sin *and* for our sin-nature—to do for us what we could not do for ourselves. The Curse on all of Creation because of Adam's rebellion has only one remedy—the death of the sinless Son of God, Himself the offended Creator! It may be that teaching this concept could provide the key to Islamic evangelism.

But what can we say to modern Christian evangelicals who hold to the work of Christ on the Cross as necessary for salvation, yet deny the foundational concepts in Genesis 1–3? Many modern evangelical seminaries give credence to the presence of a sin-nature in each one of us, all the while denying Adam as a historic person, denying the original "very good" Creation, denying Adam's sin as a historic event, and denying the Curse as passing on to all Creation (the animals, the plants, the earth, and all mankind) as a result of Adam's rebellious choice.

As you can see, denying the historic facts of Adam's sin and the resultant curse, logically undercuts orthodox Christian doctrine and places modern Christian old-earth advocates only one slippery step away from a Moslem style, works-oriented salvation, a position shared in principle by the cults and most "main-line"

denominations. A low view of sin requires no Savior to save from sin. Those presently advocating such a position may be able to maintain their *own* personal walk with the Lord, but what does their teaching communicate to their students? A world view with an illogical foundation and an error-filled revelation will not long endure.

Just as teaching on the Curse may be the key to Moslem evangelism, so clear teaching on the Biblical Curse might provide the key to returning Christianity to a truly Biblical world view.

This point, and all its ramifications, i.e., death before sin, the problem of pain, the ever-present tendency for decay in all systems, etc., occupies a major role in the ICR outreach. Perhaps there is no other single point besides this that better grabs the attention of sincere Christians who have been wrongly taught. We attribute much of the present revival of interest in Creation on the part of Christians to the communication of this point.

Often I think my evolutionary colleagues understand this issue better than my Christian brothers and sisters. Consider this quotation from an outspoken atheist:

> Christianity has fought, still fights, and will fight science [by this, he means "naturalism," ed.] to the desperate end over evolution, because evolution destroys utterly and finally the very reason Jesus' earthly life was supposedly made necessary. Destroy Adam and Eve and the original sin, and in the rubble you will find the sorry remains of the son of god. Take away the meaning of his death. If Jesus was not the redeemer who died for our sins, and this is what evolution means, then Christianity is nothing!
>
> G. Richard Bozarth, "The Meaning of Evolution," *American Atheist,* February 1978, pp. 19,30

Many Christians try to keep a foot in both camps, and accept God as Creator but still accept evolution and/or the old earth. Without a doubt, it *is* possible to be a born-again Christian and believe that fossils date from before sin. One doesn't have to be a young-earth creationist to be a true Christian. But both the old-earth idea and Christianity can't be *right*. If evolution is *true*, then Christianity is *wrong*. If the earth is *old*, then Christianity is *wrong*. These concepts are not just incompatible—they are opposites. They are mutually exclusive! As stated in the quote above, "Evolution means that Jesus was not the redeemer who died for our sins."

The Personal Battlefront

As we have seen, the rocks and fossils, which are used as evidence for evolution and the old earth, don't speak with clarity. Much evidence can be marshaled which fits far better into the young-earth scenario. The evidence, which can neither prove nor disprove, in a scientific sense, either idea about the past supports the young earth view better. And, of course, the Bible clearly teaches the young-earth concept. In fact, Christianity makes no sense at all if the earth is old.

God is not a deceiver. He would not allow a world full of rocks and fossils to "prove" a view contrary to that specifically taught in Scripture. If Scriptural history is correct and the earth is young, then the rocks must agree.

We have seen that some *interpretations* of the evidence are compatible with evolution and old-earth concepts. But these interpretations are not nearly the *best* interpretations. Only by adopting Biblical history as fact and *then* interpreting the rocks can we hope to do so correctly.

The rocks, rather than speaking of long ages, speak of death and destruction. The rocks were formed from sediments deposited by catastrophic water processes, operating at rates, scales, and intensities dwarfing those operating today. The fossils are dead things, things which died in the Cataclysm (some in lesser catastrophes, which followed the Flood).

This great watery upheaval was none other than the Flood of Noah's day. As Scripture teaches, it was a judgment on sin. God hates sin, and He saw the civilization in Noah's day, as wholly wicked.

> And God saw that the wickedness of man was great in the earth, and that every imagination of the thoughts of his heart was only evil continually.
>
> And it repented the LORD that he had made man on the earth, and it grieved him at his heart.

> And the LORD said, I will destroy man whom I have created from the face of the earth; both man, and beast, and the creeping thing, and the fowls of the air; for it repenteth me that I have made them.
>
> Genesis 6:5–7

The "wages of sin" has always been death. It was surely true in Noah's day, and God sent the Flood as a punishment for sin. Sin had so distorted God's once-"very-good" creation that God chose to annihilate it and start again. The rocks grimly remind us of the wages of sin and the wicked pre-Flood world.

But the rocks and fossils should also remind us that our present world exhibits exactly the same conditions which led God to judge the previous world.

> And as it was in the days of Noah, so shall it be also in the days of the Son of man.
>
> They did eat, they drank, they married wives, they were given in marriage, until the day that Noah entered into the ark, and the flood came, and destroyed them all.
>
> Even thus shall it be in the day when the Son of man is revealed.
>
> Luke 17:26,27,30

The apt description of our world found here and in Genesis 6 allows no other conclusion than that the coming judgment can't be far away.

These rocks and fossils will not last forever: they too will be annihilated. There will come a day when "the elements shall melt with fervent heat, the earth also and the works that are therein shall be burned up" (II Peter 3:10). But "we, according to His promise, look for a new heaven and a new earth, wherein dwelleth righteousness" (v. 13). In the New Earth, we will not have fossils to remind us of death and sin.

Just as Godly Noah accepted God's gracious provision of salvation during time of judgment, entrusting his life and safekeeping into God's hands, so we can escape the coming judgment. Our present-day Ark of safety is not a wooden vessel. Rather, it is the Eternal Son of God, Jesus Christ. Through His death on the Cross, He paid the wages

The wages of sin is DEATH . . .

victory over sin and death, offering Eternal Life to all who believe. Jesus said, "I am the resurrection, and the life: he that believeth in me, though he were dead, yet shall he live" (John 11:25).

A Christian is one who has gone to God the Father, repented of his sin, and asked God to apply the death of Christ to his own personal sin, to forgive him on that basis, since the penalty has already been paid. God responds with forgiveness, cleansing, and victory over sin, and power to break sinful habits. Most of all, He gives us life—Eternal Life—where once there was only death. And then there *will* be long ages, not millions of years of death and suffering, but innumerable years of Life with our Savior. He has done it all, "That in the ages to come He might show the exceeding riches of His grace in His kindness toward us through Christ Jesus" (Ephesians 2:7).

of our sin, and through Him we can avoid the death penalty for our sins, escape the judgment to come, and live forever with Him. "The wages of sin is death, but the gift of God is eternal life through Jesus Christ our Lord" (Romans 6:23).

A Christian is one who recognizes that he has sinned and offended the holy Creator-God, thereby separating himself from God, "All have sinned and come short of the glory of God" (Romans 3:23). Each person's sin deserves the death penalty, eternal separation from anything good and holy.

Furthermore, a Christian is one who recognizes that nothing he can do will ever change the situation. But he also recognizes that Jesus Christ, God the Son, has *already* done all that's necessary. "Not by works of righteousness which we have done, but according to His mercy He saved us" (Titus 3:5). "For He hath made Him to be sin for us, who knew no sin; that we might be made the righteousness of God in Him" (II Corinthians 5:21). "God commendeth His love for us, in that, while we were yet sinners Christ died for us" (Romans 5:8). But then He rose from the dead, in

Christ DIED for our sins

Notes

Notes

Notes

Transparency Masters

There has always been a wealth of good information in support of the young-earth position. The problem has been getting people to listen to it. First they must question their lifelong brainwashing, and then be taught the proper way of thinking about the unobserved past, as well as the evidence.

As you've noticed throughout this book, almost each major concept has been accompanied by an illustration. Actually, these are teaching tools designed to help both you and me teach others, whether in schools, Sunday schools, universities, or other arenas.

I have found that using an overhead projector usually works best for teaching. Slides are necessary for some lectures which are predominately visual, but for most, overheads are much preferred. They can be shown in lecture rooms which are not fully darkened, they give the lecturer freedom to vary the order during the lecture itself, and they allow eye contact with the audience. Thus, these illustrations are actually masters from which overhead transparencies can easily be made.

Some Pointers

The overhead masters included in this section are in the approximate order found in the book. Those within the body of the text which are one-half page or larger are not reproduced again, for most people have access to copy machines which can enlarge from the original. Since the stage on most overhead projectors is 10" x 10", I have found the optimum size for a transparency to be 8" x 10".

I would recommend that you not immediately make overheads out of all of the masters. There is more here than could possibly be covered in one lecture, and making too many could get expensive.

Actually, the cost is primarily for the blank transparency, but a good copy machine is needed to fully imprint the ink and keep it from flecking off as it is used. Many can be enhanced by permanent color markers, added to the reverse side (not the ink side). Be aware that the color tends to wash out when projected, so be generous.

As mentioned before, the photographs used in this book are not available as color slides, but let me encourage you to begin collecting your own. Color transparencies can be made from slides also, using a color copying machine with a slide projector attachment. Most large copy shops have such equipment.

(By the way, in response to the many requests, Dr. Steve Austin has compiled a set of Mount St. Helens slides which can be purchased directly from his home business. ICR, as a scientific research and educational organization, has found it impractical to be in the slide duplication business.)

Be aware that you have full permission to use these overheads (or Dr. Austin's slides) in your teaching. For that matter, you can legally use any illustration in any publication, from any source, even if you don't agree with the author. This freedom extends to your own lectures, as long as you acknowledge the source and don't misrepresent the original author's position. The permission does not extend to using the material of another in a publication or video which is to be duplicated and sold.

My prayer is that you have not only been helped by the material in this book, but that you can use it to help others. The job of education requires many educators, and may God give you abundant opportunities to build into the lives of many.

GEOLOGIC TIME SCALE

ERA	PERIOD	EPOCH	SUCCESSION OF LIFE	INDEX FOSSILS
CENOZOIC *recent life*	**QUATERNARY** 0-1 Million Years Rise of Man	Recent Pleistocene		PECTEN, NEPTUNEA, VENERICARDIA, CALYPTRAPHORUS
	TERTIARY 62 Million Years Rise of Mammals	Pliocene Miocene Oligocene Eocene Paleocene		
MESOZOIC *middle life*	**CRETACEOUS** 72 Million Years Modern seed bearing plants. Dinosaurs			SCAPHITES, INOCERAMUS, PERISPHINCTES, NERINEA, TROPHITES, MONOTIS
	JURASSIC 46 Million Years First birds			
	TRIASSIC 49 Million Years Cycads, first dinosaurs			
PALEOZOIC *ancient life*	**PERMIAN** 50 Million Years First reptiles			LEPTODUS, PARAFUSULINA, LOPHOPHYLLIDIUM, DICTYOCLOSTUS, PROLECANITES, CACTOCRINUS, PALMATOLEPUS, MUCROSPIRIFER, CRYSTIPHYLLUM, HEXAMOCERAS, BATHYURUS (TRILOBITE), TETRAGRAPTUS, PARADOXIDES (TRILOBITE), BILLINGSELLA
	PENNSYLVANIAN 30 Million Years First insects — *Carboniferous*			
	MISSISSIPPIAN 35 Million Years Many crinoids			
	DEVONIAN 60 Million Years First seed plants, cartilage fish			
	SILURIAN 20 Million Years Earliest land animals			
	ORDOVICIAN 75 Million Years Early bony fish			
	CAMBRIAN 100 Million Years Invertebrate animals, Brachiopods, Trilobites			
	PRECAMBRIAN Very few fossils present (bacteria-algae-pollen?)			

**Descent from a
Common Ancestor**

Abrupt Appearance: Stasis

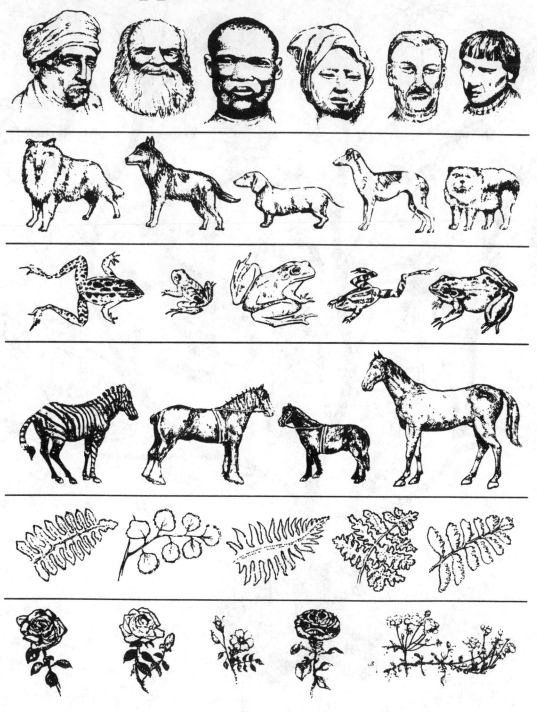

The Biblical Creation Model

1. Special Creation of all things by God in six solar days.

2. The Curse on all things because of sin. All things are dying.

3. The global Flood of Noah's day. Deposited rocks and fossils.

The Creation Model

1. Supernatural origin of all things. Design, purpose, interdependence, information.

2. Net basic decrease in complexity over time. Limited horizontal change.

3. Earth history dominated by catastrophic events.

The Evolution Model

1. Naturalistic origin of all things. Chance, random mutation, natural selection.

2. Net basic increase in complexity over time. Unlimited vertical change.

3. Earth history dominated by uniform events. Neo-catastrophism.

Assumptions

DATA

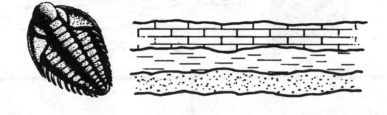

Interpretation

Assumption of evolution and the old earth.

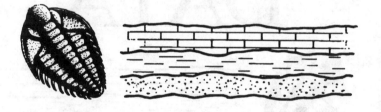

DATA

Interpretations consistent with evolution and the old earth. All contrary evidence explained away.

A circular argument arises: Interpret the fossil record in the terms of a particular theory of evolution, inspect the interpretation, and note that it confirms the theory. Well, it would, wouldn't it?

Tom Kemp, "A Fresh Look at the Fossil Record," *New Scientist*, Vol. 108, Dec. 5, 1985, p. 67.

...the record of evolution, like any other historical record, must be construed within a complex of particular and general preconceptions, not the least of which is the hypothesis that evolution has occurred.

David B. Kitts, "Search for the Holy Transformation," *Paleobiology*, Summer, 1979, pp. 353, 354.

And this poses something of a problem: If we date the rocks by the fossils, how can we then turn around and talk about patterns of evolutionary change through time in the fossil record?

Niles Eldridge, *Time Frames*, 1985, p. 52.

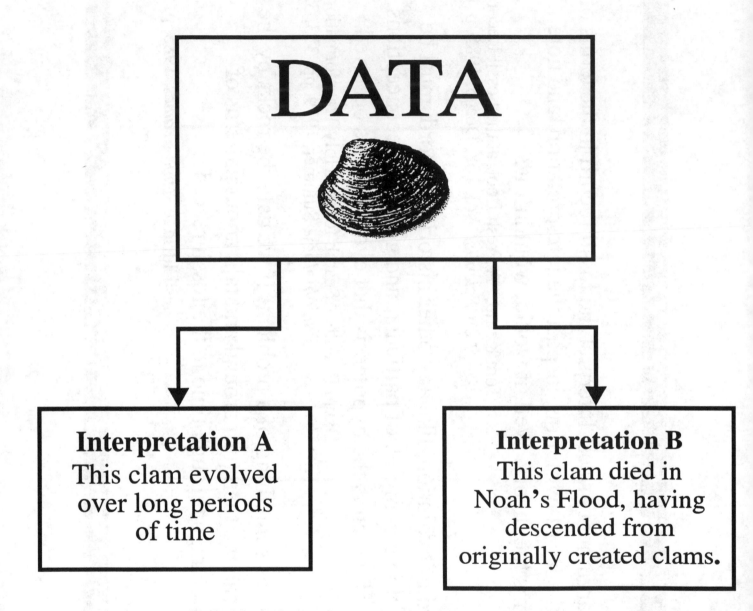

Assumption of Biblical history

DATA

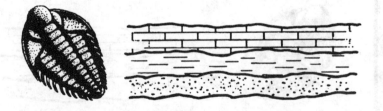

Interpretations consistent with the Bible

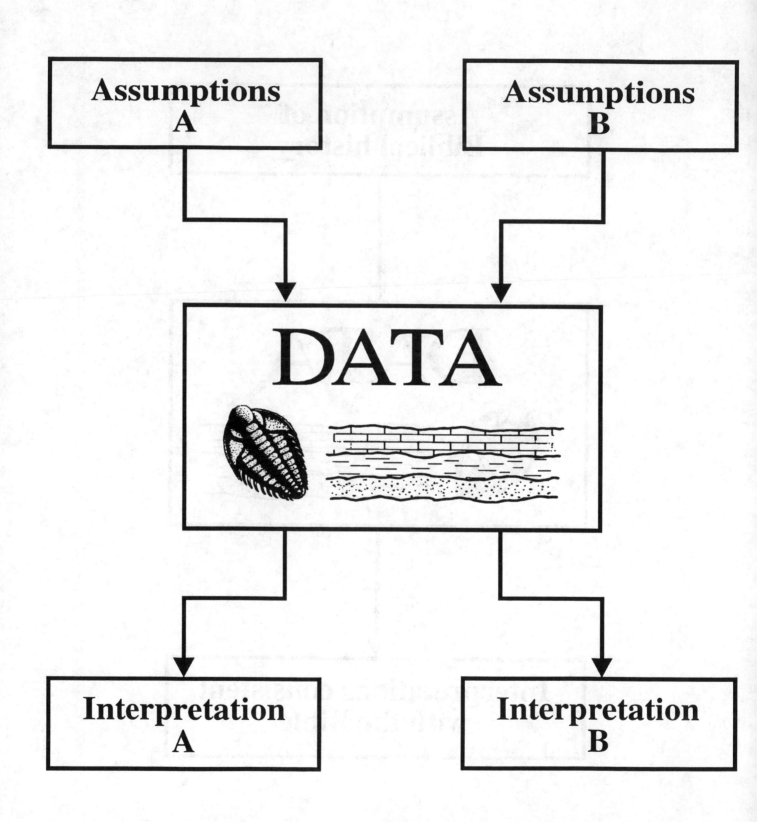

Predictions of the Evolution Model

1. Transitional forms

2. Beneficial mutations

3. Things getting better

4. New species

Predictions of the Creation Model

1. Separate, distinct kinds

2. Intelligent design in nature

3. Tendency for decay

4. Extinction of species

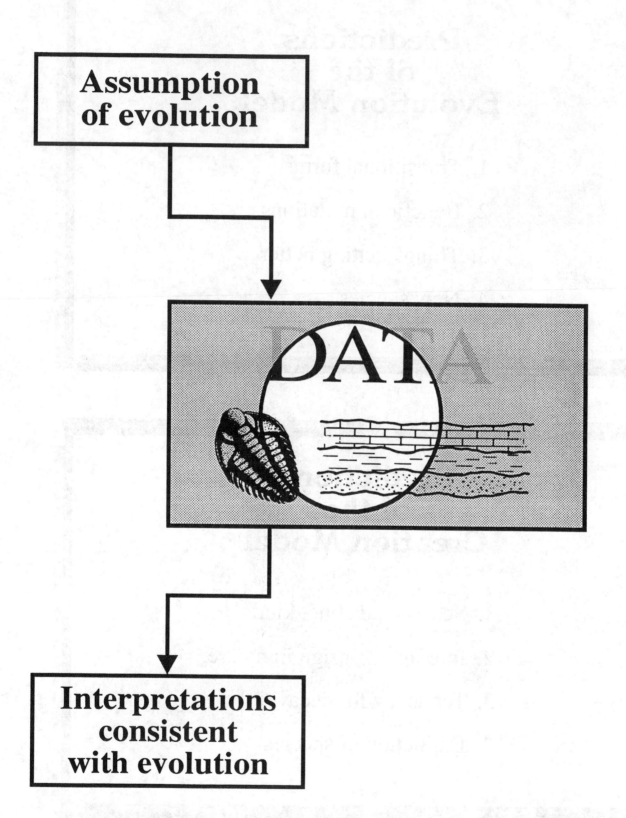

A man who has no assured and ever present belief in the existence of a personal God or of a future existence with retribution and reward, can have for his rule of life, as far as I can see, only to follow those impulses and instincts which are the strongest or which seem to him the best ones.

The Autobiography of Charles Darwin, 1887,
as republished by The Norton Library, p. 94.

For in six days the LORD made heaven and earth, the sea, and all that is in them, and rested the seventh day: wherefore the LORD blessed the sabbath day, and hallowed it.

Exodus 20:11

How Long is a Day?

- The word "day" (Hebrew *yom*) can have a variety of meanings.
  - A solar day
  - Daylight
  - Indefinite period of time

- Occurring 2291 times in the Old Testament, it almost always means a literal day.

- When used in the plural form *yamim* (845 times), it always refers to a literal day.

- When modified by numeral or ordinal in historical narrative (359 times in the Old Testament outside of Genesis 1), it always means a literal day.

- When modified by "evening and/or morning" (38 times outside of Genesis 1), it always means a literal day.

- Context of Genesis 1 is a tight chronology.

- Forms basis for our work week of 6 literal days (Exodus 20:11).

- Proper interpretation is a solar day, not an indefinite time period.

It cannot be denied, in spite of frequent interpretations of Genesis 1 that departed from the rigidly literal, that the almost universal view of the Christian world until the eighteenth century was that the Earth was only a few thousand years old. Not until the development of modern scientific investigation of the Earth itself would this view be called into question within the church.

Christianity and the Age of the Earth,
Davis A. Young, 1982, p. 25.

It is apparent that the most straightforward understanding of the Genesis record, *without regard to all the hermeneutical considerations suggested by science* [emphasis added], is that God created heaven and earth in six solar days, that man was created in the sixth day, that death and chaos entered the world after the Fall of Adam and Eve, that all of the fossils were the result of the catastrophic universal deluge which spared only Noah's family and the animals therewith.

Dr. Pattle P.T. Pun (Professor of Biology at Wheaton College),
Journal of the American Scientific Affiliation,

The Hebrew word *yom* and its plural form *yamim* are used over 1900 times in the Old Testament. In only sixty-five of these cases is it translated as a time period other than a day in the King James Version. Outside of the Genesis 1 case in question, the two hundred plus occurrences of *yom* preceded by an ordinal, *all* refer to a normal twenty-four hour day. Furthermore, the seven-hundred plus appearances of *yamim* *always* refer to a regular day. Thus, it is argued (by young-earth creationists, *ed.*) that the Exodus 20:11 reference to the six *yamim* of creation must also refer to six regular days.

These arguments have a common fallacy, however. There is no other place in the Old Testament where the intent is to describe events that involve multiple and/or sequential, *indefinite* periods of time.

Bradley, Walter L. and Olsen, Roger, in "The Trustworthiness of Scripture in Areas Relating to Natural Science," *Hermeneutics, Inerrancy, and the Bible,* (Academic Books, Grand Rapids), 1984, p. 299.

Probably, so far as I know, there is no professor of Hebrew or Old Testament at any world-class university who does not believe that the writer(s) of Genesis 1–11 intended to convey to their readers the ideas that (a) creation took place in a series of six days which were the same as the days of 24 hours we now experience (b) the figures contained in the Genesis genealogies provided by simple addition a chronology from the beginning of the world up to later stages in the biblical story (c) Noah's flood was understood to be world-wide and extinguish all human and animal life except for those in the ark. Or, to put it negatively, the apologetic arguments which suppose the 'days' of creation to be long eras of time, the figures of years not to be chronological, and the flood to be a merely local Mesopotamian flood, are not taken seriously by any such professors, as far as I know.

Letter to David Watson from James Barr, 1984.

Contradictions in Order Between the Biblical View and the Secular View

Biblical Order of Appearance

1. Matter created by God in the beginning
2. Earth before the sun and stars
3. Oceans before the land
4. Light before the sun
5. Atmosphere between two water layers
6. Land plants, first life forms created
7. Fruit trees before fish
8. Fish before insects
9. Land vegetation before sun
10. Marine mammals before land mammals
11. Birds before land reptiles
12. Man, the cause of death

Evolutionary Order of Appearance

1. Matter existed in the beginning
2. Sun and stars before the earth
3. Land before the oceans
4. Sun, earth's first light
5. Atmosphere above a water layer
6. Marine organisms, first forms of life
7. Fish before fruit trees
8. Insects before fish
9. Sun before land plants
10. Land mammals before marine mammals
11. Reptiles before birds
12. Death, necessary antecedent of man

Time is in fact the hero of the plot.... given so much time the 'impossible' becomes possible, the possible probable and the probable virtually certain. One has only to wait: time itself performs miracles.

George Wald, "The Origin of Life,"
Physics and Chemistry of Life, 1955, p. 12.

The Evolutionary View of History

1. Most recent "Big Bang," 10–20 billion years ago.

2. Our Solar System, 5 billion years ago.

3. Single-celled organisms, 3–4 billion years ago.

4. Multi-celled organisms, 1 billion years ago.

5. Humankind, 1–3 million years ago.

6. Modern Civilization, 5–10 thousand years ago.

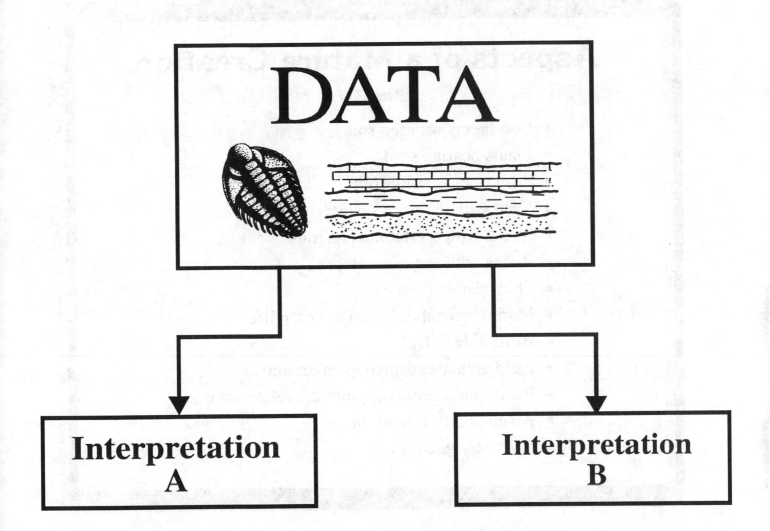

Aspects of a Mature Creation

Partial List

- Continents with top soil
- Plants bearing seed
- Fruit trees bearing fruit
- Land with drainage system
- Rocks with crystalline minerals
- Rocks with various isotopes
- Stars visible from earth
- Marine animals adapted to ocean life
- Birds able to fly
- Land animals adapted to environment
- Plants and animal in symbiotic relationships
- Adam and Eve as adults
- All "very good"

How to Date a System or Object

1. Observe the present state of the system.

2. Measure a process rate within that system.

3. Assume certain things about the past.

4. Calculate the time necessary for that process to produce the present state.

Assumptions of Radioisotope Dating

1. Constant decay rate.

2. No loss or gain of parent or daughter.

3. Known amounts of daughter present at start.

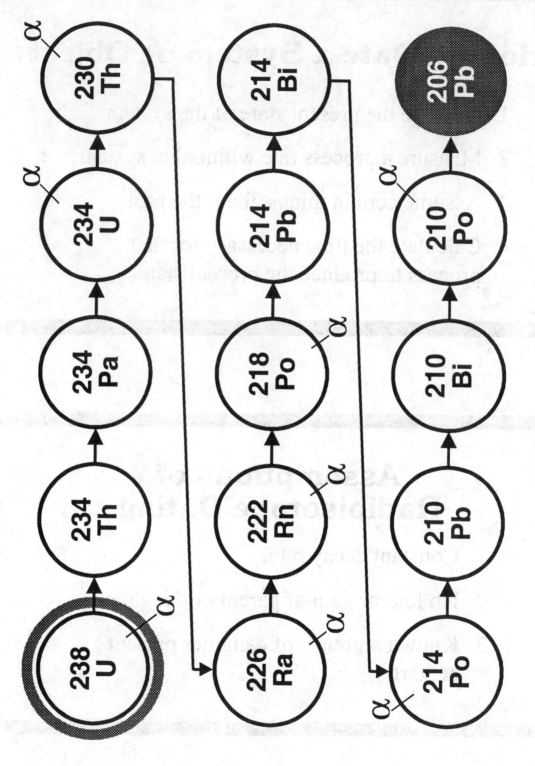

U²³⁸ Decay Series

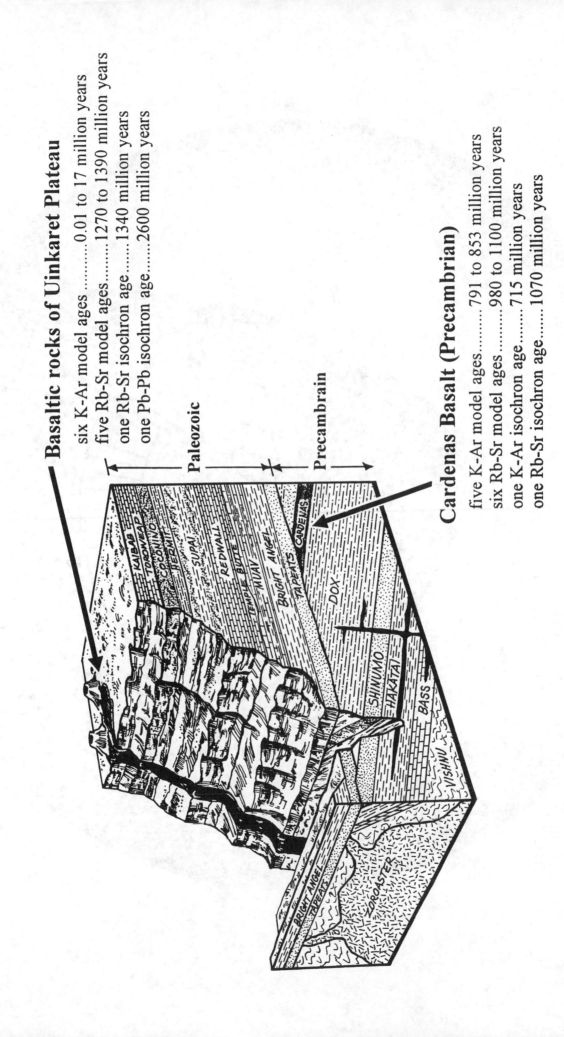

Basaltic rocks of Uinkaret Plateau

six K-Ar model ages .... 0.01 to 17 million years
five Rb-Sr model ages ...... 1270 to 1390 million years
one Rb-Sr isochron age ...... 1340 million years
one Pb-Pb isochron age ...... 2600 million years

Paleozoic

Precambrian

Cardenas Basalt (Precambrian)

five K-Ar model ages .... 791 to 853 million years
six Rb-Sr model ages .... 980 to 1100 million years
one K-Ar isochron age ...... 715 million years
one Rb-Sr isochron age ...... 1070 million years

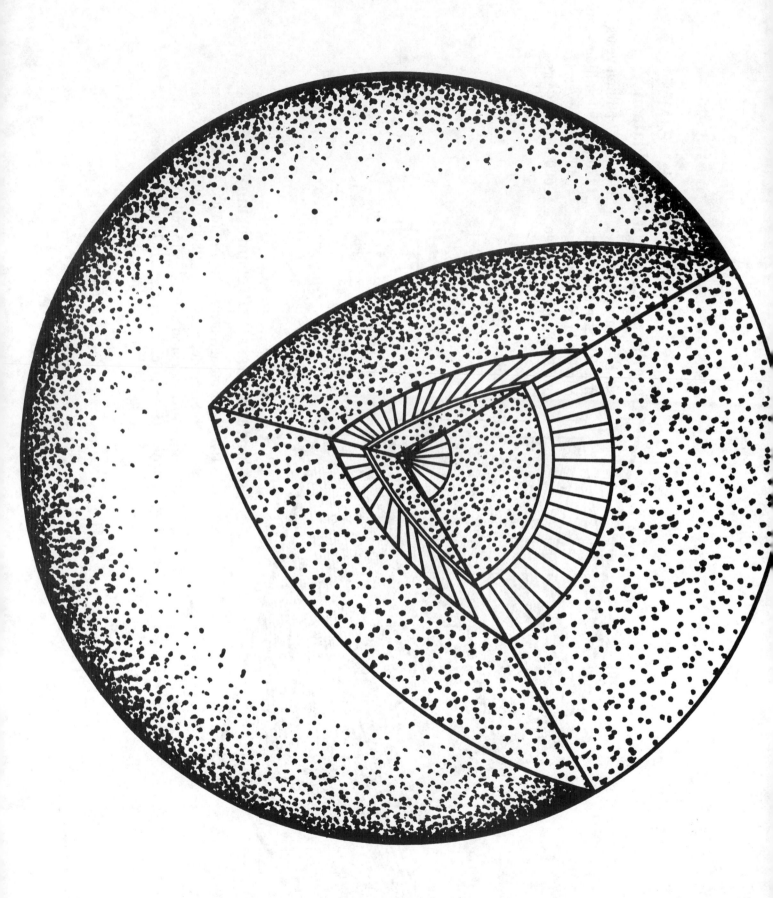

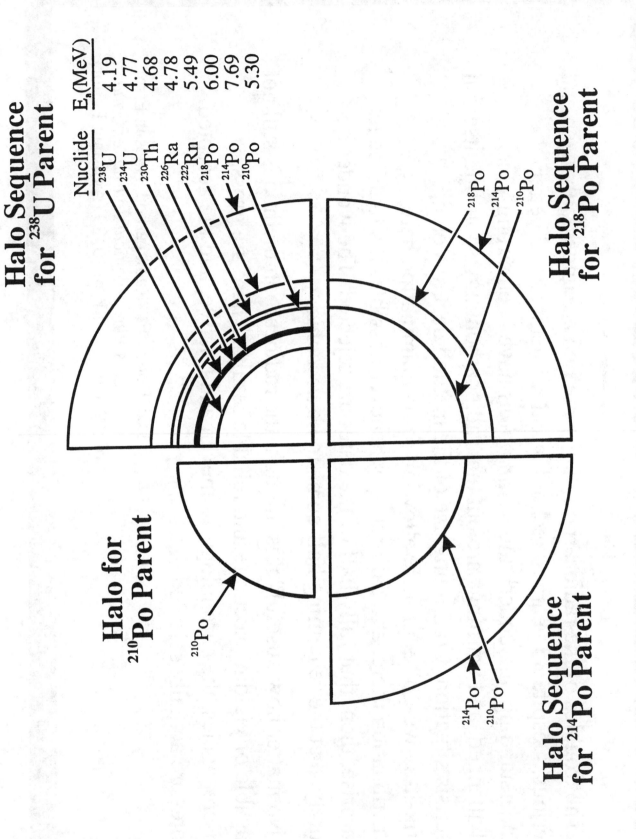

Halo Sequence for ^{238}U Parent

Nuclide	E_α(MeV)
^{238}U	4.19
^{234}U	4.77
^{230}Th	4.68
^{226}Ra	4.78
^{222}Rn	5.49
^{218}Po	6.00
^{214}Po	7.69
^{210}Po	5.30

Halo Sequence for ^{218}Po Parent

^{218}Po
^{214}Po
^{210}Po

Halo for ^{210}Po Parent

^{210}Po

Halo Sequence for ^{214}Po Parent

^{214}Po
^{210}Po

Characteristic ring configurations for different parent elements.

The troubles of the radiocarbon dating method are undeniably deep and serious. Despite 35 years of technological refinement and better understanding, the underlying *assumptions* have been strongly challenged, and warnings are out that radiocarbon may soon find itself in a crisis situation. Continuing use of the method depends on a "fix-it-as-we-go" approach, allowing for contamination here, fractionation there, and calibration whenever possible. It should be no surprise, then, that fully half of the dates are rejected. The wonder is, surely, that the remaining half come to be *accepted.*

No matter how "useful" it is, though, the radiocarbon method is still not capable of yielding accurate and reliable results. There are gross discrepancies, the chronology is uneven and relative, and the accepted dates are actually selected dates.

Lee, Robert E. "Radiocarbon, Ages in Error," *Anthropological Journal of Canada,* Vol. 19, No. 3, 1981, pp. 9, 29 (Assistant Editor).

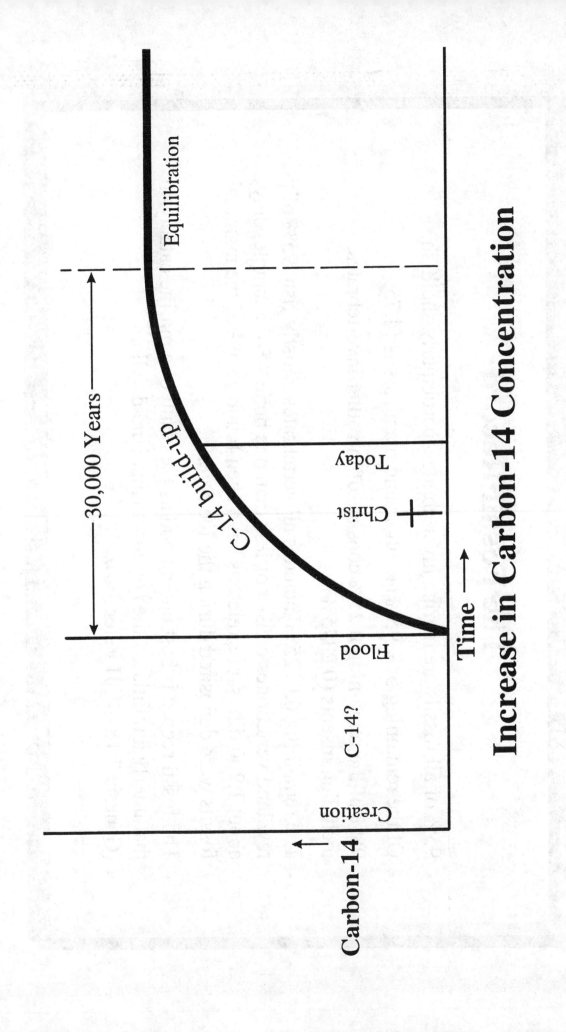

Increase in Carbon-14 Concentration

The Fossil Record

- 95% of all fossils are marine invertebrates, particularly shellfish.

- Of the remaining 5%, 95% are algae and plant fossils (4.75%).

- 95% of the remaining 0.25% consists of the other invertebrates, including insects (0.2375%).

- The remaining 0.0125% includes all vertebrates, mostly fish. 95% of the few land vertebrates consist of less than one bone. (For example, only about 1,200 dinosaur skeletons have been found.) 95% of the mammal fossils were deposited during the Ice Age.

- The fossil record is best understood as the result of a marine cataclysm that utterly annihilated the continents and land dwellers (Genesis 7:18-24; II Peter 3:6).

Why Are Human Bones So Scarce?

- Fossils are formed when buried in sediment beneath moving water.

- Land vertebrates, especially mammals, bloat when dead and float in water.

- Land vertebrates dismember easily, and disintegrate fairly quickly or are scavenged in a water environment.

- The processes acting during the Flood would destroy soft-bodied organisms, and preserve those with hard outer shells.

- The destruction of mankind was the primary goal of the Genesis Flood.

- Human bodies have a low fossilization potential.

- Of all living things, humans are among the least in number. (Some estimate that about 350 million people died in the Flood of Noah's day.)

- Even if all were preserved and evenly distributed throughout the world's 350 cubic miles of Flood sediments, the chance of exposure, discovery, recognition, and reporting of even *one* human fossil would be extremely remote.

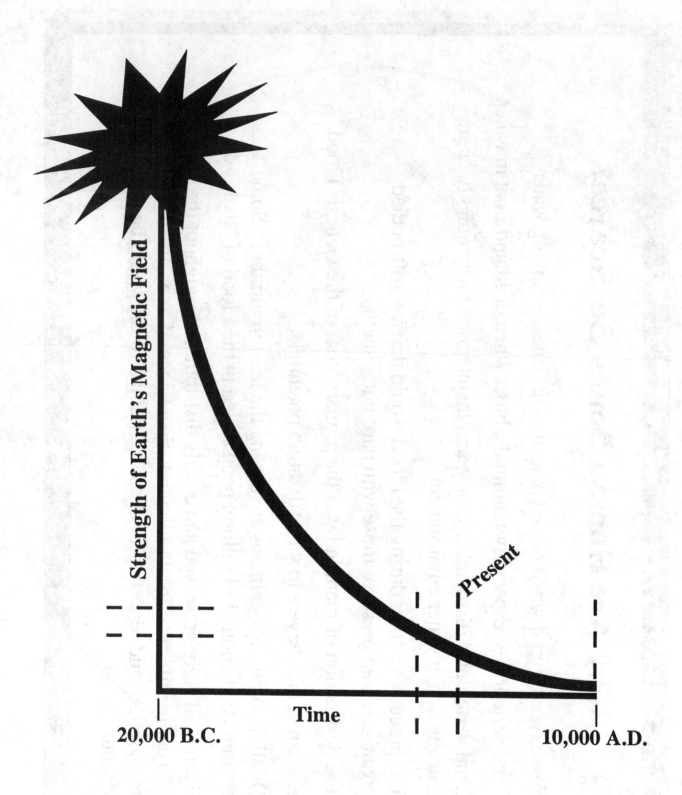

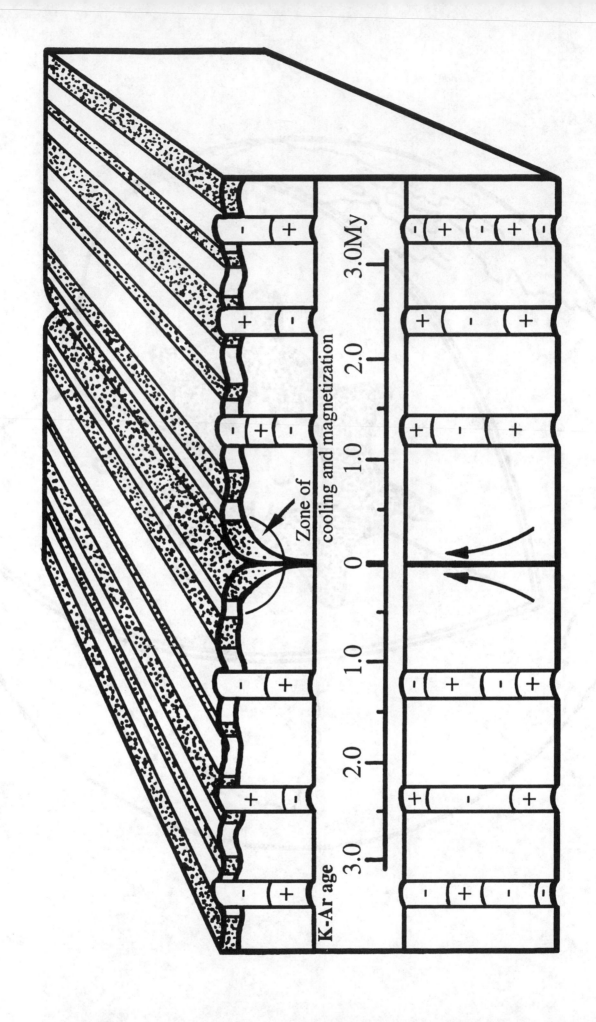

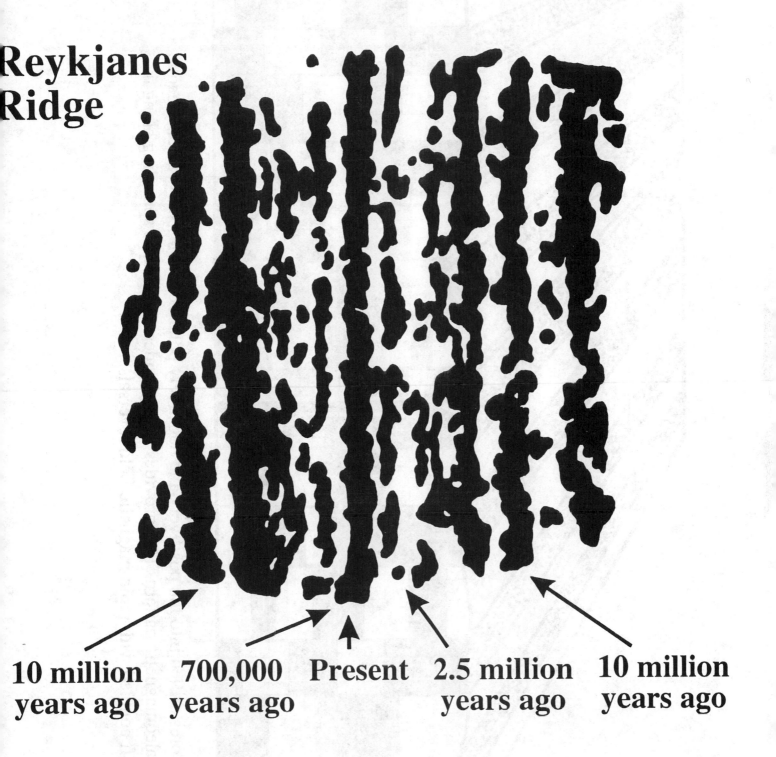

Reykjanes Ridge

10 million years ago   700,000 years ago   Present   2.5 million years ago   10 million years ago

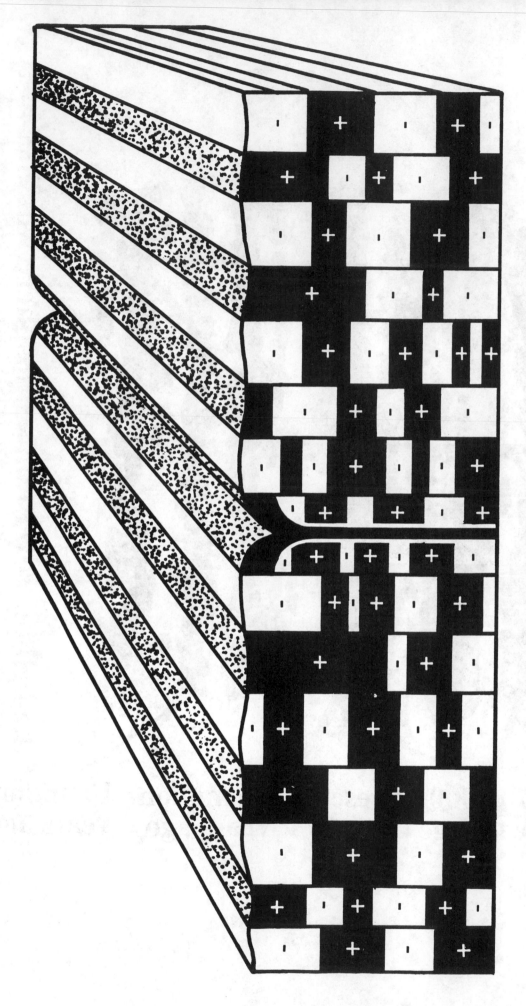

Cores drilled into the positively and negatively polarized zones show a very chaotic paleomagnetic pattern. This provides strong evidence for rapid spreading along the rift coupled with rapid magnetic field reversals.

The Age of the Atmosphere

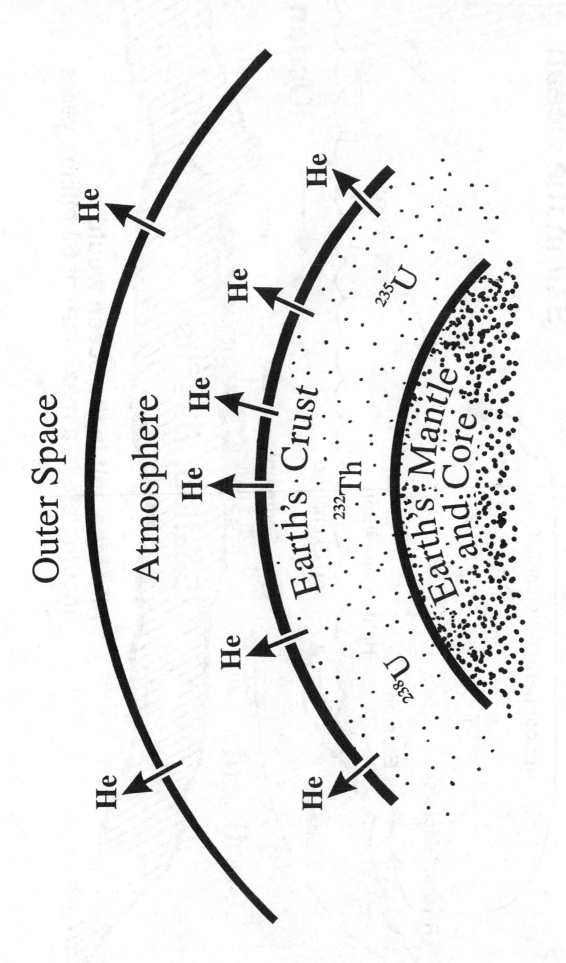

Outer Space

Atmosphere

Earth's Crust

Earth's Mantle and Core

^{235}U

^{232}Th

^{238}U

He

All of the helium now in the atmosphere would accumulate in a maximum of 2 million years!

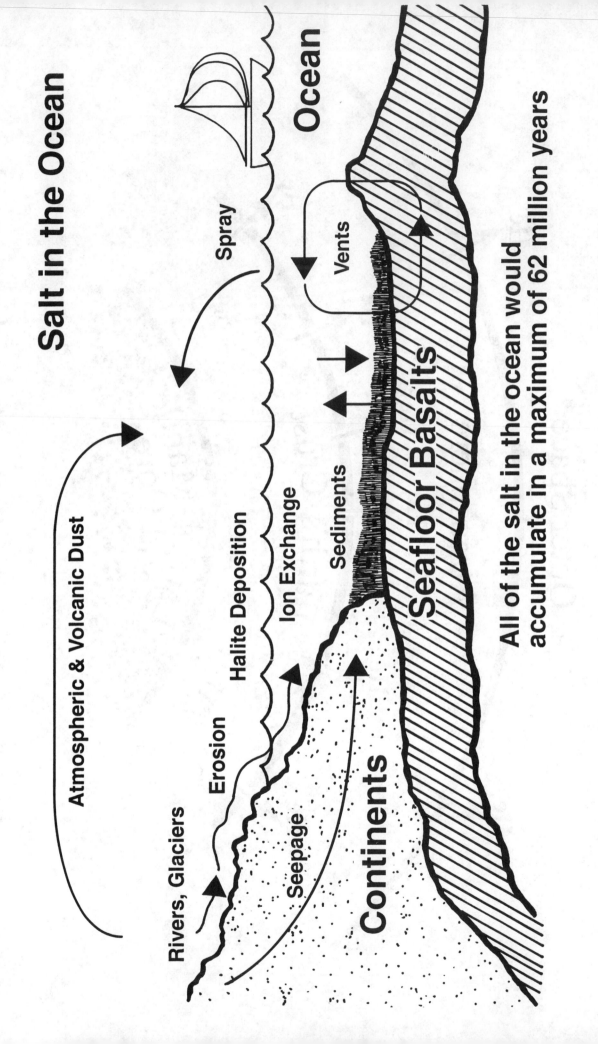

Salt in the Ocean

Ocean

Spray

Vents

Seafloor Basalts

Sediments

Atmospheric & Volcanic Dust

Erosion

Halite Deposition

Ion Exchange

Rivers, Glaciers

Seepage

Continents

All of the salt in the ocean would accumulate in a maximum of 62 million years

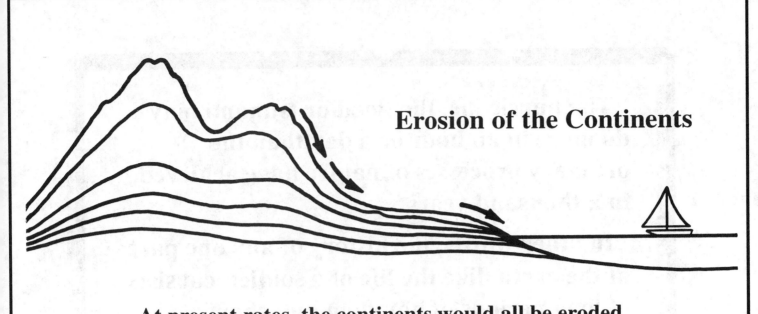

Erosion of the Continents

At present rates, the continents would all be eroded
in no more than 14 million years

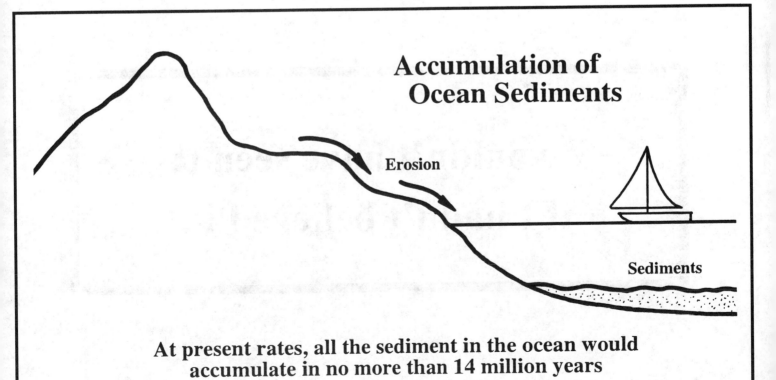

Accumulation of Ocean Sediments

Erosion

Sediments

At present rates, all the sediment in the ocean would
accumulate in no more than 14 million years

The hurricane, the flood or tsunami may do more in an hour or a day than the ordinary processes of nature have achieved in a thousand years.

In other words, the history of any one part of the earth, like the life of a soldier, consists of long periods of boredom and short periods of terror.

Dr. Derek Ager, *The Nature of the Stratigraphical Record*, 1981, pp. 54, 106.

I wouldn't have seen it if I hadn't believed it.

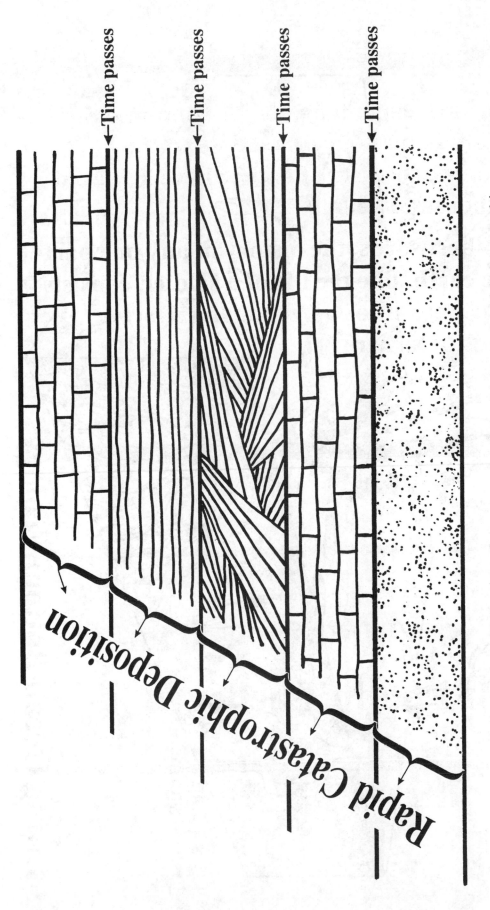

Time passes

Time passes

Time passes

Time passes

Rapid Catastrophic Deposition

To a neo-catastrophist, the rocks show evidence of rapid catastrophic processes, requiring little time for deposition. Time passes between the layers where there is no evidence.

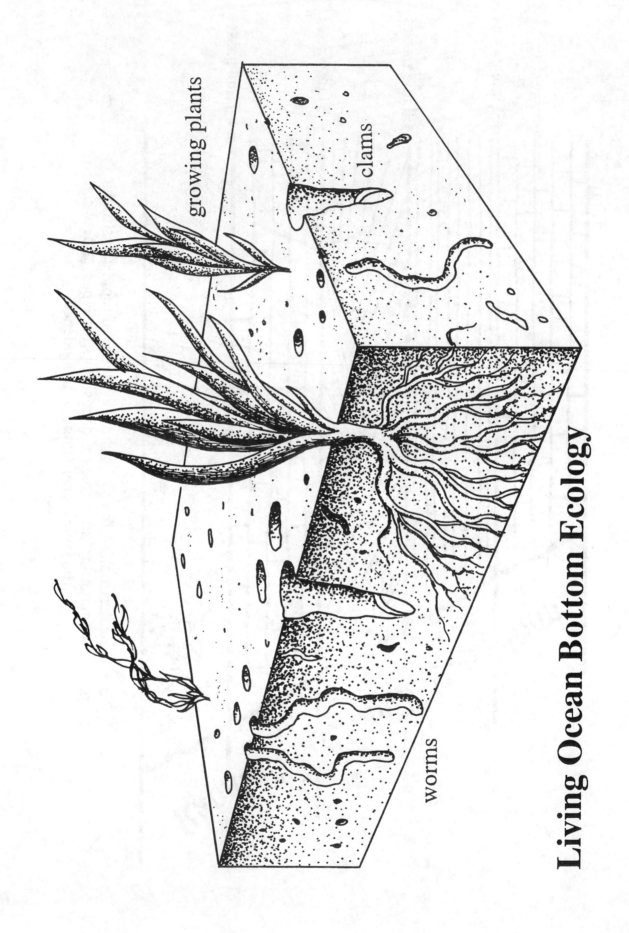

Living Ocean Bottom Ecology

growing plants

clams

worms

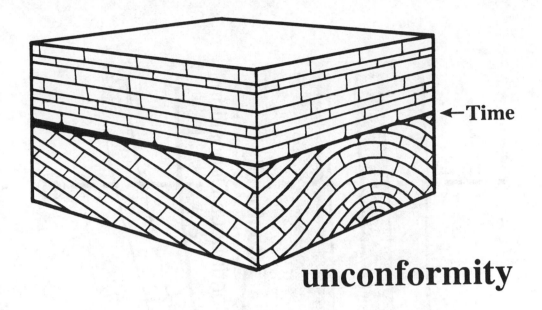

← Time

unconformity

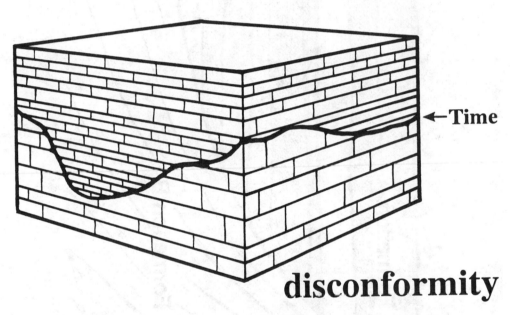

← Time

disconformity

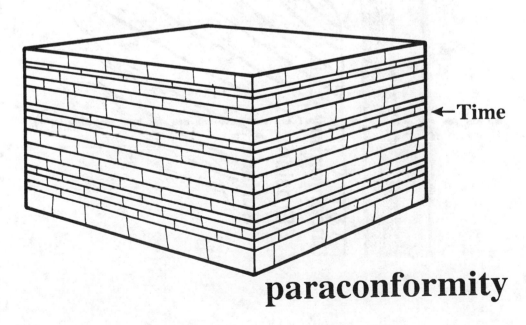

← Time

paraconformity

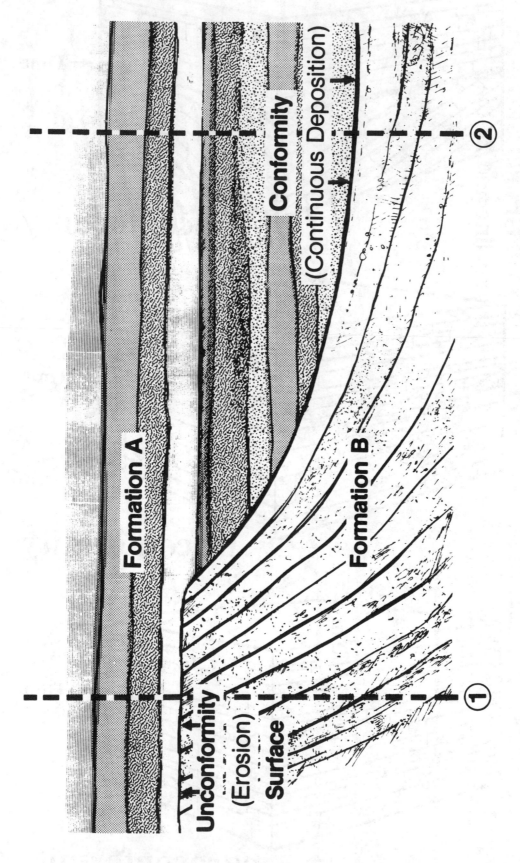

Limited Extent of Unconformities

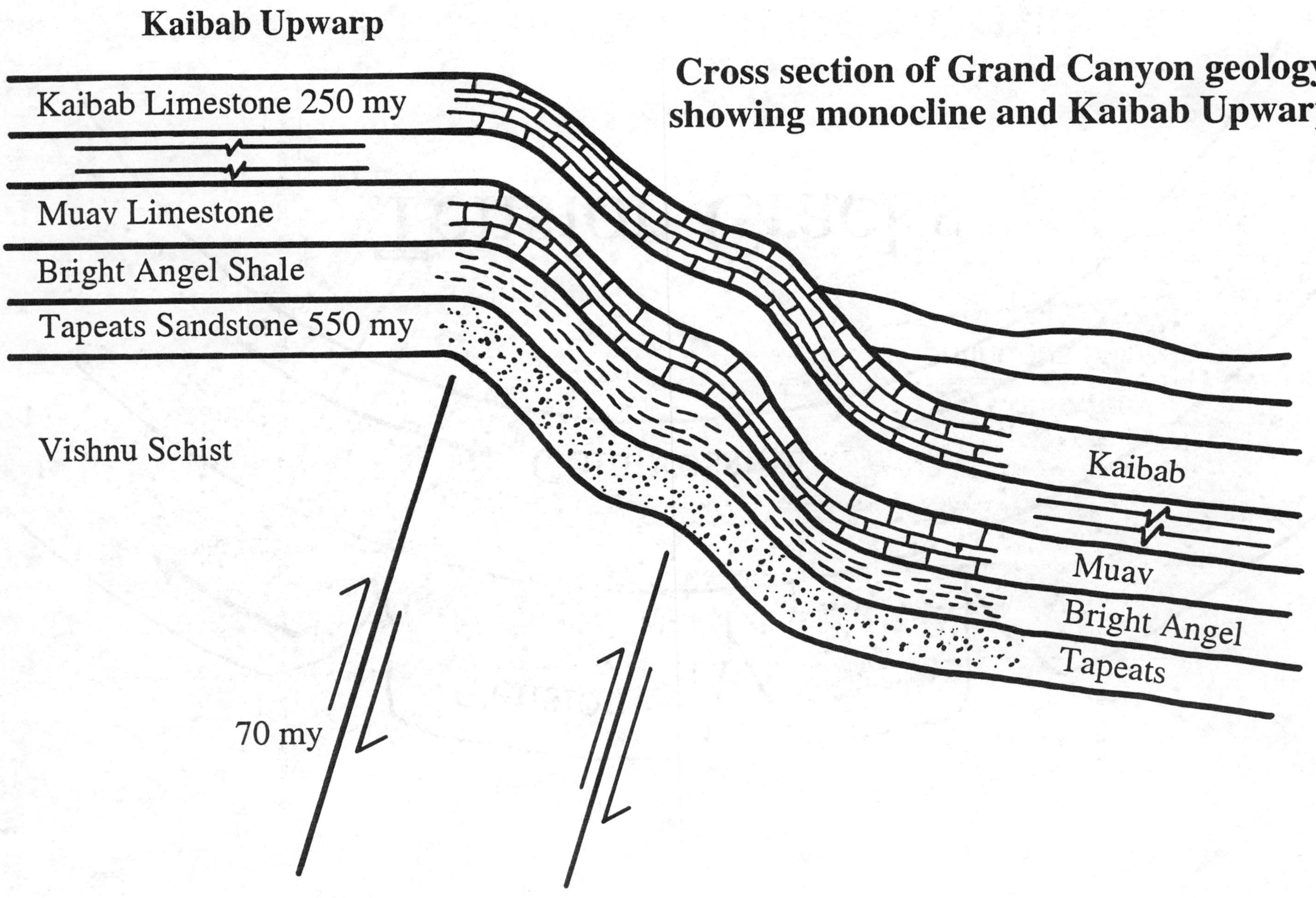

**Cross section of Grand Canyon geology
showing monocline and Kaibab Upwarp**

Kaibab Upwarp

Kaibab Limestone 250 my

Muav Limestone

Bright Angel Shale

Tapeats Sandstone 550 my

Vishnu Schist

Kaibab

Muav

Bright Angel

Tapeats

70 my

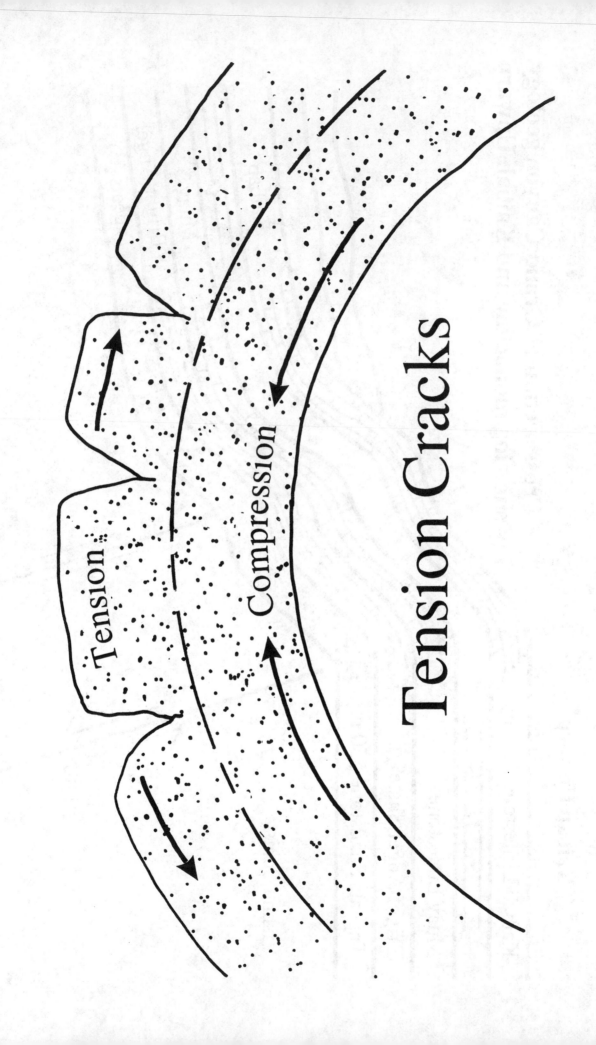

Tension Cracks

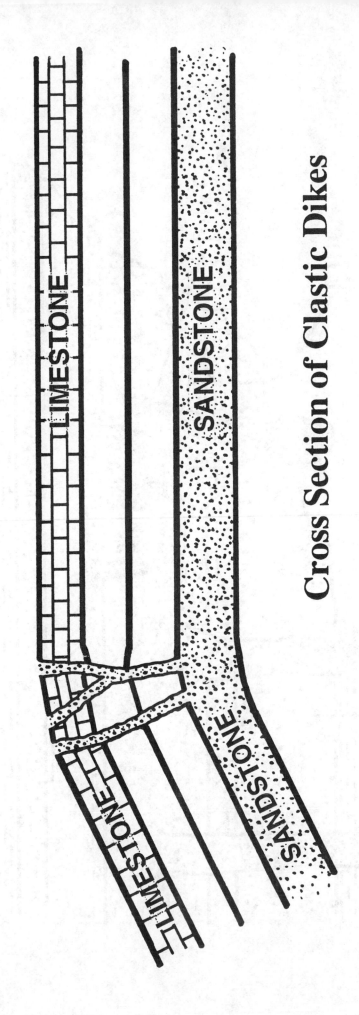

Cross Section of Clastic Dikes

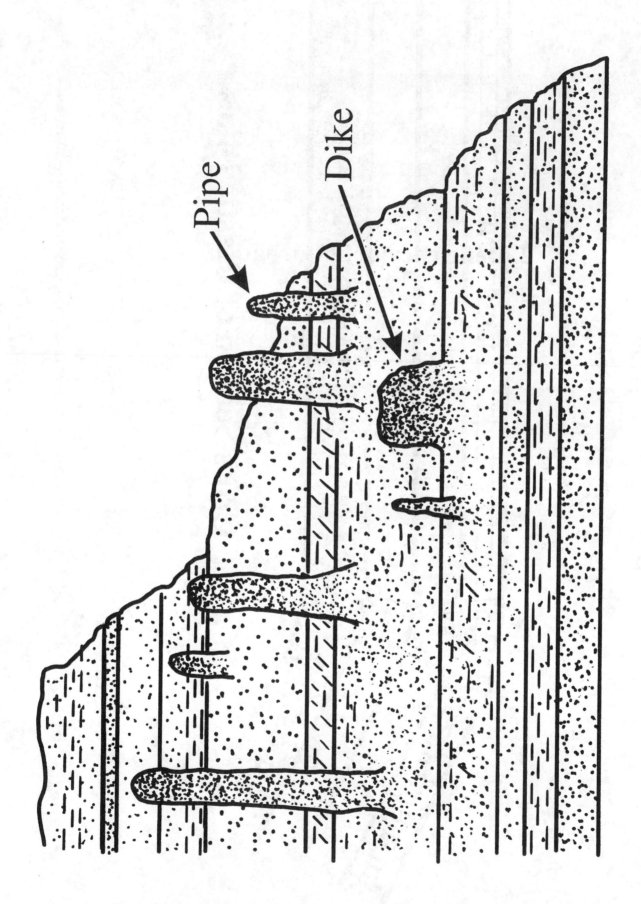

Pipe

Dike

Clastic dikes and pipes in Kodachrome Basin State Park

Geologic Evidence for the Young Earth

1. Surface features

2. Deficiency of bioturbation

3. Lack of soil layers

4. Undisturbed bedding plains

5. Polystrate fossils

6. Limited extent of unconformities

7. Soft-sediment deformation

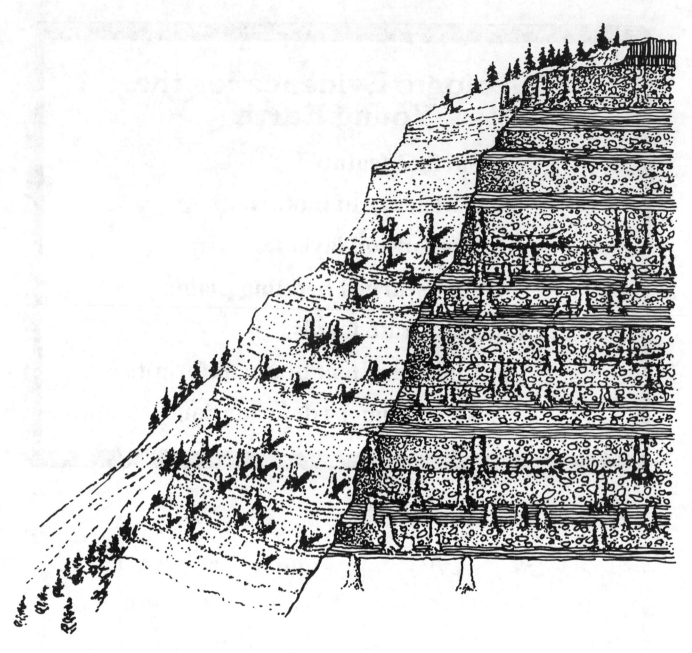

Cutaway view of Specimen Ridge

Jesus told Nicodemus, "If I have told you earthly things, and ye believe not, how shall ye believe if I tell you of heavenly things?"

John 3:12

But as the days of Noah were, so shall also the coming of the Son of man be. For as in the days that were before the flood they were eating and drinking, marrying and giving in marriage, until the day that Noah entered into the ark, and knew not until the flood came, and took them all away, so shall also the coming of the Son of man be.

Matthew 24:37–39

The world that then was, being overflowed with water, perished.

II Peter 3:6

And the flood was forty days upon the earth; and the waters increased, and bare up the ark, and it was lifted up above the earth. And the waters prevailed, and were increased greatly upon the earth; and the ark went upon the face of the waters. And the waters prevailed exceedingly upon the earth; and all the high hills, that were under the whole heaven were covered. Fifteen cubits upward did the waters prevail; and the mountains were covered. And all flesh died that moved upon the earth, both of fowl, and of cattle, and of beast, and of every creeping thing that creepeth upon the earth, and every man: All in whose nostrils was the breath of life, of all that was in the dry land, died. And every living substance was destroyed which was upon the face of the ground, both man, and cattle, and the creeping things, and the fowl of the heaven; and they were destroyed from the earth: and Noah only remained alive, and they that were with him in the ark. And the waters prevailed upon the earth an hundred and fifty days.

Genesis 7:17–24

Care for Creation
Good Science
Government Under God
Right and Wrong
Value of Human Life
Family Values
Creation
The Word of God

Homosexuality, Promiscuity
Abortion, Euthanasia
Relative Standards
Socialism, Marxism, Anarchy
Naturalism and New Age
Worship of Earth
Evolution
The Mind of Man

The wolf also shall dwell with the lamb, and the leopard shall lie down with the kid; and the calf and the young lion and the fatling together; and a little child shall lead them.

And the cow and the bear shall feed; their young ones shall lie down together: and the lion shall eat straw like the ox.

And the sucking child shall play on the hole of the asp, and the weaned child shall put his hand on the cockatrice' den.

Isaiah 11:6–8

For the earnest expectation of the creation waiteth for the manifestation of the sons of God. For the creation was made subject to vanity, not willingly, but by reason of him who hath subjected the same in hope.

Because the creation itself also shall be delivered from the bondage of corruption into the glorious liberty of the children of God.

For we know that the whole creation groaneth and travaileth in pain together until now.

Romans 8:19–22

And God said, "Behold I have given you every herb bearing seed, which is upon the face of all the earth, and every tree, in the which is the fruit of a tree yielding seed; to you it shall be for meat.

And to every beast of the earth, and to every fowl of the air, and to every thing that creepeth upon the earth, wherein there is life, I have given every green herb for meat": and it was so.

Genesis 1:29–30

The Extent of the Curse

Genesis 3:14–19

All of Creation altered because of Adam and Eve's rebellion

Earth cursed, v. 17

Animals cursed, v.14

Plants cursed, v. 18

Humankind cursed, vv. 16,17,19

Death reigns, v. 19, *Romans 8:19–22*

Wherefore, as by one man sin entered into the world, and death by sin; and so death passed upon all men, for that all have sinned.

Romans 5:12

But now is Christ risen from the dead, and become the first-fruits of them that slept. For since by man came death, by man came also the resurrection of the dead. For as in Adam all die, even so in Christ shall all be made alive.

I Corinthians 15:20–22

The secrets of evolution are death and time — the deaths of enormous numbers of lifeforms that were imperfectly adapted to the environment; and time for a long succession of small mutations that were by accident adaptive, time for the slow accumulation of patterns of favorable mutations.

Carl Sagan, *Cosmos*, 1980, p. 30.

Thus, from the war of nature, from famine and death, the most exalted object which we are capable of conceiving, namely, the production of the higher animals, [i.e., man, *ed.*] directly follows.

Charles Darwin, *Origin of Species,* last paragraph

I had no intention to write atheistically, but I own that I cannot see as plainly as others do, and as I should wish to do, evidence of design and beneficence on all sides of us. I cannot persuade myself that a beneficent and omnipotent God would have designedly created the *ichneumonidae* [a parasite, *ed.*] with the express intention of their feeding within the living bodies of caterpillars, or that a cat should play with mice. Not believing this, I see no necessity in the belief that the eye was expressly designed.

Charles Darwin in a letter to Harvard Professor Asa Gray, May 22, 1860.

Christianity has fought, still fights, and will fight science to the desperate end over evolution, because evolution destroys utterly and finally the very reason Jesus' earthly life was supposedly made necessary. Destroy Adam and Eve and the original sin, and in the rubble you will find the sorry remains of the son of god. Take away the meaning of his death. If Jesus was not the redeemer who died for our sins, and this is what evolution means, then Christianity is nothing!

G. Richard Bozarth, "The Meaning of Evolution,"
American Atheist, February 1978, pp. 19,30.

And God saw that the wickedness of man was great in the earth, and that every imagination of the thoughts of his heart was only evil continually. And it repented the LORD that he had made man on the earth, and it grieved him at his heart. And the LORD said, I will destroy man whom I have created from the face of the earth; both man, and beast, and the creeping thing, and the fowls of the air; for it repenteth me that I have made them.

Genesis 6:5–7

That in the ages to come He might show the exceeding riches of His grace in His kindness toward us through Christ Jesus.

Ephesians 2:7

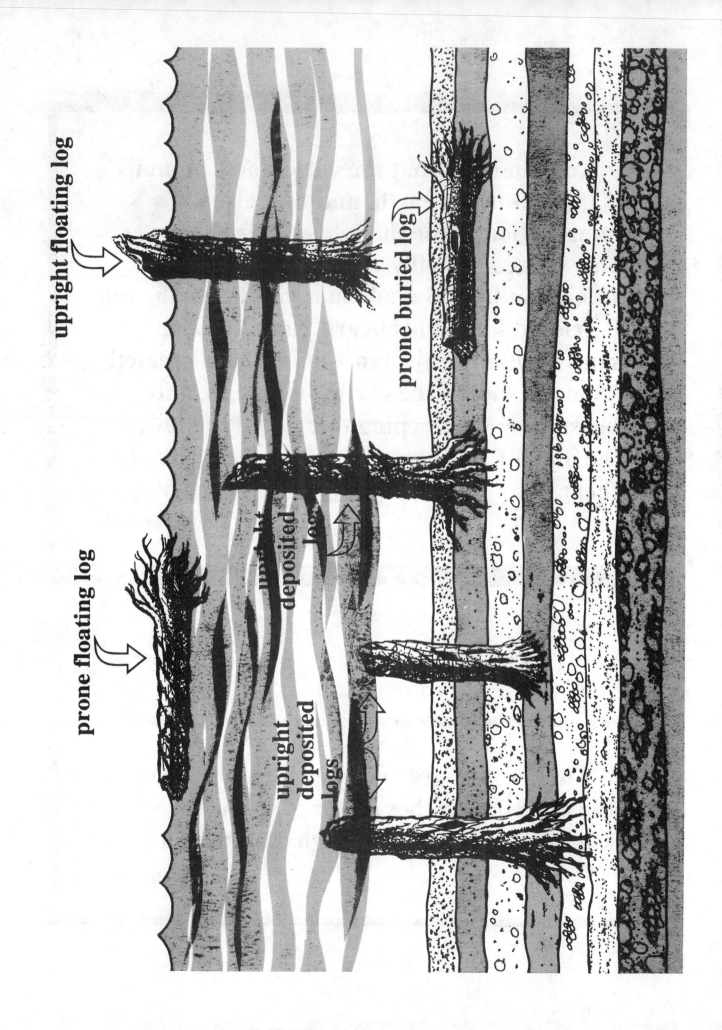

upright floating log

prone floating log

upright deposited logs

prone buried log